Literature and Ideology in
Soviet Education

Published for the Centre for Russian and
East European Studies, University of
Toronto

Literature and Ideology in Soviet Education

N.N. Shneidman
University of Toronto

Lexington Books
D.C. Heath and Company
Lexington, Massachusetts
Toronto   London

Library of Congress Cataloging in Publication Data

Shneidman, N.N.
   Literature and ideology in Soviet education.

   Bibliography: p.
   1. Russian literature—Study and teaching. 2. Communist
education. I. Title.
PG2945.S47   891.7'07'1047   73-9683
ISBN 0-669-89565-2

_c C_

Published simultaneously in Canada.

Printed in the United States of America.

International Standard Book Number: 0-669-89565-2

Library of Congress Catalog Card Number: 73-9683

Contents

Preface

My interest in Soviet literary education dates from the late sixties, when I worked on my doctoral dissertation, entitled "Russian Literature in Soviet Education," defended at the University of Toronto in 1971. The realization that communist ideology is one of the most important components of Soviet education in general, and of literary education in particular, has generated my interest in problems of the relationship of literature and ideology in the process of education in the Soviet school, and it has become the main subject of this manuscript.

I rely in this study mainly on original material, and all translations from the Russian appearing in the text, unless quoted from English sources, are my own.

The titles of Russian books appearing in the text are given first in the original with an English translation in parentheses. Subsequently the same titles appear in English.

Since any transliteration system from one language into another is arbitrary, the only binding principle must be consistency. I have adopted in this manuscript a slightly different transliteration method from that of the Library of Congress, in that "iu" and "ia" are changed into "yu" and "ya" and "ĭ" is changed into "y."

I would like to use this opportunity to express my gratitude to all those who encouraged and helped me in the course of my work on the manuscript, in particular Professors H.E. Bowman, K.B. Feuer, K.A. Lantz, G.S.N. Luckyj, H.G. Skilling, and G. Žekulin. A note of thanks is also due to the Centre for Russian and East European Studies, University of Toronto, for generous support of my research. I gratefully acknowledge the permission of the editors of the *Slavic Review* to reprint Chapter 4, which has appeared in their September 1972 issue. Finally a word of appreciation to my wife, Nina, and my daughters, Rose and Lillian, for their help, encouragement, and forbearance.

Naturally, while I gratefully acknowledge the assistance and advice of my teachers and colleagues, I accept sole responsibility for whatever inaccuracies or mistakes that may exist in the manuscript.

N.N.S.

Toronto, Canada

Introduction

With the advent of the Sputnik age the general interest in Soviet life has enormously increased. The Western reader has tried since to rediscover and to understand the manifold phenomena of Soviet reality.

Much attention has been lately paid in the West to the study of the Soviet system of education, a system which could be credited with the education and training of many high caliber scientists and specialists in different areas of scholarly endeavor. However, most Western studies in Soviet education are of a historical nature and mainly concerned with the historical background as well as with the organizational and structural foundations of the Soviet school. Without minimizing the importance of such studies, it is necessary to recognize that the proper understanding of the Soviet citizen, who is a product of a unified and centrally controlled system of education, a system that "has been consciously used for a generation or more as an agency for political socialization, to build a national political culture congruent with and supportive of existing political institutions,"[1] is impossible without studying the inner mechanics of the educational process.

A thorough understanding of the educational process in a given subject in the curriculum of the Soviet school would require, first of all, a close acquaintance with the subject matter taught. Equally important is a knowledge of the official interpretation given to the material studied, as well as of the general methodological guidelines for the subject in question, which aim to secure the most effective results in conformity with the general goals of Soviet education.

The proposed study endeavors to make up for the lack in the West of a comprehensive study of the teaching of literature in Soviet education.[2] It is not intended to be an exposition or criticism of the Soviet system of education in general. Its main purpose is to examine the basic components of Soviet literary education, with particular emphasis on the methods of ideological education in the process of teaching literature.

Literature in the Soviet schools is not only a tool of political indoctrination. It also acquaints the young generation with the cultural values of the past. It introduces the students to the language of Pushkin, Turgenev, and Tolstoy. It is a vehicle for the propagation of traditional Russian values and virtues, such as hard work, obedience to authority, and respect for parents. Notwithstanding, the main emphasis in this study is on tracing the ideological component of the educational process, a component considered more important in the Soviet Union than any other constituent part of literary education. Some difficulty may arise from the fact that there is no reliable gauge to measure the exact level of success of an educational process whose purpose is to instil certain aesthetic, ethical, or moral values. To come as close as possible to the truth I rely on official Soviet sources as well as on the opinions of those directly involved in the study and teaching of literature in the Soviet Union.

I endeavor to give in this study a concise but comprehensive outline of the programing, methodology, approach, and interpretation of Russian literature in Soviet education, with particular emphasis on the connection of Soviet ideology and politics with the educational process in literature. The main emphasis in the analysis of literary texts studied in the Soviet school is placed on Russian prerevolutionary works of literature included in the educational programs. An examination of the required school and university reading lists from Soviet literature indicates that most works are written in conformity with the Soviet method of socialist realism and they project the basic values advocated by Marxist-Leninist ideology. These Soviet works do not require any special interpretation because the social, ideological, and often political message is on the surface; it is the very essence and the main objective of these works.

The contents of this study is limited to the most essential aspects of the subject. All the tables, programs, and other relevant material that I consider integral, factual, and important illustrations of my findings are included in the Appendix.

There is much to learn from positive as well as negative experiences in the field of Soviet literary education; the more so since North American teachers of literature are now in the process of a dialogue as to the methods of study and teaching literature. While some American teachers claim that the teaching of literature must remain "objective," that "students are capable of judging for themselves and in fact responsible for making judgment,"[3] others assert that "'objectivity' or neutrality in either scholarship or teaching is taken to be inconceivable and the pretense of it immoral,"[4] and, therefore, they advocate a method of teaching which would require the instructor to deliver to the student a positive message of a definite content. The question, however, remains: What should be the content of this message in our contemporary North American conditions, and how far could an instructor drive his point without alienating the student from the subject, and without reducing the general educational value of literature to a minimum? One of the objectives of the proposed study is to examine the effectiveness of the literature teaching methods in Soviet education which do require the teacher to deliver an ideological message and to instil in the student a definite set of social, political, ideological values.

It is hoped that this study will be of use and interest to the Western student of Soviet education, literature, political science, and related fields, and that it will assist him in a better understanding of the Soviet man and of his scale of values, which is shaped and developed in the Soviet school.

1 Ideology—The Essence of Soviet Education

Fifty-six years have passed since the Winter Palace in Peterburg was stormed and the Bolsheviks, who had gained control in the local Soviets, announced the arrival of a new era. It was to be an era in which men would be equal, and society would be without exploiters and downtrodden, a society built on high ethical and moral foundations. Now, over half a century after the October Revolution, it is not difficult to see that a great deal has been accomplished. The Soviet Union has become a leading military power; its national economy is almost self-sufficient; illiteracy has been wiped out; and the living standard of the average citizen is above that of prerevolutionary days. To an outsider these achievements may seem sufficient for the building of a communist society. It may occur to the student of Soviet affairs that, as the Marxist maxim says, social being determines one's consciousness, and therefore, with the change of society and its economic patterns, the members of this society change automatically; their mentality develops and changes. Should this be the case, one of the major obstacles on the path to the creation of a communist society would be conquered. It would remain only to build new plants and factories to further mechanization and agriculture, and all the rest would come by itself. Soviet history and experience point, however, to different conclusions. With each five-year plan the Soviet national economy moves toward new and more complex targets and aims; with each decade the level of industrialization and technical achievement rises. The recent resolutions of the Soviet government and the Communist party on problems of ideology, education, and upbringing are, however, still reminiscent of those in the twenties and even before. That is not to say that the party and government do not try to change man. They do. They apply all the power available to do so, but apparently with insufficient success. This does not mean that the people in the Soviet Union have not changed. They have changed, and a great deal; but these changes are still minimal in comparison with other changes within the system. In all probability human beings, who are often irrational, whose behavior is often unpredictable and conditioned by hereditary factors, and who, besides, do not live in an isolated world, are not as easily changed as one would desire. As human beings are adaptable, so are the Soviet citizens! They conform, they agree with the system, they go along. But this is not enough: what is wanted is conformity based on conviction and the knowledge of political theory; an active conformity of citizens who live up to the word of the dogma, and who are able and ready to defend it and to fight for it.

1

The Soviet state uses everything in its power to influence the Soviet citizen and to guard him from evil burgeois influences. A whole system of political, scientific, antireligious, professional, and educational organizations and institutions serve the purpose of upbringing and educating in the spirit of Marxism-Leninism, in the spirit of devotion to the communist cause and to the Soviet fatherland.

One of the mainstays and tools of the party and the government in their continuous effort to change Soviet man has been, and remains, the Soviet system of education. Its role is of prime importance since there is only one school, centralized and supervised from above, and no Soviet youth can avoid its influence. With the existing law of compulsory secondary education, introduced in 1970,[1] the Soviet youth is exposed to the same influences throughout most of his formative years. Through a widely developed network of preschool institutions the children are influenced even before they reach elementary school.

No secret is made in the Soviet Union of the fact that the school is an arm of the party, and its main objective is the indoctrination of the growing generation. As early as 1918 Lenin reasserted the political domination of education by saying, "We state openly, that a school outside of life, outside of politics—is a lie and hypocrisy."[2] Much as Lenin valued education, he did not believe that the goals of the Bolsheviks could be achieved with the help of education only. He did not support the views of many revolutionaries who wanted to change society by changing man. For Lenin it was the other way around. He believed that it was necessary to change society and then in turn to undertake the task of changing man. Lenin maintained the "principle of political action over education . . . with perfect consistency to the end."[3]

Echoing Lenin's statements on education, L. Brezhnev, after enumerating the duties and objectives of the Soviet school, concludes by saying that all the practical objectives of the school

are only one side of the cause. There is also another side, not less important, namely, to infuse the youth with the foundations of the communist world outlook. The Soviet school does not simply prepare educated people. It is responsible for the turning out of politically literate, ideologically convinced fighters for the communist cause. The school never stood, and it cannot stand aside from politics, in the side of the struggle of classes.[4]

Developing Lenin's and Brezhnev's ideas on the primacy of politics over education, the Soviet Minister of Education, M. Prokof'ev, states bluntly

The prime task of our school is to equip its pupils with principles for a scientific understanding of the development of the modern world in its movement from capitalism to socialism to communism. In other words, in our times it is of particular importance that each school child has a profound grasp of the Marxist-Leninist theory of the development of society.[5]

It is difficult to overestimate the significance attached by the Communist party and the Soviet state to the task of educating the young generation in the spirit of patriotism and devotion to the communist cause. The party leadership endeavors to make sure that not only the subject matter taught in the Soviet school is ideologically correct, but that also the personnel involved in the educational process are politically and ideologically reliable. It is interesting to note that while in March 1971 9 percent of the country's adult population belonged to the Communist Party of the Soviet Union,[6] at the same time about 26 percent of all Soviet schoolteachers and masters (*vospitateli*) were party members.[7] The proportion of party members on the academic staff of institutions of higher learning is even higher, reaching 42 percent of the total.[8]

Party members working in educational institutions are supposed to lead the struggle for ideological purity and to serve as an example to nonparty staff members and students alike. In order to enhance the struggle against ideological diversion; to secure the development of education and scholarship in the required direction; and to strengthen the ties of the school with the party, the Twenty-fourth Congress of the Communist Party of the Soviet Union adopted a change in the party rules according to which primary party organizations in educational institutions are given the "right to supervise the activities of the management."[9] This is a privilege as well as a responsibility not given to primary party organizations of industrial enterprises.

The objectives set by the leadership of the state and the party, and the methodological guidelines laid down by the educators who are, at the same time, high party officials, predetermine the directions to be followed by each teacher, in each subject. These directions are based on the assumption that the methodological foundation of the Soviet sciences of education is the theory of Marxism-Leninism, and in particular dialectical materialism and its application to the problems of the development of society—historical materialism.[10] Soviet pedagogy assumes a class character of education. It claims that education has always experienced the influence of the relationship of people in the process of production. "Education in a socialist society is determined by the objective requirements of social development and it serves the purpose of the preparation of all-round educated and convinced builders of a communist future."[11] Soviet educational theory does not deal with education in general. The subject of Soviet pedagogy is communist education and upbringing; education relating to the realm of knowledge, and upbringing to the realm of behavior and the relationship with other people in life. Communist education is to ensure an all-round development of the young people, which should include the provision for mental and intellectual, polytechnical, moral, physical, and aesthetic education and training. One of the main objectives of mental and intellectual education in the Soviet school is to arm the young generation with a system of scientific knowledge and to form in the student's mind a communist consciousness and a communist *Weltanschauung*. The communist world outlook is based on a scientific materialistic approach to the understanding of world phenomena and it implies a "correct understanding of the role of the people's masses, political parties, and historic personalities in the process of class struggle and building of socialism and communism."[1,2]

Much attention is devoted in the Soviet school to ethical education, the foundation of which is communist morality. The moral code of a builder of a communist society includes

devotion to the cause of communism, love of the socialist motherland and of other socialist countries; work for the welfare of society, and the preservation and growth of public property; high consciousness of one's social duties and intolerance to offenders against public interests; collectivism, friendship, mutual respect; honesty, truthfulness, moral purity, modesty in public and in private life; mutual respect in the family and concern for the education of the children; irreconcilability to injustice, to parasites, to dishonesty and self-seeking; friendship and brotherhood among the Soviet nations and intolerance of national and race hatred; irreconcilability to the enemies of communism and of the cause of peace and freedom of the people; brotherly solidarity with the workers of all countries, with all people.[13]

It is suggested that ethical education, as it is understood in Soviet pedagogy, is to begin as early as possible in the life of the child. It is claimed that as the child grows he perfects and corrects acquired moral habits, but seldom develops new ethical attitudes. Hence the importance of implanting the necessary values as early as possible.

The main objective of ethical education in Soviet society is the development of socialist patriotism and proletarian internationalism; a communist relationship to labor and to public property; socialist humanism and collectivism. All these must become a part of the individual's personal convictions and manifest itself in his habits, desires, attitudes, strivings, and behavior.[14] Young children tend to worship and imitate the heroes they encounter in life and in the process of learning. It is suggested that the biography of Lenin is an excellent model for an example with the help of which it is possible to develop in the pupil a communist ethical ideal. In the forties and early fifties, the biography of Stalin, his behavior and actions, were regarded as an ethical ideal and were to be emulated. This worship of Stalin developed into a so-called "personality cult" which has been by now officially repudiated. Works of literature by Soviet writers, included into the school programs, are regarded as important factors in the formation of a communist morality. Pavel Korchagin, the hero of *Kak zakalyalas' stal'* (How Steel Was Tempered) by N. Ostrovsky, or Pavel Vlasov, the main hero of *Mat'* (Mother) by M. Gorky, are examples of young revolutionaries who embody most of the virtues required by the communist ethical ideal.

Aesthetic education, which is emphasized as an important factor in the study of literature, is also considered by Soviet literary theoreticians as an extension of ideological education. "Aesthetic education is the development of the ability to perceive fully and properly understand the beautiful and its meaning in arts, in social, daily, and personal life, and in nature; the education of love for the beautiful and the ability to embody it."[15] Soviet literary theory does not see any contradiction in the specific distinctions existing between aesthetic perception and the perception of political, moral, and other values. "Aesthetic characteristics always reveal the social contents of any phenomenon."[16] Communist aesthetics are inseparable from the general Marxist-Leninist ideals, and it might seem that the Soviet citizen is deprived of the right to admire what seems to him beautiful and wonderful, but which does not agree with the currently approved political and ideological line. "The communist aesthetic ideal is a constituent part of the communist social ideal, which includes political, moral, philosophical, and scientific views of the working class."[17]

Like Soviet ethics, aesthetics are conditioned by the relationship of people in the process of production and by class struggle. Ethics and aesthetics serve in a given society the ruling class. "Aesthetic judgment is an opinion about a certain value, but an opinion about a fixed value is the result of a selection which is determined by the social and historical conditions in which the artist finds himself. Therefore, the same life occurrence can receive opposite evaluation from different artists."[18] The aesthetic importance of an artistic image consists in the fact that the given image embodies definite human ideals. "The embodied ideal expresses the truly beautiful in life."[19] This ideal should express itself in the actions of a protagonist of a work of art. For this reason the aesthetic ideal is one of the most important in art because "it shows clearly the aims to which man strives, as well as the path which he is to follow towards these aims."[20]

In a socialist society the methodological foundation of aesthetic education is Marxism-Leninism and Lenin's theory of reflection, according to which the road to objective truth goes from live perception to abstract thinking. In Soviet psychology only the perception which appears in its unity of sensation and reflection can be regarded as valuable. The author's thinking in images and the scholar's thinking in concepts or notions are united and complement each other in order to get a full picture of these images. Soviet logic endeavors to show the inner connection between logic and intuition; between emotion and intellect, as well as between the artistic image and the idea in order to interpret the irrational forces from a rational standpoint.[21]

Soviet philosophers endeavor to minimize the element of irrationality in human intuition, an element which cannot be detached from the perception of a work of art. A proposition is put forth that "intuition is the understanding of something without actually knowing the reasons for this understanding. There is, however, a reason for every phenomenon, including intuition."[22] The introduction of a rational factor into the explanation of intuition is of prime importance for the perception of aesthetic values in art. Literature, like art in general, is perceived by our feelings as well as by our minds. The unity of the rational and the emotional and the balance between them is one of the peculiarities of artistic and aesthetic perception. Lenin's theory of reflection and cognition is presently interpreted by Soviet philosophers in a manner in which even the very first step in the process of perception has a rational beginning because our senses relate to us a message from the material world which has a logical foundation. Contemporary studies in the Marxist theory of reflection and psychology indicate that there is a rational moment in sensation and on the contrary that there is an element of sensation or feeling in an act of logical thinking. It is claimed that there is no "pure" sensation or "pure" thinking.[23]

The rational explanation of the perception of aesthetic values links Soviet aesthetic education with the ethical ideal. "The reflection in art of the beautiful in life serves the purpose of ethical education . . . materialistic aesthetics connects the teaching about the beautiful in art with ethics."[24] In contemporary Soviet literature the above is supposed to be expressed in a direct portrayal of positive characters who embody all the necessary characteristics of the aesthetic and ethical communist ideals. The aesthetic importance of most prerevolutionary literature is that it shows the obstacles on the path toward the communist ideal, and it awakens in the reader an opposition and hostility toward the described order of things. Soviet literary theory states openly that although the socialist aesthetic ideal does not reject the aesthetic norms established in the process of the historic development of humanity, all the same it is a completely new ideal. "The essence of this innovation is first of all in the fact that this ideal is inseparably linked with the great tasks and aims put forth and implemented by the Communist party."[25] The basic principle of the evaluation of a character in a work of art is his relationship to reality, judged from the standpoint of Marxist ideology and Soviet politics. It is necessary to bear in mind that these two terms have long ceased to be synonymous.

Soviet aesthetics thus are based on the Marxist-Leninist theory of cognition, which is based on socioeconomic foundations and a belief in the rationality of man. However, abstract thinking that follows the perception of a given work of art often does not lead to the conclusions desired. This is, perhaps, owing to the fact that sensation and perception are highly personal matters which are very difficult to measure, while the abstract thinking which should illuminate this sensation is highly generalized and should fit into every scheme. The relationship of logic and intuition, of emotion and intellect, is different in each human being, and it does not fit easily into preconceived patterns.

A Marxist-Leninist interpretation of the material studied is presented to students in Soviet schools at all levels, in all courses of study, be it in the humanities, the social sciences, or natural sciences. It is, therefore, surprising that some leading American educators claim that "in extent of indoctrination Soviet Union presents little that is unusual. It is the aim of all educational systems to assure the development in the nation's youth of the beliefs and values of the adult society around them. All societies indoctrinate."[26] Including under the heading of political education the subjects of language, literature, social studies, history, geography, foreign language, home room and opening exercises, and socially useful work, G. Bereday claims that while in the US in grades five to twelve almost 46 percent of school time is devoted to some form of political and social education, in the Soviet Union only 38 percent of the total school time is devoted to the same subjects. Drawing on the pedagogical axiom that there is some correspondence between exposure and learning, he alludes to the fact that the American pupil is not less indoctrinated than the Soviet one. In a formal approach to the comparison of the American and Soviet school curricula G. Bereday's conclusions may be correct. He fails, however, to take into consideration the fact that there are no *non*political subjects in Soviet education, because as one notable Soviet educator says, "in our times, ideological aspects could be detected even in what might seem the most abstract subjects."[27]

Bereday fails to take into account that not only history and social sciences, but also physics and chemistry, are projected from the point of view of dialectical materialism which is later adopted in the study of social phenomena. Natural and life sciences are taught from the point of view that the world is rational and knowable, that the cognition of man is unlimited. The examples in which quantitative changes lead to abrupt qualitative changes in science, and which are later used to prove the inevitability of revolution due to the changes in the social composition of society, are studied first in elementary science classes, and only later find their way to seminar rooms on dialectical and historical materialism. The same subjects are used to form an atheistic world outlook among the pupils and students, a weapon in their struggle with the so-called backwardness of the parents, who time and again turn to religion as they get older. Soviet educators make no secret that biology, physics, chemistry, and astronomy are of exceptional importance in the formation of a communist world outlook. "Biology discovers and demonstrates convincingly the materialistic and dialectic essence of the evolution of nature and rejects resolutely its idealistic and religious explanation and interpretation."[28]

Military training, which is not limited to universities, could be regarded as another form of ideological education. By a decree of the USSR Ministry of Education, military training has been reintroduced in many schools and the program is gradually expanding. The purpose of this course is to strengthen the patriotism of the pupils, to help them identify with the heroic deeds of the Soviet Army, as well as "to get acquainted with the soldier's actions in the basic battle situations, to learn about the structure and operation of a submachine gun, light machine gun, antitank grenade discharger; to learn shooting from a small submachine gun."[29] "Regardless of what part of the educational process we are concerned with—be it political, military-patriotic, labor, or atheistic— there is always a common denominator, which is expressed in the development of love and devotion to your motherland and an irreconcilability to its enemies."[30]

The superiority of Soviet sciences, based on a superior ideology and the priority of Soviet and Russian scholarship and discoveries, is stressed continuously and serves as a tool in the shaping of patriotic feelings in the young generation. Even in physical education, the superiority of Soviet athletes in certain competitive sports is used as evidence of the superiority of Soviet society and its way of life over the West. The Soviet pupil, in almost every class, listens again and again to the same political and ideological "truths." There are even complaints that the same material is included in the programs of different subjects. At a joint meeting of the Commission of History Education of the USSR Academy of Sciences and the USSR Academy of Pedagogical Sciences, the speakers "almost unanimously spoke of the necessity to eliminate repetition. Surely it is no secret, that the same material is covered in the courses of history, political economy, history of the Communist Party of the Soviet Union, and philosophy."[31]

At this point it is interesting to note that at the university level a council of a philological faculty is given permission by the Ministry of Higher and Secondary Specialized Education to change the number of hours assigned to separate subjects and the sequence in which they are studied, under the condition that the students acquire the scientific knowledge as determined by the curriculum, without increasing the maximum of the approved weekly study load. No such permission, however, is given for subjects in the social sciences, which usually include the history of the Communist Party of the USSR, Marxist philosophy, political economy, etc. In subjects where ideological education is the direct purpose of study, no changes or deviations in time, contents, or sequence are permitted. Uniformity, consistency, and control must be maintained at all times.

In a formal comparison of ideological and political education in the American and Soviet schools one would also have to consider the fact that the "educational system in the United States is one of the most highly decentralized in the world,"[32] whereas the Soviet system of education is one of the most highly centralized, reaching everyone of school age with the same message. The same message is also delivered in the Soviet Union by the many agencies outside the school which have a profound impact on the education of the young generation. To name just a few: the Pioneer and Communist Youth organizations, sport clubs, summer camps, etc. Every school indoctrinates and promotes the values of the society of which it is a part. The difference is only in the degree of indoctrination and in the relative freedom to choose the agency that is going to indoctrinate your child.

The extent of ideological penetration into any area of Soviet education, and the requirement of the knowledge of the dogma by any specialist, is well expressed in one of the theses of the party's Central Committee and the Council of Ministers of the USSR on education:

A knowledge of the foundations of Marxism-Leninism is indispensable for specialists in all areas. They must study Lenin and know how to apply his enormous theoretical heritage in life, to build our life in a Communist fashion. The study of Marxism-Leninism must bear creative, aggressive, and militant character. We must rear our youth in the spirit of irreconcilability with bourgeois ideology and all manifestations of revisionism. The teaching of social sciences must be connected indissolubly with the study of natural sciences; it must help the students to develop a scientific method of thought.[33]

The emphasis on ideological education in the Soviet school is as strong now as it was in the days of Stalin. The only distinction is in the necessity to adjust the ideological content of the material taught to the political requirements of the present day. Political and ideological contents continue to penetrate all areas of Soviet education. It is necessary, however, to note that the effectiveness of such education is not the same in all subjects. It is clear that the humanities and social sciences lend themselves better to indoctrination, to the creation of a certain view of life and of the world around.

2 Literature in the Soviet School

The subject of literature is not different from other subjects by virtue of being a weapon of ideological education. It is different only in the sense that it is a more powerful weapon; that ideological and ethical education is one of its main purposes. "The main aim in teaching literature in the school is the ideological and moral upbringing of the student, the formation of a worthy, active member of our society. But art is a specific form of ideology that reflects the aesthetic mastery of the world."[1] The secondary-school program in Russian literature states clearly that along with the general-educational importance of the study of literature at school, its main objective is the ideological and political, ethical, and aesthetic education of the pupils. The study of literature in school is to secure the student's understanding of the social significance of literature; the understanding of the Leninist principle of partyness of literature and the need for unmasking the ideological and aesthetic conceptions of the ideological enemies of the Soviet state. Literature lessons are to assist in the formation of a communist *Weltanschauung*; in the development of Soviet patriotism, proletarian internationalism, and communist relationship to labor.[2] In the report of the Central Committee of the Communist Party of the Soviet Union to the Twenty-fourth Congress of the CPSU, Brezhnev stated, "Workers in literature and art are in one of the most crucial sectors of the ideological struggle,"[3] because "literature, along with history, makes it possible to grasp the fundamental laws of the development of society."[4]

In the 1970-71 school year, in accordance with the new program, a formal study of Russian literature in the Soviet school was introduced in grade four. Until 1970 this study began in grade five.[5] Throughout the school literature is taught in connection with Russian language study, most of the time by the same teacher. Russian language and literature, often considered one subject, are given a prominent place in Soviet education. Each graduate of a secondary school who intends to enroll in a university or institute must take an entrance examination in Russian language and literature, regardless of the specialty chosen. The importance of Russian language and literature has been further enhanced recently by introducing a new regulation according to which the mark received at the entrance examination in Russian language and literature is equal to the mark in the selected specialty as well as to the average mark on the matriculation diploma.[6] The numerous program changes taking place in the system in the last decade have not, as far as time allotment is concerned, affected the subject of literature much. The recent shortening of the course of secondary education to ten years increased the relative weight of the subject in relation to the curriculum as a whole. In the old curriculum of 1959, 4.1 percent of the total time spent in grades one to eight was devoted to the study of literature; in the 1966 curriculum, 5 percent. On the secondary level the increase is even more visible. In the 1959 curriculum 8.9 percent of the total time spent in grades nine to eleven was devoted to literature, while in the new curriculum, in grades nine to ten, 11.7 percent of the total time is devoted to the same subject.[7]

Already in elementary school the pupils are introduced to some aspects of Russian literature. They get to know the names of some of the most important Russian and Soviet writers and poets: Pushkin, Lermontov, Tolstoy, Chekhov, Nekrasov, Gorky, Mayakovsky, and others. This introduction is not a study of literature proper. It is rather a study of the world around and its people, which is illustrated by reading what these writers had to say on these subjects. The grade one to three readers are divided into parts that deal with themes such as: the seasons of the year; the school; the family; animals; the city; the Soviet army; the past of our motherland; stories, tales, and fables; famous Soviet people; the October Revolution.[8]

The beginning of the formal literary course preserves a continuity with the elementary school. The grade four and five programs are structured on the same thematic principle, and the topics suggested are reminiscent of those studied in the younger grades.[9] The material selected, however, is more difficult and more complicated and the program includes some elementary notions of literary theory. The grade six program is planned differently. It is an introduction to the chronological study of literature in the upper grades. The basic three parts of the program deal with tales from Russian oral folk poetry and works of Russian prerevolutionary and Soviet writers. Thematically, the grade six material remains close to grade five, but in contents and organization it can be regarded as a transition to grade seven.

The program in grade seven is arranged in chronological order. It contains fewer titles, but the works are longer, and a great deal of time is devoted to literary analysis of the material read. The material studied is related to present life as well as to the Russian historic past and is drawn from nineteenth-century and Soviet literatures. In grade eight the pupils begin a systematic course of literature study which is completed at the end of grade ten. The program includes several topics from old Russian and eighteen-century literatures, but it is mainly devoted to the first half of the nineteenth century, and it is centered around the works of Pushkin, Lermontov, Gogol' (*Mertvye dushi* [Dead Souls]). For the first time literary criticism is represented in the program, by inclusion of the works of Belinsky and Gertsen.

Grade eight concludes the program of the so-called eight-year school, which is regarded as an incomplete secondary school. The methods and approach to the study of literature in the eight-year school are somewhat different from those in the older grades and are based on an aesthetic-emotional perception of literature which is united with intellectual perception, i.e., the understanding of a work of literature and its meaning, which is achieved with the help and guidance of the teacher, who bears constantly in mind that the analysis of a work of literature should not only help the pupil to master the content of the work, but above all assist him in forming communist views and convictions. Particular attention is devoted in the eight-year school to works of literature dealing with the problems of labor and workers, and the communist relationship to work, to works of art developing a sense of Soviet patriotism and friendship among the brotherly nations of the USSR and foreign countries. In the analysis and discussion of a particular work of literature the pupils are required to be able to point to the characters with whom the writer identifies; they are also encouraged to identify themselves with the positive heroes.

Upon graduation from the eight-year school all pupils are required to take a written examination in Russian literature. In the 1967-68 school year examination, the pupils were given a choice of four different topics. Two topics were related to the material covered in literature, and dealt with the works of Pushkin and Gogol'. The other two topics had strong political and ideological overtones and were little related to the material studied in the eight-year school. The topics were formulated as follows: "It is our good fortune, children, to march under the red banner!" and "I love you Russia, my Soviet land!" A random analysis of 250 examination compositions from six different Moscow schools[10] indicates that only fifty-two students selected the free topics, and it is even hinted that some chose to write on a free topic because they have not mastered the literature material required by the program. Those selecting the free topics were expected to write in a manner that would exhibit an emotional attachment and love of the motherland; a deep sense of patriotism, and a profound respect for the defenders of the socialist fatherland. Instead, the compositions read as an exposition of Soviet history from the October Revolution till now.

In what consists the good fortune of a man marching under the red banner? Why is the man fortunate who gives his life for the cause of revolution? The pupils do not write about these things. Few eighth graders speak about the happiness of being a revolutionary fighter, a builder of a new life. And those who write, do it often in a dry, generalized manner. . . . The compositions reflect little the present-day reality. Everything in them is correct, but it is colorless and bloodless. . . . It is true that there are always words of love for Russia. At times, these words sound dryly, at other times, they are written in an elated manner, but they are lacking a feeling of truly patriotic fervor."[11]

Having apparently concluded from the analysis of the examination compositions that there was not sufficient emphasis on ideology in the teaching of literature, and guided by a determination to eliminate this shortcoming, the Ministry of Education introduced a change in the examination topics for those graduating from an eight-year school. In the spring examination of 1972 the following topics were suggested: "The kind hands of a mother," "Under the banner of

Lenin, our fatherland becomes more confident, from year to year, in its march forward," "When the country bids you to be a hero, everyone becomes a hero in our country," and "Communism is the youth of the world, and the young generation is to build it." One could wonder, what do such topics have in common with the study of literature proper? They could easily pass for topics in a course in social studies or even in Soviet history, and, besides, fifteen-year-old youths lack the necessary knowledge and life experience to do justice to the suggested topics.

Teachers of literature come out openly against such a course in the teaching of their subject. The futility of such an approach is obvious to them. They demand a return to the emphasis on the works of Pushkin, Lermontov, and Gogol', which are covered in grade eight and to which there is no return in the senior grades of secondary school. The titles of letters appearing in *Uchitel'skaya gazeta* are significant in themselves: "Let's return to Pushkin," or "Clichés."[12] School inspector O. El'tseva asks in her letter: "What do we want from the youngsters? What do we examine in such compositions?" and answers herself, "It is difficult to say." She claims that the intellectual scope of grade eight pupils is too limited to be able to handle the given topics satisfactorily and, therefore, the examination compositions are full of meaningless clichés, lacking logical connection and coherence.

Teacher S. Trembitskaya complains in her letter that there is no single question, in the grade eight Russian literature examination papers, which would enable the teacher to examine the pupils' knowledge of literature proper, and in particular of the works of the nineteenth-century classics of Pushkin, Lermontov, or Gogol'. It is only possible to suspect that the increased emphasis on ideology at the expense of Russian classical literature in the eight-year school is one of the reasons for the alienation of the senior secondary-school students from the Russian nineteenth-century classics.

The grade nine program is a continuation of the systematic course of study which began in grade eight, and it is mainly devoted to the classical literary heritage of the second half of the nineteenth century. The grade nine textbook[13] includes monographic chapters dealing with one particular subject or author, and survey chapters relating the most important literary events of a given period, with which the pupils become acquainted in passing. The new grade nine program has one important addition: the study of Dostoevsky has been reintroduced.

In grades eight and nine, together with the Russian nineteenth-century classics, works by West European poets and writers are also studied in translation. In the grade eight program are included Molière's *Bourgeois Gentilhomme* and fragments from Byron's *Childe Harold's Pilgrimage*, as well as several Byron poems in Lermontov's translation. In grade nine the pupils study *Hamlet*, Goethe's *Faust*, and several short works by Stendhal and Balzac.

Grade ten is devoted to the study of Soviet literature. It deals in detail with the creative work of Gorky, Mayakovsky, Blok, Esenin, Fadeev, Ostrovsky, Tolstoy, Sholokhov, and Tvardovsky. Other writers and poets are briefly mentioned in the survey topics dealing with the impact of the Revolution on Russian literature; with the literature of the thirties; with literature of the Second World War; and with contemporary literary problems. The discussion of Soviet writers who began to write before the Revolution trace their development, with particular emphasis on their revolutionary commitments. In the study of literary theory the concept of *partiynost'* is stressed, and the creative method of Soviet literature is discussed in detail. The importance and the guiding role of the Communist party as a leading force in Soviet literature is raised to the level of a dogmatic truth, and party literary politics become the foundation of creative artistic activity.

Upon graduation from grade ten a student is required to take a written as well as an oral examination in Russian literature. For the purpose of the oral examinations, which were reintroduced in 1969, a list of over thirty examination papers is usually published by the Ministry of Education early in the year. Each paper includes several questions: one is usually devoted to Soviet literature, which is studied in grade ten, and another to Russian classical literature, which is covered in grades eight and nine. A number of papers which include questions on poetry require the student to recite passages from poetry by heart. The students are required to demonstrate

a knowledge of the studied texts and an ability to draw on the material studied in the analysis of a work of literature; an ability to base the assessment of a work of art on the Leninist principle of partyness of literature; an understanding of the ideological essence of the works studied, of the problems encountered in these works and of their meaning at the time of their creation, and at the present day.[14]

The students know fairly well what to expect on an examination, and they have ample time to review the material required, with the help of their teachers. The results of the examinations are periodically analyzed in literary and educational publications. A survey of the 1969 Russian literature oral examinations, based on the answers of over a hundred graduating students from seven Moscow schools, indicates that the students know and understand Soviet literature much better than Russian classical literature.[15] They know well Lenin's articles on literature and are able to apply Lenin's precepts to Soviet literature and Soviet conditions, but they are unable to relate Lenin's articles on Tolstoy to the latter's creative work. Most students know the literary texts required and the factual material connected with Russian history and the biographies of the authors; however, very few can relate and connect the biography with the creative writing of a nineteenth-century writer or poet. One reason for the inadequate mastery of Russian prerevolutionary literature by secondary-school students may be the overemphasis on ideology in the process of teaching literature. The requirement to connect the prerevolutionary past with contemporary Soviet problems in a harmony might seem artificial and unconvincing to a secondary-school pupil who is not yet able to apply the precepts of Marxism-Leninism and of Soviet literary theory to Russian nineteenth-century classical literature and cannot therefore identify easily with the interpretations offered.

Graduation from secondary school is the end of literary education for all those who do not intend to specialize in this field. The objective of the school course of study is, therefore, not only to familiarize the pupil with the Russian literary heritage and modern Soviet literature, but also to give him the necessary tools for proper understanding and interpretation of the works of literature which he may encounter in the future. It is understood that this must be done so as not to depart from the general objectives of Soviet education; hence it must be based on the teachings of Marx and Lenin. In other words, the pupil must be taught to approach and analyze a work of art from the Leninist point of view. He must learn to appreciate and to like what it is necessary to like, and to criticize what the official party line requires him to criticize. It is a difficult task, and for many years literature has been taught as a dogma: a subject in which all the answers are given and the pupil has just to remember them.

With the post-Stalin liberalization and educational reforms, calls for creative teaching and more freedom and experimentation were heard. Discussions and polemics appearing in the early sixties on the pages of *Novy mir* and *Voprosy literatury* indicate clearly that the methods in use of teaching literature alienated the pupils from the subject. It has become "obvious from conversations with many pupils from different classes and schools that native literature is considered by the present-day pupils as one of the most boring subjects."[16] The dogmatic approach to the subject, the requirement to memorize long passages of poetry and, at times, prose, developed in the pupils an aversion not only to the material memorized, but to literature in general.[17] The calls of the post-Stalin reformers in education for learning with understanding have been received favorably, but they have not been reflected in school programs, which are the teacher's only guide. How could a teacher change the teaching methods and substitute creative study and discussion for memorization "if in the examination papers in Russian literature published this year by the Ministry of Education of the Ukraine, for grades nine, all fifty-two papers (without exception) require memorizing?"[18]

Regardless of what the program and instructions of higher standing bodies demand, the initiative for a review of the approach to the teaching of literature has come from the older pupils themselves. The pupils, aware of the polemics around the subject of literature, have begun to question the methods used and to express their views openly, a step no one could dare take before. At a graduation examination in one of the schools the question "Why do I love Mayakovsky?" was given. One pupil began his composition, "In my opinion, the topic is somewhat naïve. Could one love the poetry of Mayakovsky? Appreciate—yes.

But to love?"[19] Another pupil asked by the teacher whether she liked Chekhov's *Vishnevyy sad* (The Cherry Orchard) replied bluntly, "It is required by the program, that is why I read it."[20]

The reevaluation of literary values taking place in the immediate post-Stalin period and the division of the Soviet literary scene into several opposing camps introduced a great deal of confusion into the minds of the pupils and teachers alike. The long-established criteria of what is good literature were challenged, and poets and writers receiving priority treatment by Stalin and his followers were in danger of being demoted. At times the opinions of the teacher, the principal, and the officials from the Department of Education as to the interpretation of the works of a certain writer varied, and the pupil would have to find his own way in the mass of information and interpretation.

An interesting occurrence is reported in *Uchitel'skaya gazeta.*[21] A pupil had handed in an essay on the poetry of Mayakovsky in which the assessment of the poet was severely critical. The teacher marked it unsatisfactory. The pupil appealed to the principal, who liked the essay and remarked it, giving it the highest possible grade. The teacher appealed to the teachers' council, which compromised and awarded the essay a satisfactory mark. One can assume that the teacher was educated in Stalin's days and kept to the old line, while the principal was of the younger breed and appreciated the pupil's original and critical approach.

The polemics dealing with the methods of teaching literature taking place in the early sixties, in which many leading Soviet literary scholars, including Gudzy, Blagoy, Timofeev, and others participated, raised many problems to which no satisfactory answer could be found within the Soviet framework of education. The revised school programs of the Khrushchev era gave the teachers and pupils some freedom in the choice of material in the field of contemporary Soviet literature, but even this little concession turned into a challenge to the established patterns of the interpretation of a work of art, and to the basic method of Soviet literature, socialist realism.

In February 1964 the Moscow Department of Public Education and the Moscow Advanced Teacher Training Institute proposed the theme "Which of the works of contemporary soviet or foreign literature I like the most and why" as a city composition from grades nine to eleven. Eleven hundred and thirty-nine compositions were written, and in some instances their contents proved shocking to the conservative educators. The fact that thirty-four pupils discussed *Odin den' Ivana Denisovicha* (One Day in the Life of Ivan Denisovich) by Solzhenitsyn and an equal number discussed *Podnyataya tselina* (Virgin Soil Upturned) by Sholokhov could be a cause of alarm in itself. The majority of pupils preferred to write about young Soviet authors. *Idu na grozu* (I Go into the Storm) by Granin, *Tishina* (Silence) by Bondarev, and *Kollegi* (Colleagues) and *Zvezdnyy bilet* (A Ticket to the Stars) by Aksenov topped the list of the works discussed, Even more significant is the way in which these works were treated. The pupils rejected the established stereotypes and favored a direct and honest description of reality without embellishment.

One concept is encountered more often than any other in the compositions in which the boys and girls ponder over the merits of a literary work. This concept is *truth*. But what does *truth* mean to the young reader? What connotation does this concept have for him? To write *truthfully*, as he sees it, means not to embroider upon life.[22]

In the discussion of Aksenov's *Ticket to the Stars* the young readers were definitely on the side of the author and against those literary critics who condemn Aksenov for his distortion of the truth and for depicting Soviet youth in an unfavorable light. The students claimed that Aksenov understands the young generation well and that he "showed the life of some Moscow kids who are about seventeen with startling exactness."[23] Taking an active stand against the conservative critics who have tried to discredit Aksenov in the eyes of the reading public, one pupil stated, "Judging by the articles, one might think that the critics do not know life, that they were never young or that they now have no young acquaintances, and that they do not go out on the street and never look about them."[24] One can see in statements similar to this the rejection of the basic concept of socialist realism, in which Soviet life is to be depicted in its revolutionary development, i.e., as it should be, rather than as it is. It appears also that a gap exists between those who write professionally and earn their bread by writing, and those who are still young and bold enough to say what they think.

The little freedom in the choice of material the teacher was given proved a hindrance on the path to the goals of Soviet education.

The arrangement in which the teacher could choose himself what work of art to teach did not justify itself in practice. Many cases were discovered in which the teachers did not exercise the necessary selectivity, and in some cases the correct approach in the choice of the work of art for study in class.[25]

Soviet ideologists and leaders in the field of education could not permit a situation in which the accepted norms are questioned, and therefore the new programs, introduced in connection with the post-Khrushchev reforms, dispense with the little freedom given to the teacher, and return to the old pattern where no deviations are possible.

It is true that the new programs cover a wider range of material. Writers and poets like Dostoevsky, Bagritsky, Esenin, who have for many years been taboo to Soviet pupils, are now studied and discussed; but probing and searching for the truth is limited to a minimum. The point of view that suggests that there is only one truth from which no deviation is possible becomes stronger, and the contention that the pupil's opinion of a work of literature is of little importance is heard time and again. In one Leningrad school, questions for a seminar in grade ten on Soviet literature of the twenties were posted on a bulletin board for the students' information. One question read: "Who is, in your opinion, the main hero appearing in the works of literature of the twenties? Justify your opinion."[26] The author of the article which quotes this question is greatly disturbed by the fact that such a formulation should even appear. He asks:

Why is "in your opinion" here? Surely it is not a matter of opinion, conjecture, or personal preference. Don't we have definite, objective, and indisputable knowledge as to who is the main hero of the literature of the twenties? This, unnecessary, elusive [*zaigryvayushchee*] word does not support the pupil's independent thinking. On the contrary it lowers him by its irrelevance and falseness.[27]

It appears that the author of this statement is behind the times, and though the liberalization of literary education has been checked, there is no return to the old dogmatic approach.

There is, however, a danger that, as one teacher suggests, the pupil will continue to give the required answers, behind which there will be no personal commitment and no sincerity. It is a fact that "most pupils get away with generalizations behind which there is no clear thought nor personal relationship."[28] Pondering on the reasons for such an attitude, the same teacher asks: "Why do many students write plain 'correct' essays in which there is no real thought? Is it because of a distrust of the teacher?"[29] This teacher is not in a position to reply to this question. The answer is suggested in another place, namely, in Solzhenitsyn's *Rakovyy korpus* (Cancer Ward). A frank discussion between two bedridden youngsters, Demka and Asya, throws some light on the teaching methods in some Soviet schools and on the teacher-pupil relationship in cases where the pupil chooses to disagree with the teacher. Asya, a grade ten pupil, discussing with Demka the meaning and purpose of life, interjects:

"We had an essay about that at school: 'What does man live for?' They gave us study material full of cotton growers, milkmaids, Civil War heroes. 'What is your attitude to the brave deeds of Pavel Korchagin?' 'What is your attitude to the heroism of Matrosov?' "

Indeed, "What is your attitude?" asks Demka eagerly. Asya does not give any straight answer, but instead tells Demka about how literature is studied at school, and how essays are written:

"Well what? Should we do what they did? The teachers said we should. So we all wrote that we would. Why spoil things just before the exams? But Sashka Gromov said, 'Do I have to write all that? Can't I write what I really think?' Our teacher said, 'I'll give you what you really think. You will get the worst mark you've ever known.' And one girl wrote—you should have been there, 'I don't know yet whether I love my country or not.' Our teacher quacked like a duck: 'What a lousy idea! How dare you not love your country?' 'Perhaps I do love it, but I don't know. I must find out for myself.' 'What is there to find out? You ought to drink in love for your country with your mother's milk.' "[30]

Literary scholars and specialists in education understand what is wrong with the teaching of literature, but they are not in a position to change it. Instead, they are on the lookout for new ways to make the study of literature more interesting, appealing, and meaningful, but ways which would, at the same time, lead to the approved and desired goals. In line with this, a new method, which is known by the name of "problem teaching" or "problem-solving approach in instruction," has been developed. The work of literature is taken as a whole, but the class is required to concentrate only on one aspect of the work, on one or several problems. The teacher is supposed to choose problems "in which the pupils can become personally involved, problems creating in the class an atmosphere of 'collective emotional experience.' "[31] The problems of "friendship, honor and conscience, love, heroism, duty, meaning of life. Problems of our age: war, culture, creative work, ideals and life, freedom and necessity—all that divides the two worlds, the two social systems," are to be studied and discussed. The questions Why? How? and What for? are encouraged and "theory from an axiom becomes a theorem, which the pupil must prove, in order to move further."[32]

The teacher, however, remains in the same unenviable situation when the answers are given, and the class must reach the necessary conclusions with the help of a creative discussion. In other words, class discussions, exchanges of opinions, are not to search for new findings and solutions; they are conducted rather with the purpose of finding new ways to the same objective, of finding additional evidence that the solution given is the only true one.

The problem teaching method in literature has been in operation for several years and the first results are available. Some teachers complain that this method leads to neglecting the study of a work of literature in its artistic and ideological unity. Instead of becoming the main object of study, the novel or poem serves as a point of departure and an excuse for a generalized discussion not related to the work studied. Others claim that this system is in keeping with the students' interests and should be used as a means of involving the pupils in the study of literature.

The problem teaching method brings another problem to the fore—students often express opinions about a work of art or offer solutions to a problem which are different from those accepted. In his discussion of literature teaching methods the notable Soviet scholar N.I. Kudryashev writes,

unfortunately, in the opinion of many senior secondary school students—not without our own guilt—the task of solving complicated problems should be left to lessons in mathematics or physics. In literature everything has been solved. If an argument develops, one simply has to express his own opinion. This should not take up too much time or effort, because there could be "no argument about tastes" and each opinion is justified.[33]

Kudryashev, of course, sharply disagrees with such approaches to the study of literature. He says, "It is necessary to change radically such dilettante notion about the study of literature. . . . The creative work of a writer is an 'examination of the truth,' and it is important to have a truthful and objectively correct opinion rather than anyone's 'personal' opinion."[34] The teacher is entrusted by the party with the task of forming in the pupil a truly Marxist-Leninist understanding of a work of art, Kudryashev goes on. The teacher is committed to this task by the partyness of Soviet literature study and teaching. The discussion of the problem teaching method, which has been going on for several years, does not lead to any sweeping conclusions. It has been even suggested that the newly acclaimed problem teaching method "is not a separate method altogether"[35] but rather a component of other methods, and provision should be made for the use of it whenever the teaching situation is most favorable.

It is not the first time that literature teachers have been forced to move from one extreme to another in order to try to get across the necessary message to the student. The situation of the teacher is indeed unenviable, because he is required, at times, to find a middle course in a situation where no middle exists. In the forties and fifties vulgar sociologism in literature was vehemently attacked and

some teachers, afraid of sociolizing, have begun to avoid sociopolitical characterization of literary phenomena, conflicts and heroes. . . . There is no need to demonstrate the harm of vulgar sociolizing. But just as harmful is an "immanent" study of an artistic work in isolation from the social struggle which it reflects and which led to its appearance.[36]

The shortcomings in the teaching of literature, as they are understood by Soviet educators, and "the dislike of literature by many students could be explained by the formal character of the information imparted in the process of teaching literature."[37] The author of the above statement decries, in an open letter to the editor of *Literatura v shkole*, the lack of communication between the top educators, scholars in literature, and the ordinary teacher. He reproaches the literary and education establishment for looking down on the teachers. He claims that the teacher is often censured for shortcomings in the teaching of literature while in reality there is very little he can do to improve it. The literature textbooks are written by literary scholars, and the ordinary teacher has little say in what is to be studied, and how.

V. Stakhov writes in the journal *Zvezda* that the poor state of literature textbooks and the odd ways in which they are published are no secret in literary and educational circles. He says that it is common knowledge that "the writing and republishing of textbooks has become a monopoly of certain people,"[38] A situation which surely has a detrimental effect on the quality of the books.

Much is being done by Soviet authorities to educate the young generation with a clear understanding of the basic party concepts on literature. All this effort is apparently of little avail. A recent report of an inspection of the Russian

Republic schools does not complain about a lack of contextual knowledge of the works of Pushkin or Tolstoy. It states, however, that "The graduates have a very remote idea about what *partiynost'* and *narodnost'* of literature are, they mastered only superficially the questions connected with the ideological and class struggle in the field of literature and art."[39] It is possible only to surmise that secondary-school pupils are simply too young to be interested in and able to cope with these highly theoretical problems, which are remote from their personal experience and not connected with their daily lives.

Notwithstanding the harsh self-criticism of Soviet teachers and educators in regard to the state of the teaching and study of literature in the Soviet school, Russian literature in general, and the nineteenth-century classics in particular, belong to the treasury of world literature. Gogol's *Dead Souls*, Tolstoy's *Voyna i mir* (War and Peace) or Dostoevsky's *Prestuplenie i nakazanie* (Crime and Punishment) are masterpieces of craftsmanship and insight. And yet, claims are being made that the secondary-school students become alienated from prerevolutionary classical literature.[40] A study and close examination of what teenagers read in their spare time indicates that the list contains very few prerevolutionary titles. The interest in classical literature is greater in the evening schools for workers and rural youths, but there the students are several years older and most of them hold full-time jobs.

The alleged alienation of teenagers from Russian classical literature has several explanations. One reason is probably the formal approach to the teaching of literature, in which a specific predetermined message of a social content is to be delivered. Another reason is apparently the peculiarity of our age. The pace of life is now much faster than a generation before. Teenagers all over the world want to be in tune with the times. They want to reach out for the future as soon as possible. They do not yet approach literature by relating to the eternal problems dealt with in the works of Tolstoy and Dostoevsky, nor are there many who are ready to appreciate the purely artistic qualities of a literary masterpiece. Therefore, they read contemporary literature which, it seems to them, takes them into the very core of pulsing life and adds a new dimension to their daily reality. In Soviet society it is a temporary process, because as soon as the young people mature and face real life they realize that there is nothing in contemporary Russian literature superior to Tolstoy, Dostoevsky, Pushkin, Chekhov, or Turgenev.

3 Literature in Higher Education

It is natural that the state of teaching literature at school is related to the personality of the teacher and the educational institution that qualifies him for his job. The number of teachers of Russian language and literature in the Soviet Union is over a quarter of a million, and over 70 percent are graduates of institutions of higher learning.[1] Each year the universities and pedagogical institutes turn out thousands of new Russian language and literature teachers who become employed in the various schools of the vast system.

There is a considerable difference between a graduate of a university and a pedagogical institute. While the first receives the qualifications of a philologist and a teacher of Russian language and literature, the latter is only a teacher. The main objective of the pedagogical institutes, which are supervised by the local ministries of education, is to satisfy the growing demand for teachers, and therefore the emphasis there is on subjects taught at school and on teaching methods. Besides, since graduates of most institutes are qualified to teach several subjects, they are supposed to carry a heavy study load, and they are left with little time for independent reading and study.

A graduate of a university with the qualifications of a philologist teacher of Russian language and literature has to cover a five-year course of study in a major department which in the larger universities is called the philological faculty (in the smaller ones, it can be united with the study of history, and called the historical-philological faculty). The study of different languages and literatures as well as linguistics is coordinated within a philological faculty. A faculty is usually subdivided into smaller departments (*otdelenie*), as in the Moscow State University, where there are departments of Russian language and literature, Slavic philology, Romance-Germanic philology, classic philology, and structural and applied linguistics. The major departments within a faculty are in turn subdivided into smaller units (*kafedra*), the chairmen of which are responsible for one particular area of study only. The Moscow State University has *kafedry* of Russian language, theory of literature, history of Russian literature, Russian oral folklore, history of Soviet literature, history of foreign literatures, general and comparative historical linguistics, structural and applied linguistics, classic linguistics, French language, English language, and German language.[2]

The structure of the Philological Faculty of Leningrad University is somewhat different. It has major departments of West European, Scandinavian, Finnic-Ugric, and classic philologies and mathematical linguistics, as well as a major department of Russian language and literature, which is in turn subdivided into three minor departments of Russian language, Russian literature, and Soviet literature.[3]

One might assume that most of the time spent in a department of Russian language and literature would be devoted to these particular subjects. Such an assumption would be erroneous—more than half of the total time is spent on the study of other subjects, some of which are just vaguely related to the student's future profession. Over 15 percent of the total time is spent on the study of different aspects of Marxist-Leninist philosophy; over 20 percent on the study of foreign languages and literatures; and up to 10 percent on subjects related to education and to future professional employment. In addition there are compulsory classes in physical education which each student must attend. The remaining time is divided between Russian language and Russian literature. This is not to say that some subjects other than Russian language and Russian literature included in the curriculum are of no use to the student. On the contrary, the study of foreign languages and foreign literatures is of prime importance; the more so since works from foreign literatures included in the school curriculum are taught by the same teacher as Russian language and literature. However, very little time remains for the study of the subject of the main specialty, leading to an "extreme overloading of the programs in history of literature at the philological and historical-philological faculties of universities and pedagogical institutes,"[4] which in turn results in a situation in which the student cannot absorb all the material covered and "in most cases he just sits listening passively to the lectures about works of art which he has not even read."[5]

This is a serious problem to which there is, so far, no solution in sight. Complaints about the lack of time to cover the program were heard time and again at the conference about teaching of literature in institutions of higher learning, organized by *Voprosy literatury* at the Philological Faculty of the Moscow State University,[6] in which many leading literary scholars participated. The authors of articles which appeared after the conference are alarmed by the trend in which "the relative weight of special disciplines (literature and native language) in the curriculum of philological departments declines from year to year."[7] In pedagogical institutes only "less than a quarter of all the study time is devoted to all kinds of Russian literary studies (including methodology)."[8] This situation has been even more aggravated by the shortening of the course of study in pedagogical institutes to four years, which was announced in the summer of 1964, and which was to be introduced over a period of three years with the incoming students in the fall of 1964.[9]

It is obvious that such a shortening of the period of study has affected the level of specialist training, and calls for the reintroduction of five-year study programs in the institutes are voiced by many scholars of high reputation. An open letter in *Uchitel'skaya gazeta*, signed collectively by the Rector of the

Leningrad Pedagogical Institute and other notable scholars, advocates the separation of joint specialization in Russian language and literature. It is claimed that the time assigned in the curriculum for the study of Russian literature is so small that "nothing, except superficial surveys, can be covered. No more than six hours are devoted to the study of the creative work of such giants as Pushkin, Tolstoy, Dostoevsky."[10]

It is not surprising that school authorities turn their criticism of the poor state of the teaching of literature at school to universities and pedagogical institutes. The situation becomes paradoxical, however, when university teachers in turn blame the middle school for their own poor performance.

It is assumed that a student who has passed the entrance examinations satisfactorily in Russian language and literature[11] and who has been admitted to a philological faculty knows the material covered at school and is prepared to carry on from the place where he has left off at school. In practice, this is not the case. Students awarded medals for excellent performance at school often show an almost total lack of knowledge of the foundations of literature. P. Pustovoyt, who examined the gold medalists applying for admittance to the philological faculty of the Moscow State University, was surprised to learn that "L.N. Tolstoy was born in . . . 1808, and that the novel *War and Peace* was written in . . . 1896, that Belinsky survived the Crimean War and serfdom, and died in 1879. It came out accidentally that one medalist did not even know when Karl Marx was born, lived, and died."[12]

It is clear that in the light of such facts it would be necessary to reexamine the university literature programs and rectify the low level of the school graduates by the introduction of a system in which the material covered at school would be reviewed and put in the proper perspective. The Soviet authorities realize that there is a glaring discrepancy between the level achieved by many school graduates and the level expected in the first-year university classes. To improve this situation the Central Committee of the Communist party and the Council of Ministers of the USSR issued a decree which envisages the establishment of preparatory departments at institutions of higher learning for those who graduate from evening secondary schools and schools in rural areas, and who have one year of practical work experience.[13] After one year of successful study, those who have passed their examinations will be admitted to normal first-year university classes without entrance examinations. It remains to be seen how this new step will affect the level of literary preparation of those who enter university. In any case, several years must pass before it will be possible to assess whether there is a positive change, while in the meantime it often happens

that a student graduates from university, passes the state examination, writes a diploma work, but he does not master the elementary skills which are a must for a literary scholar; he does not understand what a genre or an artistic form is, i.e., what it is assumed that he should know from the first year at university. Why?

Because the first-year lecturer assumes that he has learned it at school, the second-year lecturer thinks that it was taught in the first year, the third-year lecturer is sure that it was given in the second year.[14]

If this is the case with day classes, there is even more concern about evening and correspondence courses—especially since more than half of the future Russian literature teachers graduate in evening and correspondence departments of philological faculties.[15] It is of little help that it takes six years to graduate in these departments. It is common knowledge that students receive substandard education there, while their diplomas carry the same weight as received by those who study in day classes. The academic staff and administration are surely well aware of this situation since "it is no secret at the faculty that the specialist training at our [Moscow University] evening department reminds us somewhat of eyewash [ochkovtiratel'stvo]. We give diplomas to the evening students which are equal to those of the day students, but we surely give them much less knowledge."[16] In all probability the demand for Russian language and literature teachers, who may even be unqualified, is so great that this is the only way in which it is possible to train them without depriving the national economy of a substantial part of its labor force, and without going into additional expenses which would be required to train all these teachers in day classes.

Students enrolled in a philological faculty and specializing in Russian language and literature are going through a rigid course of study which includes a number of compulsory courses, both in language and literature. In language study there are introductory linguistics, general linguistics, Old Church Slavonic, Russian dialectology, history of Russian language, modern Russian language, and applied stylistics of Russian language.

The study of Russian literature includes courses in the introduction of literary study and theory, theory of literature, Russian national folklore, history of Russian literature, and literature of the peoples of the USSR. There are also elective courses in the field of specialization. The curriculum in Russian language and literature in a pedagogical institute is structured along the same lines, with the only difference that there are fewer elective courses and seminars where independent study and research are emphasized; instead, the practical sides of teaching are stressed.

The material in the literary part of the program is distributed in the four to six years of study according to the principles of chronology and historicity.[17] It begins in the first semester with the introductory course in literary study and theory (vvedenie v literaturovedenie) which is supposed to acquaint the students with some new essential notions from literary theory, as well as to fortify and to review some of the ideas learned at school. The students deal in this course with notions of form, composition, plot; with the analysis of different genres and kinds of literatures; with problems of ideynost', partiynost', narodnost', and klassovost' of literature.[18]

Another course in theory of literature is given in the last year at the university or institute. The purpose of this course is "to summarize what the students have already learned, to illuminate their knowledge with the light of the latest achievements in literary science, and to direct the attention of the future teachers to the most urgent problems of teaching literature at school."[19] This course, closely connected with the courses in Marxist philosophy, teaches the student to approach a work of literature from a Marxist point of view. It also gives in passing some attention to different "reactionary" schools and trends in literature taking root, both in prerevolutionary Russia and in the West, with the purpose of putting the students on guard in order to be able to detect works of literature which do not conform to the official party line. It is suggested that institutions of higher learning must take an offensive stand in the ideological struggle taking place on the contemporary literary scene and to introduce accordingly themes and topics which would put the problem in the proper light. As an example for the study of literary theory we might consider the topic suggested by A.I. Revyakin, from the Moscow Lenin Pedagogical Institute: "Contemporary reactionary modernism and revisionism in literature and art."[20]

The existing distribution of the theoretical courses between the first and the last years of study has resulted in a great deal of criticism. Opponents of this pattern of instruction claim that "theory of literature should be mastered by the students not episodically, but during all four years (at university—five) of study,"[21] together with the study of literary schools, trends, and texts. They claim that a study of theory which is detached from literary texts and which is not based on the immediate analysis of works of literature is irrelevant and of little practical use. Those in favor of this pattern of instruction claim that the first-year student has the necessary background in literature from the study of this subject at school, since he read and analyzed most of the works mentioned in the introductory course with his school teacher. It is very doubtful whether it is possible to build a solid theoretical literary education on the shaky foundations of a secondary-school background in Russian literature.

Between the two theoretical courses there are three to four years of study in which the bulk of Russian literature is covered. Instruction is carried out in general courses of history of literature, special literary courses, special seminars, and practical training classes.

The general courses of literary history are lecture courses in which "we first of all propagate our world outlook and affirm our conception of literary aesthetic views."[22] It is suggested that such courses "should be structured not by writers, but by trends, schools, and styles."[23] In most universities and institutes the general courses in history of literature are survey courses given in chronological order, beginning with spoken folk literature and ending with contemporary Soviet literature. The scope of each course is determined by a program approved by the appropriate ministry. The programs include lists of primary sources, literary histories, and criticism for required and suggested reading. The programs are also supplied with comprehensive introductions which outline the basic problems to be dealt with in these courses, and emphasize the necessary approach to be used in the study of the material concerned. An approved program establishes the periodization to be followed and breaks down the material into smaller units and sections. The introductory and explanatory notes to all programs for Russian prerevolutionary literature resemble each other. They have in common the requirement to study what the classics of Marxism-Leninism and the nineteenth-century Russian revolutionary democrats had to say on the subject. They require an approach to the literature of any period from a class point of view.

The obligation of a lecturer in a general course is to give the students an understanding of the basic features of the literary process of a certain period by referring to the characteristic of representative writers of that period, of their connections, differences, and struggle. It is impossible, due to shortage of time, to discuss and analyze all works mentioned in these courses. It is, however, the lecturer's duty to give *"examples* of historical and literary analysis of works of art (epic, dramatic, lyric); peculiarities of style for writers belonging to different schools; characteristic of an epoch; historical and literary background, etc."[24]

It is suggested that the main objective of literature is to "help man to change reality, understanding it in a broad sense."[25] The purpose of literary history is, therefore, to restore the initial meaning of a work of art and to relate it to the literary process taking place in a given period, and to determine the reasons that provoke the writer's reaction to reality. Since literature is a reflection of the people's different interests, it must be studied in connection with these interests; in connection with the people's ideological, economic, and social interests and problems. The lecturer's duty is to restore the initial meaning of a work of literature because "upon finding itself in a system of relationships existing in a given society, in a situation of ideological struggle, in most complex conditions, a work of art can be understood differently than it was conceived by the author; it may unexpectedly acquire new meaning, and sometimes several new meanings."[26]

Proceeding from the assumption that "an objective evaluation of a work of art is possible only when it is interpreted from an historical point of view,"[27] the interpretation of literature is based on the interpretation of history which is given, of course, from a Marxist-Leninist point of view, and which expresses itself, in literary history, in its connection with the three phases of what is termed the social liberation movement in nineteenth-century Russia. According to Lenin,[28] progressive literary leadership passed from the social revolutionaries, who were members of the nobility, and who were connected with the Decembrists movement in the beginning of the nineteenth century, to the liberal intelligentsia of the eighteen-sixties (*raznochintsy*), and later, near the end of the century, with the appearance of Gorky, to the proletariat.

Since literature is regarded as "the most active participant of the liberation struggle, its mirror,"[29] the teaching about the liberation movements becomes the point of departure for all literary studies of the nineteenth century, and the emphasis must be on works of literature that depict and foster these movements. The lecturer in the history of literature, by virtue of being also an expert in Marxist philosophy, "is an interpreter of a work of art who reconciles the contradictions between the meaning which was put into it by the author, and the meaning which was extracted by the reader."[30]

The general courses in history of literature, which are basically lecture courses without the student's active participation and without exchange of opinions, have drawn a great deal of criticism. The discussion of this pattern of instruction began with a fierce attack on the system by N.K. Gudzy,[31] who suggested cutting down the lectures to a minimum and claimed that "*special* courses are necessary, as they were in the old times at the Moscow University, and as they are up to now, in West European universities. There, no general courses are offered since their uselessness is obvious."[32] The existing system is also criticized by students, who claim that it is impossible to sit at lectures, taking notes, for six to eight hours a day.[33] Most literary scholars who have expressed their views on this question are, however, against the abolition of the general courses, though many are for a definite improvement in their content.

The special courses mentioned by Gudzy, now in practice in institutions of higher learning in the USSR, are also predominantly lecture courses in which the course topics are narrowed down to one particular writer, genre, or problem of literary theory. The instructors in such courses are encouraged to involve students in discussion, to raise controversial questions, and to assign oral reports. Nevertheless, in most cases there is no real dialogue, since the instructor is supposed, at all times, "to guide the student's thoughts, to channel it into the right direction."[34]

A Canadian exchange student at the Moscow State University, who had participated in the 1966-67 academic year in a special course entitled "Dostoevsky and the Beginning of the Age," testified that there were fifteen students in a class instructed two hours weekly by the Candidate of Science, K.I. Tyun'kin, and that the course consisted solely of lectures. At times, the instructor would ask factual questions in order to make sure that the students kept up with their reading.[35]

The special seminars, like the special courses, are aimed at a deeper study of the separate sections of the main course. Beginning with the second year at a university and the third year at a pedagogical institute, the students can choose special courses and seminars in the field of their narrow specialization. Each year one to three courses and seminars are to be taken which may run one semester or the whole year. At the end of such a course or seminar an oral test is usually given.[36] At the end of a general course in the history of literature the student takes a formal examination.

Thematically there is no distinction between special courses and special seminars. The basic difference is in methodology. A special seminar begins with introductory lectures, information on bibliographical sources, and the assignment of topics for reports. The student can choose a topic from a list suggested by the instructor. "The report (which must be in written form) is submitted to the seminar leader and to the opponent, for information, ahead of time."[37] It is suggested that it is wise to have several opponents, each commenting on a different aspect of the report. "For example, the first opponent is supposed to give a general evaluation of the report, the second to analyze its composition, the third language, the fourth bibliography in use, etc."[38]

With so many official opponents it seems that no time is left for a stimulating discussion, the more so since the opponents have an opportunity to get acquainted with the report ahead of time and to prepare themselves for their part in the seminar, while the rest of the class is handicapped in the exchange of opinions because it hears the report for the first time.[39] There is a danger that such a seminar may turn into a dialogue between the reporter and the opponents, with the instructor acting as a moderator. As it is, "one of the main shortcomings of the work of our seminars is students' passivity,"[40] and one may suspect that the official opponent system is introduced with the purpose of getting at least some action. Otherwise

a seminar looks sometimes like this: a student reads a poorly structured, or a completely loose report, from loose notes; at the same time many students, having covered themselves with purses or briefcases, are busy doing their own things: they converse, write notes to each other, study for the next class in foreign language, etc. After the report there is a tiring pause. The instructor suggests that the students discuss the report, but there are no volunteers.[41]

The same Canadian exchange student participated also in a special seminar at the Moscow State University for fourth and fifth year students on Dostoevsky's *Crime and Punishment*, in the winter of 1966-67, and he stated that the reports were usually long. Many reports were inadequate and the instructor would usually criticize them and fill in the gap left in the subject after the report. Nevertheless, the instructor required the students to keep up with their work, called them in for individual consultations, and asked factual questions. The bibliography suggested is limited to approved Russian and Soviet titles, and the Soviet students have no access to foreign sources not sanctioned for use. In the library of the Moscow University there are studies on Dostoevsky by Berdyaev, Shestov, and Ivanov, but no Soviet undergraduate student can get them. Only exchange students from the West can take them out after having secured permission from the chairman of the department.

One might suspect that a shortage of study material is the cause of students' passivity, but this is not the case. On the contrary, there is an abundance of methodological aids published in Soviet times. Over a hundred *Seminariy*[42] texts appeared after the Revolution, but it seems that they did not stimulate the learning process. Lately the authors of the *Seminariy* texts have encountered much criticism. They are accused of "forcefully thrusting upon the students certain points of view,"[43] by suggesting topics for discussion in seminar classes in which the questions predetermine the answers. For example: "Lavretsky: a characteristic representative of the progressive part of nobility intelligentsia," or "The critique of the unsound ideas in Chernyshevsky's philosophical theories: anthropologism, overestimation of power of intellect, elements of idealism in the interpretation of society development laws."[44] Questions of this kind and introductions to *Seminariy*, which give a detailed outline of the topics suggested and a depiction of the author's creative activity, make it unnecessary and impossible for the student to work independently. Indeed, what can he add that is new, or how can he challenge what has been written by a well-known authority in an official publication? It is too well known that there are no such possibilities, and hence a seminar becomes a platform for the repetition of the well-known "truths," at this time, not by the lecturer but by students in the form of "reports which are on a low scholarly level, in which description often substitutes for analysis, in retelling characters and work content, in compilation of critical works, in excessive use of clichés."[45]

The writer of these lines was fortunate to have an opportunity to visit, in the spring of 1970, a number of special course and seminar classes at the Moscow State University. One seminar on Tolstoy dealt with the topic *Anna Karenina* and *Gospoda Golovlevy* (The Golovlevs). The reporter chose to compare the two novels as histories of two families. The official opponent criticized the report severely, but not on essential issues. The main criticism was rather directed at the organization and style of the paper. Other students spoke only when asked and urged by the instructor. Their performance was limited to short statements on their attitude to the report. There were no polemics and, in essence, no discussion. A spark of animation was introduced when the only male student in the seminar made the point that he did not agree with the very principle of comparing the families in the two novels. He said that while in *Anna Karenina* there is a family problem, in *The Golovlevs* there is no true family. There is an individual who step by step destroys the family. This student obviously had the right idea, but lack of articulation and experience prevented him from explaining properly what he wanted to say, the more so since the official opponent, with the help of the instructor, did not let him even finish his thought. They attacked him by stating that according to Engels the state is formed by separate families. *Anna Karenina* and *The Golovlevs* are examples of degenerating families in a bourgeois society. Since the family is the basic unit of society, the degenerating families signify the degeneration of the bourgeois society. It sounds very simple, but the individual is lost in this approach, which fails to recognize that the family is made up of individuals, each different from the other.

After the discussion and the instructor's final remarks the reporter acknowledged and agreed with the criticism directed at his report and promised to correct the final version of his term paper. Even if the reporter had tried to argue with the opponent, he would have no chance because the opponent seemed to be better versed in the teachings of the classics of Marxism-Leninism, and at each step of the argument he resorted to their help. There can be, of course, an argument with another student, but there is no argument when Marx and Lenin come into the picture.

There is no required or suggested reading list for this seminar except the titles included in the official program of the nineteenth-century Russian literature. It is assumed, however, that the student has to know what Chernyshevsky, Lenin, and Gorky have to say about Tolstoy. In the beginning of the seminar the instructor, N.V. Nikolaeva, recommends the titles she thinks it is beneficial for the student to know, in particular those which have just appeared. She suggests the studies on Tolstoy by Gudzy,[46] Khrapchenko,[47] Bursov,[48] Kupreyanova,[49] Asmus,[50] and Eykhenbaum.[51] In preparation of the reports some students resort to the published *Seminariy*,[52] which suggest an extensive bibliography for the study of Tolstoy. These suggested reading lists often contain works on Tolstoy by prerevolutionary authors, including those by K. Leont'ev and D. Merezhkovsky.[53] In his introduction to the *Seminariy* on Tolstoy B.I. Burshov gives a critical evaluation of these sources. He has some praise for them, but he does not fail to warn the students of the general faulty approach to Tolstoy by these prerevolutionary authors.[54] The students mention the names of Leont'ev and Merezhkovsky in their reports, but they are hesitant to elaborate too much on them lest they resort to praising what should be condemned. There is a feeling that few students really study and read these sources, and those who do approach them with a preconceived notion of what to expect.

The Soviet curriculum also provides for practical training classes in literature which accompany all lecture classes from the first to the last semester. By practical training is meant the development of practical skills achieved by the reading of difficult texts, in old Russian literature in particular, collective analysis of literary works and problems, and metric analysis of poetry. In practical training classes the students are given daily homework assignments in the form of short oral and written reports dealing with the problems discussed. The subject matter studied in a practical training class depends on what course it accompanies, since it is not considered to be a separate subject but rather an integral part of a main course.

After having covered the whole course of study and passed all the tests and examinations, the student of a philological faculty is ready to graduate. In order to receive his graduation diploma he is supposed to take state examinations in several subjects, including history of the Communist Party of the USSR, modern Russian language, history of Russian literature, and methods of teaching Russian language and literature. Some students, instead of taking the state examinations, prefer to write a diploma work and to defend it publicly. The state examinations are oral and the questions to appear in the examination papers are published ahead of time. Those who prefer to write a diploma work must secure permission from the appropriate department chairman. Complaints are being voiced on the pages of the Soviet press that some students apply for permission to write diploma works in order to avoid the long and tiring procedure of the state examinations. One Soviet academician states bluntly that many poor students prefer to write diploma works because they are in danger of failing the examinations. The works such students produce are of low quality and have no scholarly value. He suggests that only the best students, in institutions of higher learning where qualified academic advisors are available, be given permission to write diploma works.[55]

Upon graduation a young specialist is, in most cases, given a Russian language and literature teacher's job, in which he must work for at least several years. The better students usually apply for admittance to the *aspirantura* (graduate department). Those who graduate from a pedagogical institute devote their graduate research mainly to problems of teaching and education in the area of Russian language and literature, while graduates from a philological faculty at a university go into graduate studies with a view to university teaching and advanced literary research.

A literature student accepted to the *aspirantura* is not required to take any formal courses. He is supposed to pass several examinations, however, known as the candidate minimum (*Kandidatskiy minimum*), which include Marxist-Leninist philosophy, foreign language and literature, and Russian literature, and to defend a dissertation. The Russian literature course is divided into four parts: old Russian literature; eighteenth-century Russian literature; ninteenth-century Russian literature; and Soviet literature, which includes also the prerevolutionary period of 1890-1917. A graduate student is examined only in the part of the literature course connected with his dissertation and his area of specialization.

There are in the Soviet Union over two thousand graduate students in philology working towards the degree of Candidate of Philological Sciences.[56] Out of this number up to five hundred are doing graduate research in philology in scientific research institutes, not connected with any teaching institutions. Here are some of the narrow specialization areas in philological sciences in which a graduate degree can be obtained at the Moscow State University: Russian language, Russian literature, Soviet literature, literature of the peoples of the USSR, Marxist-Leninist aesthetics and ethics, literature of foreign countries, theory of literature, theory of linguistics, structural, applied, and mathematical linguistics, and folklore.[57] Most students after having completed their graduate studies join the ranks of university teachers, though many remain in research institutes and continue to work there.

The highest academic degree of Doctor of Philological Sciences may be awarded to individuals holding the academic degree of Candidate of Philological Sciences or the academic title of professor, and who have publicly defended a dissertation, published works, textbooks, and advanced research. All academic degrees awarded by institutions of higher learning and research institutes must be approved by the Higher Certification Commission (*VAK—Vysshaya attestatsionnaya komissiya*), a body which examines and confirms the award of higher degrees on behalf of the Ministry of Higher and Secondary Specialized Education. The same goes for academic titles. It may happen that a degree awarded by a university is not approved by the Higher Certification Commission. The commission has the right to revoke degrees and titles "in case they have not been of concrete use in the field of research, if their works do not have value for science and production."[58]

The teaching and study of literature in Soviet universities must be considered and discussed as an integral part of the whole Soviet educational system, and therefore it would be naïve to expect drastic changes in one subject while the system as a whole remains unchanged. For that matter, the discussions and polemics taking place in the sixties about the shortcomings of university literary education were summarized by a high official of the Ministry of Higher and Secondary Specialized Education, who stated

The system of teaching, developed in our higher education—general lectures, seminars, special courses, term papers, practical training on the job, and diploma work—has been tested by many years of experience, and in its foundations, it is in keeping with contemporary requirements. The new aims in the area of specialist training improvement do not require any radical breaking of the old system.[59]

In light of the foregoing discussion one could wonder whether the Russians are not too critical of themselves; whether they do not set for themselves standards beyond their reach. It is possible only to surmise that the critical approach to the teaching of literature is a reaction to a certain change in values of the Soviet youth, taking place after the Twentieth Party Congress. This change means delivering the message in a more sophisticated manner, but the message, however, remains essentially unchanged because the university programs in Russian literature from the Stalin era are not much different from what we have today, and the interpretation of the works studied is based now on theoretical concepts similar to those in use for years.

4

The Russian Classical Literary Heritage and the Basic Concepts of Soviet Literary Education

Every effort is being made to retain all the best works of the Russian literary giants of the nineteenth century in the literature programs of the Soviet schools and universities. There is even a trend in Soviet scholarship to place the best literary work of the Soviet period in the tradition of the nineteenth-century Russian classics. Lenin repeated time and again that it was necessary "to assimilate critically all that is valuable from the preceding culture."[1] Some Soviet scholars go even further and claim that socialist realism and its best representatives are continuing the literary traditions of the great nineteenth-century Russian writers. Konstantin Fedin is thought of as one who continues Turgenev's "traditions of intellectualism" and shares his ability as "a chronicler of his epoch, a creator of unforgettable women characters,"[2] and Sholokhov is regarded as a writer who further develops Tolstoy's style. Some Soviet critics even complain because there is no visible link in the educational programs to connect Mayakovsky with Pushkin and Lermontov.[3]

As far as the teaching of contemporary Soviet literature is concerned, the emphasis is on authors and works well known and approved by political and party leaders. The latest works appearing in Soviet literary magazines and journals do not find their way into programs of educational institutions. It is little wonder, since much of contemporary Soviet literature passes unnoticed: "Four-fifths of the new works of literature receive no mention in literary criticism."[4] The same is true of the literary groups that continued to exist in the early postrevolutionary period: "Their aesthetic platforms are treated in an obscure manner."[5]

Thus, the teaching of literature and the humanities is "mainly turned to the past, toward the study of the history and literature of the presocialist epoch,"[6] and the teacher must possess the necessary skill to extract from a work of art created in a bourgeois society, and by an artist alien to the socialist order of things, the components most useful for Soviet education. This skill is based on a knowledge of the basic precepts of Marx and Lenin. In practice these precepts are narrowed down, by Soviet literary theory, to a number of guidelines according to which every work of literature is to be judged. These principles are discussed in the Soviet theory of literature under the headings *klassovost'* (class character), *ideynost'* (moral substance), *narodnost'* (national spirit), and *partiynost'* (partyness, party principles and spirit). Soviet literary history and criticism make use of these principles in different combinations and proportions depending on which work of art is being discussed.

It may seem to the uninitiated student of Russian literature that the principle of *klassovost'* is the least complicated, and that by proceeding from the Leninist assumption that there are several cultures in each contemporary bourgeois nation (*natsional'nost'*) it would be enough to establish the class background of a writer and to go on from there. The fact is, however, that "the analysis of the class direction of the writer's creative work presents one of the most difficult problems in the study of literature."[7]

The dilemma in applying the principle of *klassovost'* is that if the class background of a writer were to be the only measure of his *klassovost'*, there would be no room in Soviet education for the works of most prerevolutionary writers. The principle of *klassovost'* is that a member of a certain class expresses the class consciousness of his own stratum: "Whether the artist wants it or not he is connected with his epoch; but he is always an offspring of his class, and certain class interests, certain forms of class struggle, are always reflected in his work."[8] The efforts to demonstrate this very truth and to find evidence that the nineteenth-century classics expressed the views of a bourgeois society are objectives of the so-called vulgar sociologists in literature. In connection with the denunciation of vulgar sociologism and with the increased effort to emphasize the link between socialist culture and the best writing of the past, this proposition has been put forth:

In reality classes are not isolated one from another, but find themselves in a complex interaction. Owing to this, the ideologies of writers belonging to different classes often have, along with marked differences, similar, common traits. These similar, sometimes common, traits are the reason for the fact that a writer, while being a representative of a certain class, also expresses to a degree the feelings, moods, strivings, and interests of persons belonging to other classes.[9]

Thus, it is hinted that a member of one class can express to a degree the views of another class. According to Marxism-Leninism this does not mean, however, that the artist adopts a nonclass position. He remains consciously or unconsciously a member of his own class, and he speaks in the name of his class: "Even if an artist, as has happened many times, has become convinced of the historical injustice of the interests of his class, and, being honest with himself and with others, refuses to defend them, it does not mean in the least that by doing so he is going over to the position of another class."[10]

The nineteenth-century Russian classical writers were members of a class whose interests were far from those of the radicals and revolutionaries, and although some of these writers were progressive for their time and age, their aims and philosophy of life did not come near the aims of the working class and the proletariat, in the sense in which these terms are understood today. The accepted (in Marxist-Leninist theory) division into classes can hardly be adopted for the purpose of analyzing the class character of Pushkin and his contemporaries.

With the denunciation of vulgar sociologism, coupled with the effort to reestablish the nineteenth-century classics in a prominent place in Soviet education, the importance of *klassovost'* as a guiding principle for the evaluation of a prerevolutionary work of art diminishes. In the latest textbooks on the theory of literature the discussion of *klassovost'* as such is omitted altogether. "Class struggle," it is suggested, "has different stages and degrees of development. On the higher stages, in the conditions of highly developed contradictions, it assumes a political character and it shapes itself into a struggle of parties."[11] The class character of literature is thus associated with political struggle—an association which may be of some use in the interpretation of a Soviet work of art, but which is useless in the treatment of prerevolutionary literature retained in the programs.

A close similarity exists in Soviet literary theory in the treatment of the notions of *klassovost'* and *ideynost'*. There is hardly a textbook on literature that would have no mention at all of the *klassovost'* and *ideynost'* of a work studied. The program for the university course Introduction to the Study of Literature (*Vvedenie v literaturovedenie*) requires in the first chapter a discussion of *ideynost'* and *klassovost'* along with *narodnost'* and *partiynost'*.[12] To the students' dismay, however, no clear-cut definition of *klassovost'* or *ideynost'* is to be found in the approved textbook on literary theory.

It is difficult, if not impossible, to regard *klassovost'* and *ideynost'* as Marxist philosophical categories, since these notions were introduced into the Marxist-Leninist terminology in the post-Marxian period. But it is possible to deduce the meaning of *ideynost'* from the Marxist explanation of ideas and perception. According to Marxism the creation of ideas has to do with man's participation in the process of production. Since ideas change along with the changes in the process of production, there is only a semblance of independence and "objectivity" of ideas.[13] Thus, literature, which is regarded as "one of the forms of social consciousness, one of the forms of ideology,"[14] is conditioned by the existing economic situation, which expresses itself, in a given society, in the existing relation between the productive forces and the means of production: "*Ideynost'* is perceived in the context of Lenin's literary judgment as something that has already been discovered in the *Weltanschauung* of the writer, something that has already been formed into a system of his views."[15] In Soviet society communist *ideynost'* conditions "the main task of the literature of socialist realism—the active struggle for the building of a communist society and a qualitatively new approach to all social problems: labor, peace and war, happiness, love and marriage, and so forth."[16]

Soviet philosophers also consider *ideynost'* as an ethical category characteristic of man's activity and his self-consciousness. It signifies the adherence of an individual to a certain idea that guides him in his actions, and to which he devotes his life. The highest historical form of *ideynost'* is considered to be communist *ideynost'*, which is, in turn, connected with the most progressive and humane ideals which embody the strivings of the working people and which are based on a scientific understanding of the laws governing history. The lack of *ideynost'* spreads philistinism, commonplaceness, bureaucratism, political short-sightedness.[17]

In Soviet terminology to subscribe to the principle of *ideynost'* simply means to adopt the position of the party by subscribing to its ideology. In this sense *ideynost'* must be regarded not only as a strong weapon of literary criticism but also as an indicator of how literature is to be written, and therefore it must reflect the latest theoretical and political developments in world communism. Since *ideynost'* as applied to contemporary Soviet literature would mean the reflection in a work of art of Marxist-Leninist ideology as it is understood today by Soviet leaders, one must be aware of the latest developments on the "ideological front," which are often connected with political events, in order to project a proper point of view in a work of art. No longer is there a single source for the development and interpretation of Marxist dogma. In the present era of polycentrism in world communism the Soviet author must be more careful than ever if he is to stand up to rigid scrutiny in the light of *ideynost'* and not be accused of deviating from the party line.

But what about the nineteenth-century Russian classics? Such an application of the principle of *ideynost'* to them would be unsuitable because "the objective content of a work of art is determined by the author's subjective point of view concerning the society depicted by him."[18] And the author's point of view is, in turn, determined by the conditions of his own society. It seems that the solution to this apparent contradiction is to apply to the nineteenth-century classics a concept of *ideynost'* that is divorced from the philosophical *Weltanschauung* of the writer, speaking of it in a broad sense. *Ideynost'* in this context is regarded as a moral quality connected with the writer's character and his personal philosophy of life, which expresses itself in his attitude toward the weak, humiliated, and downtrodden, and manifests itself in the positive deeds of the heroes in his works.

The only term discussed here which has been inherited by Soviet culture together with the works of the Russian classicists is *narodnost'*. The word was introduced into Russian literature by the poet and critic P.A. Vyazemsky, who used it in a letter to A.I. Turgenev in November 1819, and later in his article "A Conversation of a Classic Writer with an Editor" (1825). Some of Vyazemsky's contemporaries ascribe the introduction of this term to A. Bestuzhev (apparently without sufficient ground).[19] Of course Vyazemsky could not predict, nor could he expect, that the term would become so popular in the years to come. He simply chose to use the Russian word *narodnost'* for the French *nationalité*.

With Pushkin this term received new meaning. After stating that to different people the word means different things, Pushkin called *narodnost'* "a virtue which can be fully valued only by one's own fellow countrymen." He said that it was a "climate, a way of ruling, a faith giving each nation its particular physiognomy, which is, more or less, reflected in the mirror of poetry."[20] In his commentaries on Pushkin as a poet, Gogol' often used the terms *nardonost'* and *natsional'nost'* (nationality) interchangeably. He claimed that it is not important what a writer depicts, but how he depicts it, and whether the spirit of his people is conveyed. He said that a poet could be national even in depicting other peoples and nations; he only has to look at them with the eyes of his own people, his own nation.[21]

V.G. Belinsky, whose use of the term *narodnost'* is closer to the contemporary Soviet interpretation, gave this definition: *"Narodnost'* is not a virtue, it is a necessary condition of a true work of art, if under *narodnost'* we are to understand a truthful depiction of a people's or country's disposition, customs, and character. The life of any nation is expressed in its own unique form. Consequently, if the depiction is *truthful*, it complies with the requirements of the term *narodnost'*."[22] Though his interpretation of *narodnost'* is fairly close to the current one, Belinsky confused *narodnost'* with *natsional'nost'*. For the young Belinsky *narodnost'* in literature was connected with its national originality, and he could not reconcile the aristocratic background of some writers with the *narodnost'* of their works. Thus, he criticized the tales of Pushkin, claiming that they contained "Russian words, but no Russian spirit."[23]

Soviet texts on the theory of literature, approved for use in institutions of higher learning, endeavor to give a contemporary definition to the term *narodnost'*. L.I. Timofeev examines it as an aesthetic category in its chronological evolution and finds it the highest form of artistry (*khudozhestvennost'*). In other words, no work of art can stand up against the measure of *narodnost'* unless it has high artistic value. The transition from artistry to *narodnost'* is determined by the conditions of *narodnost'*, which are "revealed in the stating of problems of general national concern by the author, in an approach to these problems which favors the interests of the people, in a depiction of man which would contribute to the spiritual growth of the people, and in the democratism of form which would make sure that the masses understand the given work."[24]

Timofeev says that in the past an author seldom expressed ideas that were a direct reflection of the people's interests. He claims, however, that the truthful and sensitive depiction of reality can "lead to correct conclusions, even though the writer himself has not done so."[25] This is the key to the use of *narodnost'*. The Soviet literary historian is given a free hand in the interpretation of a nineteenth-century work of literature, and he sometimes arrives at conclusions the author himself would never have dreamed of.

Thus, regardless of what attitudes Turgenev, Tolstoy, and Dostoevsky had toward the aims and means of the revolution, they are still considered to be connected with the liberation movements in Russia, if only because their works depict members of society who were involved, in one way or another, in these movements and struggles. It has been assumed by Soviet literary historians that Tolstoy, Dostoevsky, and Turgenev were afraid of the tragic outcome of a bourgeois revolution in Russia and therefore looked for other paths in their search for the liberation of mankind—for justice and happiness. In most cases the path led toward moral self-improvement, a solution far from acceptable to the radicals and revolutionaries: "But the power of these writers did not express itself in their preaching of moralism and utopia, but rather in artistic exploration of life. Realism helped to discover the terrible and real truth of social and political life in imperialist Russia."[26] Thus, it is claimed that without even realizing it both Tolstoy and Dostoevsky joined hands with the revolutionary forces and supported them.

According to Lenin, no great writer could avoid touching upon some of the essential aspects of the revolutionary movement. It is therefore the duty of Soviet literary history, "in the field of the interpretation of Russian classics, to search in nineteenth-century literature for the reflection of preparation for the twentieth century—the century of the victorious revolution in Russia."[27] This approach to the nineteenth-century Russian classics limits the need to tamper with the original texts. It remains only to put them in proper perspective by emphasizing what is important and overlooking the rest.[28] The use of *narodnost'* makes it possible to retain the Russian classical heritage in the Soviet school curricula, and to emphasize the connection between socialist culture and the best that was written before the Revolution.

Not all literary scholars fully agree with Timofeev's definition of *narodnost'*. For F.M. Golovenchenko, for example, along with other requirements, the "*narodnost'* of a writer is always connected with a progressive ideology."[29] If the term "progressive" is used in its contemporary Soviet application, this prerequisite could disqualify many great nineteenth-century writers, including Gogol' and Dostoevsky, from those approved in light of *narodnost'*. L.V. Shchepilova, on the other hand, connects *narodnost'* with the national character of a work of art, which in turn depends on the patriotism of the writer.[30] Such an interpretation of *narodnost'* could, perhaps, be of some use in the analysis of a postrevolutionary work of literature; but in the interpretation of *narodnost'* of a nineteenth-century work of art it is dangerous to proceed from the patriotism of the writer.

The connection between *narodnost'* and *natsional'nost'* is also confusing. Lenin's statement about the presence of two national cultures in each contemporary nationality partly clarifies the distinction between these two terms in literature.[31] This clarification, however, was sufficient for Lenin's own time, when there still were different classes in the young Soviet state. In our own day, when there are said to be no antagonistic classes in Soviet society, there is a tendency for these two notions to converge. Those who state that the two terms are synonymous regard the new Soviet nation as a homogeneous people, qualitatively different from a bourgeois class society with several cultures. The opponents of such an approach claim that national consciousness does not develop simultaneously with the changes occurring in the social sphere, and therefore these two terms should remain distinct even in Soviet society, the more so since there is no need to confuse sociological and aesthetic categories.[32]

At the present time the most important concept in Soviet art, which includes much that has been known until now under the notions of *narodnost'*, *klassovost'*, and *ideynost'*, is the principle of *partiynost'*. It is not a new principle, and some theoreticians of Marxism try to trace it back to Marx and his ideas of tendentiousness in literature.[33] With Marx, however, the tendentiousness, or *partiynost'*, of literature worked only in the interests of a class or party, while in the Soviet Union, where the ideologies of the party and the state are synonymous, *partiynost'* has become an official policy of the state.

Lenin used the term *partiynost'* for the first time in his work *Ekonomicheskoe soderzhanie narodnichestva i kritika ego v knige g. Struve* (The Economic Content of Populism and Its Criticism in the Book of Mr. Struve) (1895).[34] A more detailed elaboration of the relationship between the party and its literature appeared after its defeat in the 1905 revolution, when literature remained, for a while, the only political weapon of the party. In the article "Party Organization and Party Literature,"[35] published in the November 13, 1905, issue of *Novaya zhizn'*, Lenin clarified the relationship between the party and its literature. He stated that newspapers must become party organs, and writers must join the party. He called for the creation of a free press—free from the control of capital, and free from anarchic bourgeois individualism. Lenin added, however, that he spoke only of party literature, which was subject to party control, while every writer outside the party was free to write and say whatever he pleased, without the slightest restriction. Indeed, in those days no one outside the party had to ask Lenin's permission when and how to write. It was rather the tsarist censorship that imposed restrictions, and thus was to be feared.

Nowadays it is different. The censorship of the tsarist state is replaced by a new Soviet censorship. The fact that party literature has actually become state literature makes it impossible to publish anything that is not in agreement with party ideology and party politics. It becomes obligatory for those who are not party members to subscribe in their writings to the same ideals as party members, because they are citizens of a state controlled and ruled by the party. Lenin himself gave the term *partiynost'* different meanings at different times: it could mean belonging to a party, or the defense by a philosopher of a certain ideology, or a conscious political struggle in the defense of the interests of a certain class.[36]

After Lenin's death and with the development of Stalin's "cult of personality," which dominated all aspects of party and Soviet life, there was less emphasis on Lenin's principle of *partiynost'*, since all achievements of the Soviet state were associated with the name of Stalin. In the rare instances when the principle of *partiynost'* was brought to the fore it was referred to as a Leninist-Stalinist principle developed by both of them. According to A. Belik, the principle of *partiynost'* would first of all mean the depiction of reality in its revolutionary development; to see in it constantly a struggle between the new and the old, to participate actively in this struggle with the means of one's creative work on the side of the new; it would mean constantly to affirm Soviet reality and to criticize passionately, reject the old, capitalist, conservative—everything that hinders the victory of the new, communist reality.[37]

With the affirmation of collective leadership in the party after the death of Stalin, different steps were taken to bolster the image of the party and to make it possible for the party to fill the vacuum left by the demise of its leader. In the arts this function was assigned to the principle of *partiynost'*, which was to permeate every aspect of artistic, creative, and critical activity. Lenin's article "Party Organization and Party Literature" was quoted time and again, and after the Twentieth Party Congress Stalin's name was left out altogether from the references dealing with the development of Soviet literary theory.

The little intellectual freedom granted to artists after Stalin's death was immediately felt in the field of literary theory, and the first to be attacked was the very principle of *partiynost'*. Some Soviet literary critics, along with several East European Marxist scholars of high repute, including the Yugoslavs I. Vidmar and B. Zicherl,[38] began to question whether the application of Lenin's concept of *partiynost'*, as practiced in Eastern Europe today, was really what Lenin had meant. They emphasized that Lenin's article made a clear distinction between those who were party members, and thus obliged to follow party policy, and those who were not party members, and therefore could write as they wished. The Soviet critic Ya. Strochkov wrote in *Literaturnaya gazeta* that Lenin's article had been addressed to the writer "who called himself a party member but conducted himself in his literary activity as a nonparty, not accountable to any one person."[39]

This was, of course, too much. All those who have tried to keep the principle of *partiynost'* from being applied to writers who are not party members have been severely attacked by official party spokesmen and accused of revisionism. The principle of *partiynost'* has received new political coloring. Previously it was mainly identified with the method of socialist realism in Soviet literature, but now it is also identified with fundamental party policy.

The Soviet approach in which literary theory is regarded as an exact science calls for a precise definition of the term *partiynost'*. But though all Soviet literary theoreticians agree that *partiynost'* is the very foundation of Soviet literature, "there exist as many definitions of the notion of 'partiynost' of literature' as there are scholars writing on this topic."[40] Such a state of affairs is, of course, unacceptable in Soviet education, and therefore literary educators have worked out their own definition of the term.

In Soviet publications used for educational purposes the essence of Communist *partiynost'* in literature is frequently described as "an open, consistent defense of party ideology; the participation of literature with its own specific means in the solution of the fundamental aims of the working class; the leadership of the party in the development of literature."[41] Having apparently become aware of the existing differences in the definition and interpretation of the term *partiynost'*, the Secretary of the Central Committee and member of the Politbureau of the Communist Party of the Soviet Union, M. Suslov, found it necessary to come out with his own, what might seem official, definition of *partiynost'*:

Marxist-Leninist *partiynost'* is a principle which implies a consistent implementation of a scholarly, objectively truthful analysis of social phenomena. At the same time it guides scholars and helps them to take up the most correct social-class positions and to combine scholarship with the interests of the revolutionary struggle of the working class and of all workers, and with the aims of the building of communism."[42]

The political nature of the principle is explicit. Nevertheless, Soviet literary theory tries to connect it with the principles of *narodnost'* and *klassovost'*, and undertakes to show that the principle of *partiynost'* is the development of *narodnost'* and *klassovost'* in new Soviet conditions. *Partiynost'* is considered to be a development of *klassovost'* in a sense in which the artist becomes aware that he belongs to a class;[43] it is a conscious realization of one's membership in a class and a readiness to fight for its aims. *Partiynost'* is also considered to be "the highest form of *narodnost'* in literature."[44] The communist *partinyost'* of a writer is claimed to be the very foundation of the *narodnost'* of his creative activity. The striving toward *narodnost'* leads, in turn, toward *partiynost'* in literature.[45] The aims of communist *partiynost'* are seen as fundamentally national. All the same, even Soviet scholars have to agree that not all expressions of *narodnost'* in Soviet literature reach the level of communist *partiynost'*. In other words, not all Soviet works of art can stand up to its requirements. On the other hand, *partiynost'* is the only criterion one should use to determine the level of *narodnost'* in a work of art.[46]

Some Soviet scholars claim that in Soviet reality "the notions of *narodnost'*, *klassovost'*, and *partiynost'* lose their distinctions and definitely merge."[47] This union between *klassovost'*, *narodnost'*, *ideynost'*, and *partiynost'* is a convergence in which the interests of the working class itself are rather neglected. It is well known that according to Lenin "class political consciousness can be brought to the workers only from without."[48] Workers now, as in the past, are more interested in improving their economic conditions than they are in political theories that offer no immediate benefits. To advocate in Soviet literature a struggle to improve the economic conditions of the working class would mean a departure from the political goals of the revolution, and a substitution of trade-unionism for political struggle—a trend which was vigorously opposed by Lenin, because "trade-unionism means ideological enslavement of the workers by the bourgeoisie."[49]

Thus, it is suggested that most workers lack the class consciousness and active ideology to carry on a political struggle. The task of arming the working class with a revolutionary ideology is carried out by the vanguard of the proletariat, which is organized in a political party. The party, which includes the most politically conscious workers, takes upon itself the task of developing an ideology which is to be considered not only the ideology of the party but also of the class. It becomes apparent, therefore, that the principles of *klassovost'* and *ideynost'* as applied to Soviet literature must be linked to the principle of *partiynost'*, since the party is the only spokesman for the class, and the ideology of the party is the only ideology permitted in the Soviet state.

Some authors and teachers tend to use these terms interchangeably. Indeed, how can one expect students to be able to disentangle this mess when "even some lecturers are unable to understand it fully,"[50] and one of them, a certain A.I. Smirnov, even adds Tolstoy, Chekhov, and Korolenko to the list of party writers.[51]

Considering the close connection between the principle of *partiynost'* and the method of socialist realism in Soviet literature, which received new emphasis after the Third Congress of Soviet Writers in 1959, it is not surprising that the works which stand up to the scrutiny of *partiynost'* are ones written in the manner demanded by the theoreticians of socialist realism and are usually included in the school and university programs. To name just a few: *Mother* by Maxim Gorky, *Chapaev* by Dmitriy Furmanov, *How Steel Was Tempered* by Nikolay Ostrovsky, and *Virgin Soil Upturned* by Mikhail Sholokov.

The new theories of peaceful coexistence and competition between different social systems, developed in the face of the new realities of the atomic age, have profoundly affected the growing generation of Soviet youth. The rapprochement between the East and West in the areas of economics, politics, and trade has also influenced the ideological sphere. It is difficult, however, to promote coexistence in one area and wage war in another. But this is exactly what is demanded by party ideologists. It is not surprising, therefore, that with the development of East-West relations there is a growing effort to increase vigilance against alien penetration. In art it is done by reemphasizing the principles of *narodnost'* and *partiynost'* as the basic literary concepts of Lenin's legacy.

A special plenary meeting of the board members of Soviet creative artistic associations, including writers, painters, composers, and architects, was called in December 1969 to discuss the problem of the embodiment of the Leninist principles of *partiynost'* and *narodnost'* in Soviet literature and arts. The speeches delivered by many leading artists and party ideologists could hardly qualify as contributions to the theory of art. The emphasis was mainly on the political aspects of literature and the arts, and on the need to guard and promote Lenin's ideological heritage. There is no doubt that the aims of the meeting were to raise the ideological and political consciousness of the younger generation and to remind the students and teachers of the true goals of artistic education in the Soviet Union. The time for such a meeting was considered ripe, because foreign ideological influence was on the increase, and because the hundredth anniversary of Lenin's birth was a most appropriate time for such a gathering.

It is sufficient to quote from a speech delivered by Sergey Mikhalkov to realize that there are serious shortcomings in the methods of Soviet ideological education in literature. Speaking for the higher echelon of writers and literary politicians, Mikhalkov made an apparent attack on the literary educational establishment by saying,

Alarming signals are coming from schools and institutions of higher learning. It happens that pupils in the senior grades and even students in philological faculties know more about the problems of the theater of the absurd, about the novel without a hero, about all possible contemporary, bourgeois, reactionary trends in literature and the arts in the West than about the past and the present of the literature of their own motherland.[52]

It is doubtful that Soviet students know more about Western literature and art than about Russian writers and poets. All the same, there is a growing interest among Soviet young people in Western life and culture, not because Russian literature is poor in content or quality, but because the Soviet student is tired of the stifling atmosphere in which literature is taught. He is tired of applying the same clichés and searching for the same truths in every work of literature he studies.

5 Lenin's Articles on Tolstoy and the Development of the Approach to Russian Classics in Soviet Education

The connection of ideology and politics with the evolution of the Soviet approach to the nineteenth-century Russian classics could be illustrated best by the example of Tolstoy. It seems logical that in the interpretation of Tolstoy Soviet literary theoreticians would be guided from the very first postrevolutionary days by the articles on Tolstoy written by V.I. Lenin. However, "the works of the twenties devoted to Tolstoy, take no notice at all of Lenin's articles on Tolstoy."[1] It is natural, therefore, that this gap should have been filled by contributions of Marxists with what they thought would be the right Marxist interpretation of Tolstoy.

One of these Marxists is the well-known G.V. Plekhanov,[2] whose articles on Tolstoy, written before the Revolution, were widely read and discussed in the twenties. Plekhanov makes a clear distinction between Tolstoy the artist and Tolstoy the thinker; he claims that the proletariat could accept only Tolstoy the artist, at the same time rejecting Tolstoy the thinker. Plekhanov stresses the fact that the conscious representatives of the working people love Tolstoy just "from here and to here": the workers

value in Tolstoy the writer who, regardless of his misunderstanding of the struggle for the reshaping of social relationships to which he has remained entirely indifferent, has all the same deeply felt the dissatisfaction with the present social order. And most of all—they value in him the writer who made use of his enormous artistic talent in order to depict clearly this dissatisfaction, even if he has done so only episodically.[3]

Plekhanov is not alone in his efforts to throw a shadow of doubt on the value of Tolstoy's creative writing due to the total unacceptability to the revolutionaries of Tolstoy's philosophy of life. Even after the Revolution Tolstoy's doctrine of nonresistance to evil and his calls for self-perfection as a means of changing society are severely attacked. As late as 1925 A.V. Lunacharsky finds it necessary to repeat many of Plekhanov's accusations of Tolstoy and to regard Tolstoyism as the ideological public enemy number two of the Revolution. Lunacharsky claims that only Menshevism is more dangerous than Tolstoyism, because Tolstoyism "strongly influences the intelligentsia, and what is in some cases even more important, it can turn out to be our competitor in the efforts to influence the better peasants, not only in Europe but also deep in Asia."[4]

The late twenties was a time of ideological instability in Soviet Russia, and it is not surprising that some politicians and literary critics went to extremes in order to demonstrate their devotion to the party and the working class. Such a course was taken by the literary critic M. Ol'minsky, who came out in *Pravda*[5] against the publication of the collected works of Tolstoy because the latter was allegedly counterrevolutionary and served the cause of reaction with his journalistic as well as artistic writings. Ol'minsky went even further than Plekhanov and Lunacharsky. By assuming that no member of a bourgeois class could contribute anything worthy of the attention of the working people, he refused to acknowledge even Tolstoy the writer. Such an approach to literature is symptomatic of the development which in the thirties has grown into what it is now known as vulgar sociologism. It is an analysis in which the social aspects of a work of literature and the class position of the writer are overstressed while form and aesthetics receive no attention at all.[6]

This development in literary theory and criticism had far-reaching consequences for literary education in general and for the teaching of Tolstoy in particular. "The sociological approach to the study of Tolstoy was drying out the lectures; it made them meaningless, and, in a way, abstract, bare—the works on literature were falling short of literariness."[7] In the thirties the social determinism of a work of art "which could be understood only in connection with its social nature"[8] continued to be stressed. The preoccupation with the social aspects of literature and with the class background of the writer prompted sharp criticism of Tolstoy the man as well as of his writings. Tolstoy was attacked because his writings "were not nourished by the consciousness of the 'inevitability of a forthcoming revolutionary struggle of the masses' and were not directed towards the education in the masses of a sense of such inevitability. L.N. Tolstoy's creative work reflected the unpreparedness of the masses for such a struggle."[9] It was stated that Tolstoy, who was alien to the cause of revolution, and who did not recognize the revolutionary methods of class struggle, turned to the wealthy and the rich, who shared with him the same background and position in life, with a call to renounce their privileges. Tolstoy was also ridiculed for his efforts to convince the oppressed and the exploited that there are no guilty in this world; that all are brothers. The development of capitalism in Russia and the rise of revolutionary consciousness in the masses allegedly led Tolstoy to the search for a solution to all social evils in the person of Karataev, a character in *War and Peace*. "Two themes become dominant in Tolstoy: the theme of affirmation of the Karataev consciousness among the socially oppressed and the victory of the Karataev humility over the spirit of Pugachev's revolt; and the second theme—the theme of the enlightenment of the rich, the resurrection of those in power."[10]

Tolstoy's artistic writings, even those written after his conversion in the eighties, are condemned as depicting only the nobility and the wealthy. He is criticized for dealing with strata of society with no relevance to contemporary Soviet life. A discussion of *Kreytserova sonata* (The Kreutzer Sonata) states, "In essence Tolstoy criticizes here only the family life of the wealthy. His criticism by-passes proletarian life. Indeed, there is little in common between the family of a working man and all that Pozdnyshev has to say about the balls, at which marriage partners are attracted, about dowry, about playing the piano, etc."[11]

Only after the Second World War, and in particular after the death of Stalin, do some changes occur in the approach to literature and in the methodology of teaching Tolstoy. Lenin's articles become the guiding authority in the analysis of Tolstoy's work, and Lenin's view that Tolstoy must be approached in the unity of Tolstoy the artist and Tolstoy the thinker-prophet becomes binding. That is not to say that Lenin identifies Tolstoy the artist with Tolstoy the thinker. On the contrary, just as Plekhanov does, Lenin sees a clear distinction between them, but "the narrow-mindedness of Plekhanov manifests itself in the fact that while developing his formula 'from here and to here' he does not display any unified understanding of Tolstoy as a thinker and a writer, allowing thus a mechanical division between these notions and making a schematic imprint on the whole conception."[12]

In less than three years, from September 1908 to January 1911, Lenin wrote seven short articles on Tolstoy. Most of them appeared in illegal publications and were without signatures or signed with Lenin's pseudonyms. The articles were connected with two important dates in Tolstoy's life. The first article, "Leo Tolstoy as the Mirror of the Russian Revolution,"[13] was written in connection with Tolstoy's eightieth birthday, which was celebrated in 1908. The remaining articles were written in connection with Tolstoy's death, which occurred in 1910. Lenin does not analyze the literary heritage of Tolstoy. The articles are provoked not by Lenin's academic interest in literature but rather by the political and social struggle taking place around Tolstoy's personality. The articles are repetitious and constitute a part of the ideological argument between Lenin and the Mensheviks as well as the representatives of the liberal-bourgeois political parties.

Lenin begins his first article by saying that the juxtaposition of Tolstoy with the Revolution could appear to many as artificial and strange, and he states that "a mirror which does not reflect things correctly could hardly be called a mirror." But Lenin explains further that "if we have before us a really great artist, he must have reflected in his work at least some of the essential aspects of the Revolution."[14] Lenin makes no secret of the glaring contradictions in Tolstoy; he says, however, that these contradictions are a reflection of the contradictory conditions in the Russia of the last decades of the nineteenth century. "Tolstoy's ideas are a mirror of the weakness, the shortcomings of our peasant revolt, a reflection of the flabbiness of the patriarchal countryside and of the hidebound cowardice of the 'enterprising muzhik.' "[15]

Lenin sees the importance of Tolstoy's views in the fact that as a whole they reflect the peculiarities of the Russian Revolution, which at that stage was a bourgeois-peasant revolution. Lenin's first article on Tolstoy is directed against the Mensheviks, in particular against Plekhanov, who minimizes the role of the peasantry as an ally of the working class in the forthcoming revolution, and who is prepared to give up the initiative and the leadership of the bourgeois-democratic revolution to the bourgeoisie. Plekhanov and the Mensheviks are accused of not understanding Tolstoy because they could not understand the role of the peasant in the first Russian Revolution, and they could not envisage Tolstoy as a reflection of Russian peasantry.[16]

After Tolstoy's death Lenin wrote six articles in three months. In "L.N. Tolstoy," the first article appearing after and in connection with the writer's death, Tolstoy is hailed as one of the greatest artists in world literature. Lenin writes that although Tolstoy does not solve a single problem in his works, he poses many important questions and reflects in his works correctly the mood of the oppressed masses. According to Lenin, Tolstoy belongs to the period of 1861-1904, the period of the growth of the peasant-bourgeois revolution in Russia. The passing of Tolstoy reflects the passing of an era, with all its weaknesses and shortcomings reflected in the works of Tolstoy.

In "L.N. Tolstoy and the Modern Labor Movement" Lenin makes a point that the old patriarchal Russia begins to break up after the abolition of serfdom in 1861. The process of the destruction of Russia's old foundations is reflected in Tolstoy the artist as well as in Tolstoy the thinker. Lenin claims that the criticism directed by Tolstoy against the existing order of things is not new. In fact, he says, there is nothing in Tolstoy's criticism that has not been said before him, in foreign or Russian literatures, by those who are on the side of the working people.

But the uniqueness of Tolstoy's criticism and its historical significance lie in the fact that it expressed, with a power such as is possessed only by artists of genius, the radical change in the views of the broadest masses of the people in the Russia of this period, namely, rural, peasant Russia. For Tolstoy's criticism of contemporary institutions differs from the criticism of the same institutions by representatives of the modern labor movement in the fact that Tolstoy's point of view was that of the patriarchal, naïve peasant, whose psychology Tolstoy introduced into his criticism and his doctrine.[17]

"Tolstoy and the Proletarian Struggle" explains the shortcomings and inner contradictions in Tolstoy's ideology. Lenin says that Tolstoy speaks for the masses which hate the oppressor but which lack the necessary consciousness and determination in order to wage a successful struggle against its social enemies. "By studying the literary works of Leo Tolstoy the Russian working class will learn to know its enemies better, but in examining the *doctrine* of Tolstoy, the whole Russian people will have to understand where their own weakness lies, the weakness which did not allow them to carry the cause of their emancipation to its conclusion."[18]

In his last article on Tolstoy, "Leo Tolstoy and His Epoch," Lenin sums up much of what he has said before. It is, however, the first time that Lenin uses names of specific characters and titles of works by Tolstoy to illustrate his own ideas. Lenin quotes Levin, one of the protagonists of *Anna Karenina*, who says "Here in Russia everything has now been turned upside down and is only just taking shape."[19] Lenin adds that it is a most accurate characteristic of the period between 1861 and 1905. According to Lenin, however, Tolstoy's positive ideas outlived their usefulness completely with the passing of 1905, and the latter's conception of how things should be arranged after the old foundations of society have been destroyed is of no use to the working class.

Tolstoy's doctrine is certainly utopian and in content is reactionary in the most precise and most profound sense of the word. But that certainly does not mean that the doctrine was not socialistic or that it did not contain critical elements capable of providing valuable material for the enlightenment of the advanced classes. There are various kinds of socialism. In all countries where the capitalist mode of production prevails there is the socialism which expresses the ideology of the class that is going to take the place of the bourgeoisie; and there is the socialism that expresses the ideology of the classes that are going to be replaced by the bourgeoisie. Feudal socialism, for example, is socialism of the latter type, and the nature of *this* socialism was appraised long ago, over sixty years ago, by Marx, simultaneously with his appraisal of other types of socialism.[20]

Further Lenin states that a quarter of a century ago the critical elements of Tolstoy's teaching could be of some practical use despite their reactionary and utopian essence. He concludes, however, by pointing to the dangers of Tolstoyism: the usefulness of utopian ideas is in reverse proportion to historical development, and, therefore, with the rise of class and political consciousness and struggle, Tolstoy's ideas become more harmful to the cause of revolution than ever before.

The one hundredth anniversary of Lenin's birth, celebrated in 1970, prompted further emphasis on Lenin's articles on Tolstoy. Lenin's and Gorky's interest in Tolstoy's creative work and their appreciation of the latter's artistic genius received wide mention. Much has been also made of the fact that Tolstoy had allegedly been acquainted with some of Lenin's works. There is no indication that Tolstoy read "Leo Tolstoy as the Mirror of the Russian Revolution," the only article on Tolstoy written by Lenin before the writer's death. There is, however, in Tolstoy's personal library in Yasnaya Polyana a legal bolshevik publication entitled *O boykote tret'ey Dumy* (On the Boycott of the Third Duma) which contains two articles, one of which, "Protiv boykota," (Against the Boycott) is written by Lenin. It is assumed that Tolstoy read this article since several sentences and separate words are underlined by the reader.[21]

The importance of Lenin's articles on Tolstoy for the study and teaching of literature in the Soviet Union is presently not limited to the interpretation and approach to Tolstoy only. These articles are considered to be a part of Lenin's ideological legacy which is to be constructively applied to problems of art in general and to prerevolutionary works of literature in particular, becoming thus a part of what seems to be the foundation of Soviet literary theory.

Lenin's articles on Tolstoy do not add much to aesthetic theory as such, since they "are concerned with social questions rather than with problems of art."[22] The application, however, of Lenin's approach to Tolstoy in the contemporary treatment of this writer, an approach in which Lenin finds it possible and useful to draw from both Tolstoy the artist and Tolstoy the thinker, could be considered as one of the reasons for the greater freedom in the study of the artistic values of Tolstoy's work. Once it is established that a work of literature should be studied in the unity of the contents and form and in the unity of the ideological and the aesthetic, it becomes possible for the student of Tolstoy's artistic heritage to turn directly to the analysis of the text in which the "text does not serve as an illustration of one thought or another, of the lecturer's theoretical propositions, but a direct source from which this thought and proposition are derived."[23] It also becomes possible to devote more time to the study of style, genre, composition, and other problems of aesthetics, connected with Tolstoy's work, which have, so far, been totally neglected. This is not to say that the social and ideological aspects of Tolstoy's work are to be overlooked. Not in the least. The primacy of contents over form in the analysis of a work of art is to be maintained with full consistency.

Lenin indicates that there are positive and negative traits in both Tolstoy's artistic and journalistic writings, and that these traits are to be judged on their own merits depending on how useful they can be to the cause of the working class. This indication makes it possible to reassess some aspects of Tolstoy's teaching in the light of Soviet experience and to look for new areas in which the teaching of Tolstoy and the socialist dogma come into close proximity. One such area is Tolstoy's teaching of moral self-perfection. Tolstoy's proposition that it is necessary to change man in order to affect a change in society was severely attacked by prerevolutionary Marxists, including Lenin, who assumed that a revolutionary change of the social order in which a just relationship between the means of production and the productive forces would be established (in other words, in which the exploitation of one human being by another one would be eliminated) would be sufficient to change man. Soviet experience suggests that the change of social order does not necessarily lead to a simultaneous change in man and, therefore, Soviet ideologists could, perhaps, acknowledge that there are some merits in Tolstoy's idea of self-perfection, but "to some Soviet researchers and critics the idea of the acceptance, in our day, of Tolstoy's teaching of moral perfection of man occurs as all but a deviation from Marxism."[24] These critics seem to belong to the old Stalinist school and fail to recognize reality behind the word of the dogma.

Nevertheless, time and again the idea that there is some use in Tolstoy's teaching of self-perfection for the Soviet man comes up in Soviet literary criticism. M.B. Khrapchenko, for one, takes issue with the critics mentioned above and, by resorting to the help of the New Program of the Communist Party of the Soviet Union, tries to imply that there are some merits in this particular fragment of Tolstoy's teaching.[25] Similar ideas come to the fore in articles dealing with the correlation of aesthetics and ethics in the works of Tolstoy where the problem of moral perfection is approached from new positions.[26] Leading Soviet scholars are careful in dealing with problems in which everyday experience comes in conflict with Marxist dogma. The simple Soviet people, and among them some teachers, are less versed in the theories of Marxism and more aware of what is happening around them. They, therefore, see that the Soviet man is in essence in his daily life not much different from the man of the prerevolutionary period. One teacher states bluntly that most important in Tolstoy's teaching, as far as its relevance to contemporary Soviet life is concerned, is his teaching about the striving for self-perfection.[27] The teacher claims that man can, and should, become better if he wants to build a better future; that the idea of moral perfection could help the education of the young generation.

It is not difficult to see that these efforts to bring Tolstoy's teaching closer to the problems of contemporary reality are in line with the general tendency, beginning in the fifties, to show the nineteenth-century classics in a positive light. There is always, however, the danger that the underestimation of the negative can lead to distortions. And indeed, in the late fifties, after the Twentieth Party Congress, the danger of the so-called revisionism in the Soviet brand of Marxism-Leninism becomes apparent in the study of literature, and the emphasis on the ideological aspects of Tolstoy's work is made with new force. This inclination is propelled by some articles of Soviet and East-European literary scholars on the reinterpretation of Lenin's articles on Tolstoy. Among these scholars stands out the Yugoslav critic I. Vidmar, who tries to deduce from Lenin's interpretation of Tolstoy that since an artistic work with reactionary ideas can be great, it could mean that ideas are irrelevant as far as the definition of the artistic value of a work of art in general is concerned.[28] Such an approach is, of course, considered a distortion not only of Lenin's articles but of the works of Tolstoy himself, a distortion peculiar to the Western approach to Tolstoy and "in a peculiar manner supported by the revisionists, Lukács and Vidmar in particular, who are trying to underestimate the role of ideology in the work of Tolstoy, with the purpose of setting off the great Russian writer against Soviet literature, the *partiynost'* and high ideological substance of which they try to minimize in every possible way."[29]

It is not surprising that Soviet literary theory and criticism devote much room to the proper interpretation of Tolstoy. Tolstoy is one of the most widely published writers in the Soviet Union and one of the most widely read writers in the world. "According to the number of translations to foreign languages, as the figures of UNESCO indicate, his works are in first place among the works of all other writers."[30]

The official guidelines in the approach to Tolstoy and the directives for further research in different areas of Tolstoy's literary heritage continue to stress the importance of Lenin's articles on Tolstoy. They demand new works which would deal with the problems connected with the breaking point in Tolstoy's *Weltanschauung,*[31] so far insufficiently developed in Soviet literary history and criticism. It is claimed that "little has been done in the study of Tolstoy's creative method [*tvorcheskiy metod*] on the background and in connection with world and Russian literary developments."[32] These guidelines are of prime importance to Soviet literary education since, first of all, many leading scholars working on Tolstoy are connected with institutions of higher learning (to name just a few: B.I. Bursov, Ya.S. Bilinkis, N.N. Naumova [Leningrad], K.N. Lomunov, N.V. Nikolaeva [Moscow], A.V. Chicherin, L.A. Lebedeva [Lvov]). It is obvious that the interests and the direction of research conducted by the teaching staff affects in great measure the students, who in turn after graduation become teachers of literature and who usually continue to teach Tolstoy at the secondary-school level along the lines developed at the Institute or University.

Besides, there is a practice in Soviet higher education that members of a seminar contribute their own research to the scholarly and research objectives of the leader of the seminar,[33] serving thus as unofficial research assistants who have little room for divergence from the direction taken by the instructor. It follows that there is a kind of unity between the scholar and the researcher, who is at the same time the professor and author of the textbook on literary history, with all levels of education—at the university through direct confrontation with the student, at school through the student who has just graduated and has become a teacher, and through the textbook, the use of which cannot be evaded.

The guidelines for the study of Tolstoy encountered in literary journals are often veiled in scholarly language which obscures their true meaning. Some authors are, however, more outspoken and state clearly where Tolstoy's importance to the contemporary reader lies. V.I. Arkhipovsky states bluntly that the "shattering criticism of the basic principles of the sociopolitical life in tsarist Russia develops in Tolstoy's work into a denunciation of world imperialism, which is extremely important also in our time."[34] Arkhipovsky states further that Tolstoy's work is of great significance due to its enormous educational value. He points to Tolstoy's criticism of class society, of organized religion, and to the possibility of using Tolstoy's work in developing Soviet patriotism. As far as elementary and even secondary school is concerned, these remarks are perhaps of more use to the teacher than the theoretical elaborations of notable scholars, because the teacher begins the introduction of Tolstoy to Soviet students precisely along these lines.

The emphasis on ideology in the teaching of Tolstoy's works in the Soviet schools is implemented with the help of a variety of methods. One method is a selective approach, in which many works by Tolstoy, as well as critical works on Tolstoy, are not included into the educational programs. Thus, secondary-school students know nothing about Tolstoy's *Ispoved'* (Confession), and university students are not required to read *Chto takoe iskusstvo?* (What Is Art?). There are also a number of important critical studies by Russian and Soviet scholars which have failed to impress the educational authorities and have not found their way into the educational programs. To name just a few: *Analiz, stil' i veyanie. O romanakh gr. L.N. Tolstogo* (Analysis, Style, and Atmosphere in the Novels of Count L.N. Tolstoy) by K. Leont'ev,[35] *L. Tolstoy i Dostoevsky* (L. Tolstoy and Dostoevsky) by D. Merezhkovsky,[36] *Mater'yal i stil' v romane L'va Tolstogo "Voyna i mir"* (The Material and the Style in Leo Tolstoy's Novel "War and Peace") by V. Shklovsky,[37] and *Molodoy Tolstoy* (The Young Tolstoy), *Lev Tolstoy. 50-ye gody* (Leo Tolstoy in the Fifties), and *Lev Tolstoy. 60-ye gody* (Leo Tolstoy in the Sixties) by B. Eykhenbaum.[38] All these studies have one common trait: the sharp critical approach to Tolstoy, the refusal to regard him as superhuman or faultless. But this is an approach for which the leading Soviet Tolstoy scholars have little sympathy, because they have created their own image of Tolstoy which they guard jealously.

Thus, the emphasis in the study of Tolstoy's creative writings, including *War and Peace* and *Anna Karenina*, is placed, on the one hand, on the writer's criticism of the tsarist government, the church, the judicial system, and the corrupted social order, and on the other hand, on the patriotism of the Russian people and the army in its struggle against Napoleon and other foreign enemies. The patriotism of the Russian soldier is to be identified by the Soviet student with the patriotism of the Soviet citizen, and there is no need to elaborate on the fact that the Russian soldier is a serf who is forced to serve the corrupted tsarist regime, the same regime which was soon to suppress the Decembrist uprising of 1825 in Russia.[39]

It may seem a paradox but one may conclude that precisely because of the unified approach to Tolstoy suggested by Lenin, it becomes possible to teach Tolstoy's creative work and his philosophy in a proportion required by the goals of Soviet education which emphasizes one aspect of Tolstoy while it utterly neglects and overlooks the other one. The approach in which Tolstoy the thinker and Tolstoy the writer are dealt with in a combined, integrated manner makes it possible to ignore Tolstoy's positive ideas and to seek out, with the help of the principles of *narodnost'* and *ideynost'*, the elements in Tolstoy's writings which are most useful and suitable for the purpose of Soviet education.

Lenin's articles on Tolstoy are of immense importance to the contemporary Soviet interpretation of the Russian prerevolutionary literary heritage because the requirement for an integrated approach to a creative artist makes it possible to ignore all the material and evidence which is contrary to the officially accepted image of any prerevolutionary writer and to create in the student's mind a picture of an author which could serve the aims of Soviet education but which may be regarded as one-sided and incomplete.

6 The Basic Principles and Literary Practice

Literature is often referred to in the Soviet Union as *chelovekovedenie*, the study of man, and the saying that writers are engineers of human souls is often attributed to Stalin. There is a measure of truth in both statements. Literature does influence the reader, and it leaves a certain mark on his attitude to a given situation and even on his behavior and actions. Books read and studied at school help in forming the student's *Weltanschauung* and his attitude towards the surrounding world. In this respect the Soviet writer who writes for a given audience and with a certain purpose helps indeed in shaping the character of the young Soviet citizen.

But what about the prerevolutionary writer? Is he also an "engineer," as the Soviet writer is? A prerevolutionary writer, who exercises a certain degree of literary craftsmanship, could influence his reader and mold his character as much as a Soviet writer does. However, the prerevolutionary writer, who was in most cases not a radical, would shape the character of his young Soviet reader in his own image—an image far from socialist reality. The adjustment between the reality projected by the prerevolutionary writer and the aims of Soviet education is being achieved with the help of a textbook of literature in which reality is projected from a certain point of view, and in which a work of literature is interpreted in accordance with the basic principles of literary education and Lenin's articles on Tolstoy.

The task of a Soviet writer of a textbook of literature is not as easy as it may seem at first sight. It was much easier right after the Revolution. That was a time when everything connected with the tsarist past was outrightly condemned—a time when leftist extremism in politics had reached a point where Lenin himself had to warn against the dangers of the so-called leftist "infantile disorder" in communism. There was no need in these circumstances to resort to the help of the principles of *narodnost'* and *partiynost'* in literature, since the principles of *klassovost'* and *ideynost'* were the main guidelines in use. How could a member of a defeated class be right? And what other ideology beside the victorious Marxist ideology could have anything positive? The defeat of the revolutionary movements in central Europe after the end of the First World War, and the isolation of the USSR which followed, led to the development of the theory of the possibility of a victory of socialism in one separate state only. Under these new conditions it became necessary to draw on the Russian past and on its historical mission as a leading nation in East Europe. The connection with the Russian historical past and with the spiritual resources of the Russian people became even stronger during the Second World War when, at times, Russian patriotism became synonymous with the patriotism of a Soviet citizen.

It is sufficient to follow through the evolution taking place in the treatment of Gogol' to realize to what degree the political situation in the USSR influences the teaching of literature, and to see how the application of Lenin's articles on Tolstoy to the interpretation of any prerevolutionary writer makes it possible to reassess the Russian classical literary heritage. In the thirties Gogol' was regarded as a great writer but was looked upon as a "romantic and utopian, the bard of a dying class"[1] who dreamed of the reestablishment of a regenerated feudal society and who took refuge in an idealized past such as that described in *Taras Bul'ba* because the present has become too oppressive and menacing. No secret was made, in the thirties, of Gogol's fear of a revolution. It was stated openly that the purpose of *Revizor* (The Inspector General) and of the first volume of *Dead Souls* "was to fight for the capitalization of the economy; an economy which should, however, retain as its foundation a relationship established in the system of serfdom."[2] The purpose of the second volume of *Dead Souls* "was not to depict ideal landowners but to wage war against class struggle; to fight against the danger of revolution; to preach a reconciliation with reality."[3]

In the fifties the old Gogol' is no more recognizable; he becomes a

"writer-patriot" whose work became a radical indictment of feudalism. . . . *Taras Bul'ba* is said to present a people's collective united by strong feelings of comradeship and patriotism. Its romanticism, far from being condemned, is said to make the story lifelike and convincing. On the other hand, Gogol's *Selected Passages,* the book containing his conservative and moralizing political views that so provoked the critic Belinskii, are mentioned only briefly and with notable restraint so as to detract little from the created impression of him as a whole.[4]

Little has changed since. In the late sixties[5] the essence of Gogol's *Inspector General*, which is studied for eight hours in grade seven, lay in his intention to unmask the existing tsarist system and to expose the callous suffocating atmosphere of the Russia of his days. It is claimed that the power of Gogol's satire was directed not against separate officials but rather against Nikolay's Empire as a whole.[6] In support of this allegation an argument is put forth that since the city to which Khlestakov arrives is not named, this occurrence is not localized and is therefore typical for all Russia. It is assumed that Gogol', who was known to be a fervent patriot, became disappointed with the tsarist system after his arrival at Peterburg and turned his attack against the *chinovnik*, or official bureaucrat, whom he considered to be the embodiment of the tsarist regime. It is not surprising, therefore, that *The Inspector General* is considered to be not a moral satire but a social one with some political implications.[7] The more so "since according to Gogol' *Nedorosl'* (The Minor) and *Gore ot uma* (Woe from Wit) represent a new type of comedy—political comedy,"[8] something similar to what Gogol' had allegedly wanted to create in *The Inspector General.*

Of course, *The Inspector General* is presently viewed as a work fully complying with the requirements of *narodnost'*, which is manifested "first of all in its *ideynost'*."[9]

Gogol's art is considered to be realistic and typical for the Russia of his own day. Very little stress is placed on the writer's great power of creative imagination. The fact that Gogol' could not be a realist in a true sense because he simply did not know Russian provincial life is hardly mentioned. He is made out, on one page, to be a patriot, unable to stay away from Russia when he went abroad after the publication of *Gants Kyukhelgarten* (Hanz [sic] Kuechelgarten),[10] while a few pages later it is mentioned in passing that after 1836 Gogol' lived abroad, only coming to Russia several times in connection with the publication of *Dead Souls.*[11]

It is worthwhile to note that publications intended and approved for the use in schools and universities as well as research papers appearing in the so-called *Uchenye zapiski*, or scholarly notes, published by institutions of higher learning, are usually orthodox and biased. The sacrifice of high scholarship to the needs of the didactic ends of education is apparent. The more so since many opinions expressed in these publications meet with profound criticism and disapproval from leading Soviet literary scholars not connected directly with the educational establishment.

To take just one example, there is in Gogol's story "Shinel' " a fantastic ending, in which The Important Person is robbed by the ghost of Akaky Bashmachkin. The epilogue was added after the story was already finished, and it may be regarded as a moral condemnation of The Important Person. Some of Gogol's contemporaries interpreted the robbing of the coat from The Important Person by Akaky's ghost as the fate awaiting the Russian ruling class if it did not repent of its ways; an interpretation that could hardly have occurred to Gogol' himself.

R.Z. Kanunova goes even further. She claims that the epilogue of "Shinel' " "is not a struggle of Akaky Akakievich with The Important Person but that of the author himself," and she states further that Akaky's protest and moral victory are so important because "they express Gogol's innermost thoughts about the superiority of the people over their oppressors, about the people's enormous terrible inner strength."[12]

One can look at this interpretation of the epilogue of "Shinel' " as at a good effort in the use of one of the preconditions of *narodnost'*, in which conclusions can be drawn in the interests of the people even if the author himself does not intend to do so. It is gratifying to know that not all Soviet scholars indulge in such scholarly acrobatics by trying to deduce certain conclusions without any reasonable foundation. G.A. Gukovsky states bluntly that "it would be a big mistake to see in the posthumous reprisal of Akaky Akakievich against The Important Person any hint of revenge of the people oppressed by the rulers against their oppressors, in other words—any revolutionary symbol. Gogol' did not have any revolutionary ideas."[13]

The appearance of divergent opinions by different authors dealing with the same subject is a healthy sign. However, these opinions are directed to different readers, and it happens, at times, that an author has to adjust his own conclusions if his work is intended for use at school. The authors of textbooks are put in such a position by the requirements of the approved programs which enumerate, point by point, what is to be discussed and what is to be emphasized. Gogol's biography, for example, is to be studied from the point of view of the "conditions of class struggle, home upbringing, and school education [Nezhin gymnasium] which predetermined the progressive ideological direction of the writer."[14] The first part of *Dead Souls* is to be regarded as "realistic satire on the Russia of serfdom and nobility bureaucracy."[15] The university program requires the student to know Belinsky's letter to Gogol' about *"Vybrannye mesta iz perepiski s druz'yami,"* (Selected Passages from Correspondence with My Friends) but there is no such requirement to know the letters themselves.[16]

Thus, one might conclude that the student knows more about what has been said and written about Gogol' by a particular group of critics than he knows about Gogol' himself. The more so since there is a trend in Soviet literary education to emphasize the positive in the writer studied by not exposing his negative traits. One can only agree with F. Lilge, who concludes his comparison of the accounts given of Gogol' in the thirties with those of the fifties by saying, "The earlier one stays somewhat closer to the truth in acknowledging Gogol's social views and the inner conflict between the comic artist and the social missionary."[17]

The tendency to present the nineteenth-century Russian classics in a positive light in which their sympathy to the people and hatred of the tsarist system is constantly emphasized, and in which their democratic inclinations are stressed, is not limited to Gogol' or Tolstoy. Dostoevsky *who* has been reintroduced into the school curriculum after almost thirty years, and the study of his writings has received more attention after Stalin's death than at any other time after the revolution.[18] Dostoevsky is, however, a special case, and the struggle for his place in Soviet education is far from finished. The literary educational establishment, while pointing to the artistic values of Dostoevsky's works, and while stressing the importance of his aims of uplifting the distressed, the downtrodden, and the poor, still cannot forgive him the choice of the path to salvation which leads through suffering to redemption in Christ. As a matter of fact, grade nine pupils do not really find out about this path. They are repeatedly told that "Dostoevsky does not know how to get rid of tyranny, because he sees the essence of it in human nature, and not in the degenerated social order."[19] Of course, Dostoevsky believes in the irrationality of man and wants to change society by changing man, while Marxism advocates exactly the opposite. It believes in the rationality of man, and it claims that it is necessary to change, first of all, the social and economic orders, the relationship between the productive forces and the means of production, and only later, in these new conditions, to change man.

Lately those who want to regard Dostoevsky first of all as a writer have, at least for a while, the upper hand. It is worthwhile to note that at a meeting of the executive of the Literature and Language Department of the USSR Academy of Sciences at which new textbooks for grades eight and nine were discussed, the chapter on Dostoevsky was severely attacked by M. Khrapchenko, who stated that Dostoevsky "is discussed in the book from one point of view—that of unmasking,"[20] and he quoted a passage from the book in which all mankind is identified with the underground man of Dostoevsky. Khrapchenko considered it slander on the human race; it would be inconceivable to imagine that all people are like the underground man. The editor of the grade nine book, B.I. Bursov, was forced to delete this passage. It does not appear in the 1968 edition. Doubtless other changes have been introduced in the same book.

University textbooks on Dostoevsky are full of inconsistencies and ambiguities. On the one hand, an effort is made to present him in a positive light, going to extremes such as stressing his connection with the Petrashevsky circle and claiming that "he was recognized as one of the most dangerous political criminals,"[21] while on the other hand pointing out that the at-times-truthful pictures of reality given by Dostoevsky in *Besy* (The Possessed) are "drawn in the clearly expressed reactionary tendency to discredit the revolutionary movement."[22] While given credit for his attack on the bourgeois-nobility society in *Brat'ya Karamazovy* (The Brothers Karamazov) Dostoevsky is at the same time accused of tendentiousness; of desire to extol suffering and humility; of the premeditated leading of man into a dead end from which there is no way out. "The Legend of the Grand Inquisitor" is regarded as Dostoevsky's attack not only against Roman Catholicism but also against socialism, "because according to him it is impossible to govern people without coercion, and this is incompatible with socialism."[23]

On one hand Dostoevsky is claimed to be the "spokesman of the petty bourgeois consciousness from the period of the rapid growth of capitalism,"[24] while on the other hand it is explained that Dostoevsky fears revolution because it supposedly leads to capitalism. Dostoevsky's trip to Western Europe in 1862-63, where he saw the "terrible face of capitalism,"[25] supposedly led him to the conclusion that capitalism had been brought about by the French Revolution, and therefore it was necessary to fight revolution in order to avoid the pitfalls of capitalism in Russia. (This argument may be regarded as a straight contradiction of the claim that Dostoevsky is the mouthpiece of the petty bourgeoisie because the petty bourgeoisie is the very class which has benefited most from the rapid growth of capitalism.)

The efforts of those who want to use a new approach in the study of Dostoevsky and who want to see in him primarily a great artist, leaving philosophy and politics to philosophers and politicians, are not unnoticed by the leaders of the literary educational establishment. It is well known, for example, that the 1929 edition of M.M. Bakhtin's study of Dostoevsky is considered one of the best in this field.[26] In 1963 a new revised and corrected edition of the same study appeared.[27] In the preface to the new edition the author states clearly that so far most studies of Dostoevsky are primarily concerned with the ideological aspects of his creative activity and it is often forgotten that "Dostoevsky is first of all an *artist* (it is true, of a peculiar kind) and not a philosopher and not a pamphleteer."[28] Having this in mind, Bakhtin embarks upon a study of Dostoevsky's poetics with the purpose of finding out all that is new in the great writer's creative work, and emphasizing in particular all the new artistic devices and methods which have changed, to a great extent, the old previously accepted artistic forms.

One rarely encounters a Soviet study of Dostoevsky in which Bakhtin, who is regarded as a leading authority on the writer, is not quoted or mentioned. All this obviously annoys A.I. Revyakin, who is against the use of aesthetic analysis without any connection with problems of ideology, of social causality, and class nature as a means of education. He considers such tendencies alien to Marxism-Leninism, and he points to Bakhtin's study of Dostoevsky as an example in which formalism encounters a liberal reception from the critics. He claims that "M.M. Bakhtin's *Problemy poetiki Dostoevskogo* [Problems of Dostoevsky's Poetics] (1963), in which the concrete observations, in particular, of the language are interesting, is in essence methodologically harmful and has received in our press an obviously exaggerated positive response."[29]

It is clear that the place of Dostoevsky in Soviet education is still in a state of fluctuation. The possibility is not excluded, however, that with time Dostoevsky's works will, with the help of the principle of *narodnost'*, assume a place similar to that of other nineteenth-century Russian classics. Indeed, it is quite possible that a metamorphosis will take place in the treatment of this writer similar to that which has taken place in the approach to Gogol' and Tolstoy. The tendency to stress the positive in Dostoevsky is the first step in this direction. A comparison of the two editions[30] of L. Grossman's study of Dostoevsky seems to confirm this assumption. It is interesting to note that in the 1965 edition there are several new chapters which deal with Dostoevsky indirectly, but put him in a more favorable light from a Soviet point of view than he seems really to deserve. One new chapter deals with the trial of Vera Zasulich, who made an attempt to assassinate the Governor of Peterburg, Trepov. We find in this chapter a description of the trial, of the feelings and relationship of the masses to the trial, of the political situation in Russia in those days, but very little about Dostoevsky, who was present in the courtroom during the trial. Grossman concludes the account of the trial with a remark that "Dostoevsky feels sympathy to the acquital of the girl,"[31] a feeling which is in accord with the feelings of a Soviet citizen, and which brings the writer, as a man, closer to the contemporary reader.

The one hundred and fiftieth anniversary of Dostoevsky's birth, celebrated in November 1971, stimulated further attempts to portray Dostoevsky as one of Russia's great writers who is of immense importance to the contemporary generation. Soviet literary scholars have assumed the role of Dostoevsky's defenders. They claim that Western critics falsify and attack Dostoevsky because the latter criticized the West after having lived there for several years.[32] There is little mention now about Gorky's articles on Dostoevsky in which Dostoevsky is called a philistine and is compared to the Grand Inquisitor.[33] *The Possessed* is no more a critical pamphlet of the revolutionary movement but a denunciation of the existing evil. It is stated by many critics that Dostoevsky is justified in criticizing the shortcomings of the vulgar metaphysical materialism;[34] that he did not attack socialism in general but rather its utopian vulgar brand. It is hinted that had Dostoevsky known Marxism and true scientific socialism his attitudes would surely have changed, since at heart he was a socialist.

It is possible to change an interpretation of a work of literature, but there is little one can do with Dostoevsky's journalistic writings, which are mainly antisocialist, pro-tsarist, even reactionary. It is easier to embellish Dostoevsky the artist than Dostoevsky the man. The Soviet scholar Yu. Kudryavtsev, however, makes an effort to make Dostoevsky appear as almost antigovernment. He minimizes the importance of Dostoevsky's relationship with the chief procurator of the Holy Synod of the Russian Orthodox Church, K. Pobedonostsev, and with the editor of the progovernment journal *Russkiy vestnik*, M. Katkov. Kudryavtsev claims that Dostoevsky published in *Russkiy vestnik* because no one else wanted to published his works or give him money in advance, which he always demanded. This might be true, no progressive journal would accept Dostoevsky's novels unless he would be prepared to change their contents. Kudryavtsev implies, however, that when the editor of *Otechestvennye zapiski*, Nekrasov, offered for the novel *Podrostok* (The Raw Youth) more than Katkov did, Dostoevsky was happy to agree to this offer.[35] The truth of the matter is, as Dostoevsky's wife relates in her memoirs, that Dostoevsky agreed to Nekrasov's offer only after having communicated with Katkov, and after having made sure that *Russkiy vestnik* did not require the novel. *Russkiy vestnik* was at that time publishing *Anna Karenina*, but Katkov, having offered Dostoevsky the same honorarium as Nekrasov did, refused to give the two thousand rubles in advance required by Dostoevsky.[36]

Some recent Soviet literary scholars, carried away by their desire to extol Dostoevsky's virtues, began to overemphasize the latter's importance to the revolution and to socialism. At a meeting called by the editorial board of *Voprosy literatury* in order to discuss the trends in Dostoevsky scholarship in connection with his one hundred and fiftieth birthday, Dostoevsky was lauded by academician B. Suchkov as the "greatest critic of capitalism."[37] Sober voices in Soviet literary scholarship, however, warn of the danger of jumping from one extreme to another; from total repudiation to complete vindication. B. Meylakh,[38] for example, sees a danger in covering up Dostoevsky's true image and in showing him in a better light than he deserves; a phenomenon which has become almost common in connection with the writer's jubilee. Another Soviet scholar,

U. Gural'nik, criticizes Kudryavtsev for "improving history and leaving out from his book certain facts which are not in keeping with his conception of Dostoevsky."[39] Speaking at the conference at *Voprosy literatury*, G. Berezko sharply disagrees with B. Suchkov, and says:

I cannot visualize in Dostoevsky, as B. Suchkov says, the greatest critic of capitalism in world literature. This is simply incorrect. I do not know any other writer in whose works the feeling of compassion to the downtrodden, the oppressed, the unhappy and the alienated would be stronger than in Dostoevsky's works, but this is not a denunciation of capitalism (just as Gogol's 'Shinel' " is not a denunciation of capitalism). . . . Dostoevsky did not call for a struggle with the unjust society, and there is no need to attribute to Dostoevsky what cannot be found in his novels.[40]

Suchkov should be considered one of the official spokesmen on Dostoevsky scholarship at the present time. He was the main speaker at the Dostoevsky Jubilee Celebrations taking place in November 1971 at the Bol'shoy Theatre in Moscow in the presence of Politbureau and the Communist Party Central Committee members. Berezko is closer to the truth, however. Dostoevsky was indeed more concerned with the fate of the individual than with social schemes. He was, as he called himself, a realist in a higher sense. He was able to probe and to dissect the dark sides of the human soul. He was far, however, from criticizing the existing order and from preaching socialism; he claimed that

it is clear and intelligible to the point of obviousness that evil in mankind is concealed deeper than the physicians-socialists suppose; that in no organization of society can evil be eliminated; that the human soul will remain identical; that abnormality and sin emanate from the soul itself, and finally that the laws of the human spirit are so unknown to science, so obscure, so indeterminate and mysterious, that as yet, there can neither be physicians nor *final* judges, but there is only He who saith: 'Vengeance belongeth to me; I will recompense.' He alone knows the *whole* mystery of the world and man's ultimate destiny.[41]

While the formulation of a new Soviet approach to Dostoevsky is in process, the teaching of Dostoevsky's works at school continues in the old spirit, because it is based on previously accepted programs and on old textbooks. It may take several years before new guidelines on the teaching of Dostoevsky at school will be worked out.

The subject matter and the strata of society with which the nineteenth-century classics deal in their works lend themselves fairly well to an interpretation as required by the goals of Soviet education. The case is different with 1890-1917 literature, in particular, with those writers who are known as decadents and symbolists. Even in the fifties D. Merezhkovsky, Z. Gippius, F. Sologub are still grouped together under the heading of "literature of the reactionary trend."[42] No clear distinction is made between symbolism, futurism, acmeism; they are all regarded as nihilistic and reactionary. Of course, apolitical art for art's sake is regarded as reactionary. And if for Gogol' and Dostoevsky evil is the negation of good behind which the possibility of the opposite exists, for the decadents evil is basic, the essence of life. If in Dostoevsky there is always the background of potential, in Sologub all is flat. Life is evil. It is not surprising, therefore, that little is found in these works which could be extracted for the use of Soviet education, even with the help of the flexible principles of *narodnost'* and *partiynost'*.

The attitude toward the artists of these groups did not change in the sixties. There was, however, an effort to make a distinction between the different groups and to deal with each on its own merits. Instead of calling them reactionary, they are united under the heading of "antirealistic trends in Russian literature of the pre-October period."[43] An effort is also made to separate those who have later supposedly accepted the Revolution from the literary groups with which they were previously associated.

A case in point may be A. Blok, whose poem "The Twelve" is considered an end of an era of the "humanistic traditions of Russian classical literature" and at the same time a beginning of a new tradition, that of a "fighting humanism, the humanism of struggle and overcoming."[44] The study of Blok in universities and pedagogical institutes is artificially divided into two parts and is dealt with in two different courses—Russian prerevolutionary and Soviet literature. In grade ten of secondary school the pupils are told that "Blok belonged to those poets who welcomed and immediately accepted the October Revolution,"[45] and that the figure of Christ appearing in "The Twelve" is "the symbol of the holiness of the revolutionary cause."[46]

High-school students have no access to Soviet studies of Blok which claim to the contrary. They study, however, the poem "Khorosho" by V. Mayakovsky, in which there is a clear allusion to Blok's association with and longing for the values of the past. With all due regard to Mayakovsky, "the pupils of the older grades could be, of course, told that in reality Blok's attitude to the Revolution was different from the description given in Mayakovsky's poem."[47] University students who learn more about Blok's past, about his connection with the symbolist movement, and about his poems written before the revolution begin to realize the tragedy of Blok's duality, and consequently the whole truth cannot be hidden from them. They are told that "Blok did not comprehend the true essence of the proletarian revolution till the end of his days. But rejecting the old world, he stretched out a friendly hand to the new proletariat rebuilding life."[48]

This is true, but it is not the whole truth. Blok indeed reached out toward the proletarian revolution, but "in doing so, he broke down. . . . The convulsive and pathetic break with the whole past became for the poet, a fatal rapture."[49] It is not the break with the past that caused the poet's breakdown; it is rather the disillusion with the new. There have been, in the past, other infatuations which carried the poet away and with which he had to break, and still he could find the inner strength to recuperate. Writing about Blok and the Revolution, the American literary scholar V. Erlich asks: "Was the revolution then another love object?" and he answers "In essence—yes."[50] The difference between the poet's previous objects of love and the Revolution is that there is no choice in the latter case. If the poet wants to stay in Russia he must continue loving the Revolution and its product, or face destruction. The poet's love of the Revolution is short-lived and the break destroys him, both spiritually and physically.

Blok is first of all a poet; to look for any political commitment in his work should be regarded as a serious blunder. All his creative work, beginning with "On the Crossroad," where he begins to doubt his feelings for the Beautiful Lady, is a constant succession of different emotions and feelings, at times for a single person, at other times for Russia and its people. When Blok becomes absorbed by a feeling he surrenders himself wholly to the new emotions. With Blok everything is spontaneous. It is tragic that the very spontaneity, which is considered by the Bolsheviks to be the greatest evil of the labor movement in the prerevolutionary period,[51] is used in order to attract the poet to the aims of the Bolshevik party, and later in the effort to prove that Blok is on the side of the October Revolution.

Blok's commitment to the aims of the Revolution is often deduced solely on the basis of the interpretation of his greatest work, "The Twelve." He wrote the poem at a time when a political message was sought in every written word. But did Blok intend a message? In all probability not. The duality and complexity of his character seldom permitted the poet to create on a rational level. Besides, the poet himself gave an explicit reply to this question: "Those who see in 'The Twelve' political verses are either very blind to art, or deep in political mud, or possessed by spite—be they friends or enemies of my poem."[52] And indeed if a political message had been sought, would it not be better, as A. Lunacharsky suggests, to have Lenin instead of Christ marching in front of the twelve?[53] But "Blok overlooked Lenin. He heard no 'music' in Lenin's speeches."[54]

Comparing the approach to Blok in the immediate postrevolutionary period with the treatment of Blok in today's Soviet school, one can conclude that step by step the picture of the poet has been made more attractive. This is not to say that there is approval for Blok's true beliefs. It is rather an effort to emphasize the positive by overlooking the negative. After the Revolution, when the class struggle was still on and when the principle of *klassovost'* in literature was applied with force to all survivors of the tsarist regime, "Blok is a spokesman of the nobility . . . with certain reservations he may be considered the last great artist of the Russian nobility."[55] He was a product of the disintegration of his class who by being a nobleman felt despair over the destruction of the nobility and at the same time repugnance to the growing bourgeoisie, and who looked to the Revolution for an outlet for his feelings and emotions. The Revolution did not save him because Blok was, due to his class background, as Lunacharsky says, alien to its true cause. Regardless of the fact that he "exhibited the maximum revolutionary impulse of which the consciousness of nobility was capable . . . it left Blok on the threshold of the Revolution, amazed, bewildered, unable to appreciate the real rhythm of its march."[56]

Soviet textbooks and methodological aids make use of different means and ways in extracting positive, optimistic notes from the works studied at school. One method is the particular emphasis on understanding of the undercurrent (*podtekst*) of a work discussed. It is claimed that, at times, the second plan or undercurrent is more important than the text itself, and that the true meaning of a work can be fully understood and appreciated only if one can read between the lines. It is obvious that between the lines different readers see different things. The textbook makes sure that the student sees what he should see, though it is not always as easy to do as it may seem.

Chekhov's *Cherry Orchard* "is first of all a play about the motherland, about the alleged and real landlords of the Russian soil, about the approaching renewal of Russia."[57] This renewal is not shown; there is no hint how this change is to take place, and there are no positive heroes in the play. If the "trashy student Trofimov,"[58] as Gorky calls him, is the only representative of the future, it is very doubtful whether Chekhov is optimistic about what is in store for Russia. The play ends on a tragic note. The cherry orchard is destroyed. The student, however, who is armed with the understanding of the dialectic process of the development of society, is to read between the lines and to deduce from the destruction of the orchard, which symbolizes an end of an era, that a new era is coming, and "that the time is not far when all Russia will become a wonderful orchard."[59]

Chekhov was criticized in his time by those who believed that literature should contain a message. He was accused of not making clear on whose side his sympathies were, of not indicating whether he was a liberal or a conservative. Chekhov defended himself by saying that it is not the duty of a writer to solve problems. He claimed that in such great works as *Anna Karenina* or *Evgeniy Onegin* not a single problem is solved, but they completely satisfy the reader because they present all their problems in the right way.[60]

In the late eighties and nineties, as Chekhov approached maturity, his stories did tend to suggest a positive message, which remains, however, always under the surface. The university program suggests studying Chekhov as one of the greatest representatives of Russian critical realism from the end of the nineteenth century. His creative work is to be regarded as a reflection of the progressive democratic ideology in the period of transition from political reaction, in the eighties, to the rise of the social movements before the 1905 revolution. Chekhov's early works should be considered as a "critique of philistinism and social depravity in the autocratic Russia of the period of social and political reaction."[61] In Chekhov's later stories his growing interest in social problems should be emphasized; the depiction of ideological vacillations; the search for social ideals and for a comprehensive world outlook. *"Chelovek v futlyare"* and *"Palata 6"* should be regarded as a "critique of the despotic regime and bureaucratic system of tsarist Russia at the end of the nineteenth century."[62] It is claimed that in the stories *"V ssylke," "Dom s mezoninom," "Zhena," "Palata 6,"* Chekhov is "unmasking the illusions of the liberals and the populists," as well as Tolstoyism. The motif calling for the struggle for a bright future and for human happiness is considered to be the most important aspect of Chekhov's latest works. Little time is devoted in the program to the characters' personal problems and relationships; to the unexplained reasons for their personal unhappiness. There is no mention of the dominant theme in Chekhov of the mutual lack of understanding between human beings; as D. Mirsky puts it, of the impossibility for one person to feel in tune with another,[63] of their mutual unsurpassable isolation, the impossibility of understanding each other.

The importance of the undercurrent is also stressed in the interpretation of *Tikhiy Don* (The Silent Don) by M. Sholokhov. It is claimed that the author's sympathy to the main hero of the novel is a misunderstanding, that "the shades of sarcasm, pain, and sympathy in the author's characteristic of Grigoriy distinctively contradict its straight meaning," and that the "secondary plan [*podtekst*] is quite often more important and introduces in it essential correctives."[64] The student is thus induced to read between the lines, and to notice things he could not, perhaps, see while reading the original text. The textbook tries to make up, it seems, for what Sholokhov himself missed in the novel. It tries to make the student forget about the main hero and to think rather about what follows after the novel. This is where the optimism of the novel comes in.

Not the sad end of Aksin'ya and Natal'ya, nor the tragic fate of Grigoriy Melekhov lead Sholokhov to a pessimistic interpretation of the events. On the whole the novel is deeply optimistic. In the process of the irreconcilable struggle of the old with the new, in the process of transformation of the people's life, the triumph of the Revolution and the inevitable destruction of all that is against it are vividly shown.[65]

The problem is, however, that the optimism of Sholokhov and the optimism of the novel are two different things. The novel is so contrived that the student identifies and sympathizes mainly with Grigoriy Melekhov. The epilogue of the novel, in which our hero is back home, standing bitter and disillusioned on the ruins of the past, with little hope or knowledge of what the future holds in store for him, could be regarded rather as a tragic end by Melekhov's well-wishers, regardless of what political camp they belong to. One leading American literary historian claims,

The Silent Don is not a happy or hopeful book. Life's movement we sense in it, but we do not have a sure sense of its direction. The interpretation of the novel according to which Gregor's individualism is "wrong" and the outlook and behavior of the communist Koshevoy "right" belongs to Soviet critics rather than Sholokhov.[66]

The Silent Don was written after the Revolution, but it deals with the period of transition and transformation in Russia, and it is natural that a certain interpretation is required in order to make it seem to be a work complying with the requirements of socialist realism and *partiynost'*. As far as contemporary Soviet literature is concerned, the problem of interpretation has been lately simplified by excluding from the school programs anything that runs counter to the approved line and that does not lend itself easily to the interpretation required. At the university level the existence of such works cannot be concealed; even if the works of V. Aksenov, V. Nekrasov, or E. Evtushenko are not included in the required reading lists, they are discussed in survey courses, and these authors are often accused of subjectivism and aestheticism, of the propagation of these tendencies under cover of a struggle with dogmatism.[67]

It is worthwhile to note that at the time of Khrushchev's attack on Stalin's personality cult, Solzhenitsyn's *One Day in the Life of Ivan Denisovich* was on the required university reading list in the course of Soviet literature.[68] But it has disappeared since—when a writer is purged in the Soviet Union, so are his works.[69] One of the great Russian poets B. Pasternak, is hardly mentioned at all in the course of Soviet literature. The Soviet student knows nothing officially about *Doktor Zhivago* (Doctor Zhivago), nor does he learn much about Pasternak's poetry. Pasternak is mentioned in the program only once, in connection with his poetry of the early twenties.

The analysis of school and university programs and textbooks, as well as the acquaintance with the methods and principles of Soviet literary education, makes it possible to suggest that there is in the Soviet school a well-designed and structured system of literary education the objective of which is to help the student to master the material required and to become familiar with the historical background of the periods dealt with in different literature courses. The understanding of historical events, however, is shaped in one way—that of the inevitability of a socialist revolution—and the interpretation of literature runs along the same lines. Thus, all evidence which does not support the basic historic and economic premises of Marxism is left out or, at times, given a one-sided interpretation in order to obtain the effect desired.[70]

Does the Soviet student accept without misgivings what he is taught in the literary course? It is difficult to give a definite reply. Some students surely accept what they are taught at face value. Others argue and contradict, but in the long run are forced to accept the official interpretation if they do not want to risk failing the course. Still others choose to remain silent. Without knowing in what direction the winds of the future blow they remain indifferent and prefer to keep quiet. One Russian literature teacher complains, "A student demonstrates praiseworthy obedience, he repeats in his composition everything you have passionately pronounced in class, but you know very well that he thinks differently."[71] And what he thinks we will, perhaps, never know. To keep quiet on touchy matters has become a way of life with the Russians—a habit developed and nourished through centuries of oppression, persecution, and suspicion.[72]

Conclusion

It seems to have been established beyond doubt that one of the main objectives of Soviet literary education is to imbue the young generation with a spirit of devotion to the Soviet state and the communist cause. In order to achieve the desired goals Soviet educators select for inclusion in the educational programs only those authors and works which lend themselves easily to the required interpretation, and they approach these works in a manner to secure the extraction of the values most pertinent to the goals of Soviet ideological education. Since the purpose of Soviet literary education is not to expose the student to the whole variety of literary material available, but to create instead in the student's mind an image of a writer or poet which would conform with the purpose of Soviet ideological upbringing, the principles and methods of Soviet literary education often sacrifice true scholarship for indoctrination. Many works, nineteenth-century classics in particular, receive a one-sided treatment.

The examination of the effectiveness of the method of teaching literature, in which a preconceived social message is sought in each work studied, is conducted by juxtaposing the two basic levels involved in the educational process of teaching literature. The first level is mainly theoretical and it deals with the official Soviet view of how literature should be studied; how it should be approached and dealt with. The second level is the practical level on which the theoretical premises of literary education are tested in their practical application. On the theoretical level I concentrate on the programs and on Soviet textbooks on theory and history of literature approved for use at school and university. On the practical level we learn about the opinions of teachers, methodologists, and students, who comment on, agree with, or criticize the officially approved line in literary education. The juxtaposition of these two levels, which is conducted throughout the study, makes us aware of an existing discrepancy between the theory and practice of literary education which is often expressed in a poor mastery by many students of the ideological content of the material required, and in numerous requests by students and teachers alike to change the approach to the teaching of literature.

The Soviet approach to the study of literature, in which the ideological aspect of education is overemphasized, and in which only one definite solution to the problems encountered in literature is possible, often runs counter to the student's inherent craving for freedom of expression and to his desire to find for himself a solution to the problems discussed in literature classes. Instead of developing love for and attachment to literature, Soviet methods of instruction in literature often lead to opposite results. One leading Soviet literary scholar even claims, "We will not surprise anyone if we say that the students become, at times, so sick and tired of the best works of literature which have been singled out for inclusion in school programs that it is very seldom that someone would touch, from his own good will, any of these works after school."[1] The apparent alienation of some students from literature, and in particular from nineteenth-century classical literature, is in all probability due to the fact that the Soviet student does not see much relevance or importance in the interpretation of a work of art as it is required by the program and the textbook, and because he often has difficulties in identifying with the nineteenth-century hero, who becomes dehumanized by being turned into a vehicle of ideas and a representative of a certain class.

Soviet teachers, educators, and methodologists try hard to change the existing situation. So far, the efforts are of little avail, since the teachers are permitted to work only within a certain framework, limited by the goals of Soviet education. It appears that it is difficult, if not impossible, to institutionalize aesthetic perception, personal feelings, and appreciation of artistic values which may simply appeal to one reader, leaving the other one uninterested, uninvolved, and totally unmoved.

Taking the example of Soviet literary education, it is possible to suggest that when the teaching of literature is turned into a definite ideological weapon it loses much of its general educational significance and ceases to play the role of an important factor in the upbringing and educating of the young generation.

At this point one could ask: What is the relevance of the above conclusions to American schools and to our methods of teaching literature? One thing is clear: one should not force upon the student one's own social, political, or philosophical views and try to compel him to accept them at face value. This does not mean in the least that literature should be taught in a vacuum. On the contrary, an effort should be made to instil in the student certain moral, aesthetic, and other values, accepted by a given society, but this should be done in a spirit of tolerance and in a manner which would not restrict the student's personal freedom of dissent or stifle his curiosity and interest in literature.

Appendix

Table A-1
General Educational Secondary School—Curriculum[1]

Subject	Weekly Classroom Hours										Total Classroom Hours	
	1	2	3	4	5	6	7	8	9	10	New Plan	1959 Plan
Russian Language	12	10	10	6	6	3	3	2	2/0	—	53	57
Literature	—	—	—	2	2	2	2	3	4	3	18	19
Mathematics	6	6	6	6	6	6	6	6	5	5	58	59
History	—	—	—	2	2	2	2	3	4	3	18	20
Social Science	—	—	—	—	—	—	—	—	—	2	2	2
Natural History	—	2	2	2	—	—	—	—	—	—	6	2
Geography	—	—	—	—	2	3	2	2	2	—	11	12
Biology	—	—	—	—	2	2	2	2	0/2	2	11	11
Physics	—	—	—	—	—	2	2	3	4	5	16	17
Astronomy	—	—	—	—	—	—	—	—	—	1	1	1
Drawing	—	—	—	—	—	1	1	1	—	—	3	4
Chemistry	—	—	—	—	—	—	2	2	3	3	10	11
Foreign Language	—	—	—	—	4	3	3	2	2	2	16	20
Fine Arts	1	1	1	1	1	1	—	—	—	—	6	7
Singing and Music	1	1	1	1	1	1	1	—	—	—	7	8
Physical Culture	2	2	2	2	2	2	2	2	2	2	20	22
Labor Training	2	2	2	2	2	2	2	2	2	2	20	58
Total required lessons	24	24	24	24	30	30	30	30	30	30	276	330
Optional lessons	—	—	—	—	—	—	2	4	6	6	—	—
Total	24	24	24	24	30	30	32	34	36	36		

Grade 4 Program in
Literature (70 hours)[2]

Russian folk stories: "Ivan-krest'yanskiy syn i chudo-yudo," "Tsarevna-lya-gushka" (5 hours).

Riddles (2 hours)

Proverbs and sayings (2 hours).

A.S. Pushkin. "U lukomor'ya dub zelenyy . . . " "Skazka o mertvoy tsarevne i o semi bogatyryakh" (4 hours).

G.Ch. Andersen. "Snezhnaya koroleva" (4 hours).

N.A. Nekrasov. "Krest'yanskie deti" (2 hours).

L.N. Tolstoy. "Kavkazskiy plennik" (3 hours).

I.S. Turgenev. "Mumu" (5 hours).

M.Yu. Lermontov. "Borodino" (2 hours).

N.I. Rylenkov. "Vse v tayushchey dymke . . . " (1 hour).

K.G. Paustovsky. Sketches from "Meshcherskaya storona": "Obyknovennaya zemlya," "Lesa," "Luga," "Moy dom," "Beskorystie" (4 hours).

A.A. Fadeev. "Metelitsa" (3 hours).

K.M. Simonov. "Syn artillerista" (2 hours).

V.P. Kataev. *Syn polka* (7 hours).

A.T. Tvardovsky. "Lenin i pechnik" (2 hours).

S.Ya. Marshak. "Lenin." V.M. Inber. "V etot den' " (2 hours).

A.P. Gaydar. *Timur i ego komanda* (4 hours).

For Independent Reading[3]

(For each part of the program)

Folk stories: "Muzhik i tsar'," "Skoryy gonets."

Sh. Perro. "Zolushka."

S.Ya. Marshak. "Dvenadtsat' mesyatsev."

A.P. Chekhov. "Mal'chiki."

A.N. Maykov. "Moy sad s kazhdym dnem uvyadaet . . . "

I.S. Nikitin. "Vstrecha zimy."

S.A. Esenin. "Bereza."

N.A. Zabolotsky. "Ottepel'."

A.N. Pleshcheev. "Vesna."

F.I. Tyutchev. "Neokhotno i nesmelo . . . "

A.A. Fet. "Zreet rozh' nad zharkoy nivoy . . . "

I.A. Bunin. "Gustoy zelenyy el'nik u dorogi . . . "

M.M. Prishvin. "V krayu dedushki Mazaya" (Sketches: "Zharkiy chas," "Belich'ya pamyat'," "Lyagushonok").

V.D. Bonch-Bruevich. "V pervye dni Oktyabrya."
M.V. Isakovsky. "Zdes' pokhoronen krasnoarmeets."
N.S. Tikhonov. "Ruki."

For Memorization

Riddles and proverbs according to the pupil's choice.
A.S. Pushkin. "U lukomor'ya dub zelenyy . . . "
"Skazka o mertvoy tsarevne i o semi bogatyryakh" (to be chosen from several
    fragments).
M.Yu. Lermontov. "Borodino."
N.A. Nekrasov. "Krest'yanskie deti" (the fragment: "Odnazhdy v studenuyu
    zimnyuyu poru . . . ").
K.M. Simonov. "Syn artillerista" (one fragment to be chosen).
S.Ya. Marshak. "Lenin."

Total Hours

For the study of literary texts—54 hours.
For the development of speech—8 hours.
For the discussion of home reading—8 hours.

Grade 5 Program in
Literature (70 hours)[4]

Grade four switched to the new program in literature in the 1970-71 school year, while grade five switched to the new program in 1971-72, resulting in a certain overlapping. The program has been adjusted since, so there is no repetition of the same material in different classes.

Stories, Riddles, Proverbs

"Morozko" (folk story) (2 hours).
A.S. Pushkin, "Skazka o mertvoy tsarevne i o semi bogatyryakh" (3 hours).
Riddles about labor, nature, and animals (2 hours).
Proverbs about labor in the past and about the work of Soviet people; about the defence of the motherland; antireligious proverbs; proverbs about the character and actions of people (2 hours).

For Independent Reading

"Tsarevna-lyagushka" (folk story).
Stories of the people of the USSR and of foreign people (to be selected by the teacher from the textbook).
P.P. Bazhov. "Kamennyy tsvetok" (Ural tale).
A.P. Gaydar. "Goryachiy kamen'."
G. Longfello. "Piroga Gayvaty."
Proverbs of the people of the USSR and foreign proverbs (to be selected by the teacher from the textbook).

Summer and Autumn Nature

I.S. Nikitin. "Utro" (2 hours).
A.S. Pushkin. "Osen' " (a fragment) (1 hour).

For Independent Reading

A.N. Maykov. "Letniy dozhd'."
F.I. Tyutchev. "Est' v oseni pervonachal'noy . . . "
S.A. Esenin. "Nivy szhaty, roshchi goly . . . " (the first two stanzas).

M.A. Sholokhov. "Osen' v lesu" (from the novel *Tikhiy Don*).
M.M. Prishvin. "Osinkam kholodno," "Listopad" (from the chapter "Vremena goda" in the book *Lesnaya kapel'*).

Russian Writers About the Past of Our Fatherland

M.Yu. Lermontov. "Borodino" (2 hours).
I.A. Krylov. "Volk na psarne," "Kvartet" (3 hours).
I.S. Turgenev. "Mumu" (5 hours).
V.G. Korolenko. "Deti podzemel'ya" (6 hours).
V.P. Kataev. "Gavrik i Petya" (from the story "Beleet parus odinokiy") (3 hours).

For Independent Reading

I.A. Krylov. "Oboz," "Svin'ya pod Dubom," "Dva mal'chika."
S.V. Mikhalkov. "Polkan i Shavka."
A.V. Kol'tsov. "Kosar'."
A.P. Chekhov. "Kashtanka," "Mal'chiki."
K.M. Stanyukovich. "Maksimka."
A.M. Gorky. "Mal'chiki" (from *Detstvo*).

Winter Nature

A.S. Pushkin. "Buran v stepi" (from *Kapitanskaya dochka*) (2 hours).
S.A. Esenin. "Bereza" (1 hour).

For Independent Reading

F.I. Tyutchev. "Charodeykoyu-zimoyu."
M.M. Prishvin. "Zazimok." "Osennee utro" (from the chapter "Vremena goda" in *Glaza zemli*).
S.Ya. Marshak. "Kak porabotala zima."

Soviet Writers About the Soviet Fatherland

S.V. Mikhalkov. "V muzee V.I. Lenina" (2 hours).
A.A. Fadeev. "Metelitsa" (4 hours).

K.M. Simonov. "Syn artillerista" (2 hours).
S.Ya. Marshak. "Rasskaz o neizvestnom geore" (1 hour).
P.A. Pavlenko. "Stepnoe solntse" (abridged) (4 hours).
V.V. Mayakovsky. "Kem byt'?" (2 hours).

For Independent Reading

V.D. Bonch-Bruevich. "Nash Il'ich."
Yu.P. German. "Rasskazy o Dzerzhinskom."
V.I. Lebedev-Kumach. "My Rodinu slavim trudom."

Spring Nature

F.I. Tyutchev. "Vesennie vody" (1 hour).

For Independent Reading

M.M. Prishvin. "Cheremukha," "Berezy" (from the chapter "Vremena goda" in
    Glaza zemli).
L.N. Tolstoy. "Vesna" (from *Anna Karenina*).
M. Dzhalil. "May."
I.Z. Surikov. "Vesna."
A.A. Fet. "Eto utro, radost' eta."

Total Hours

For the study of literary texts—50 hours.
For the development of speech—12 hours.
For the discussion of home reading—8 hours.

Grade 6 Program in
Literature (70 hours)[5]

Oral Folk Poetry

Byliny: "Il'ya Muromets i Solovey Razbovynik," "Vol'ga i Mikula" (5 hours).
Folk songs: "Iz-za lesa temnogo, iz-za sadika zelenogo" (1 hour).

For Independent Reading

"Sadko" (bylina).
Folk songs: "Ne shumi, mati, zelenaya dubravushka," "Akh, kaby ne tsvety da ne morozy."

Works of Russian Writers

I.A. Krylov. Fables: "Volk i yagnenok," "Osel i solovey" (2 hours).
A.S. Pushkin. *Dubrovsky* (8 hours).
M.Yu. Lermontov. "Parus" (1 hour).
N.V. Gogol'. *Taras Bul'ba* (8 hours).
N.V. Gogol'. "Dnepr" (from the story "Strashnaya mest' ") (1 hour).
I.S. Turgenev. "Bezhin lug" (4 hours).
N.A. Nekrasov. "Na Volge," "Zabytaya derevnya" (3 hours).
A.P. Chekhov. "Khameleon" (2 hours).

For Independent Reading

S. Ayni. "Shkola."
N.V. Gogol'. "Ukrainskaya noch' " (from the story "Sorochinskaya yarmarka").
S.A. Esenin. "S dobrym utrom."
I.A. Krylov. "Slon na voevodstve," "Trishkin kaftan," "Dem'yanova ukha," "Lzhets."
M.Yu. Lermontov. "Tri pal'my."
S.V. Mikhalkov. "Slon-zhivopisets."
N.A. Nekrasov. "Kalistrat," "Plach detey."
A.S. Pushkin. "Pesn' o veshchem Olege," "Poltavskiy boy" (from the poem "Poltava"), "Besy."
I.Z. Surikov. "Ya li v pole da ne travushkoy byla," "Dolya bednyaka."
I.S. Turgenev. "Shchi," "Golubi" (from "Stikhotvoreniya v proze").

A.A. Fet. "Ya prishel k tebe s privetom . . . "
K. Khetagurov. "Ne ver', chto ya zabyl."
A.P. Chekhov. "Detvora," "Nalim," "Loshadinaya familiya."
N.M. Yazykov. "Plovets."

Works by Soviet Writers

A.M. Gorky. "Strast' k chteniyu" (from *V lyudyakh*) (2 hours).
A.T. Tvardovsky. "Lenin i pechnik" (2 hours).
N.S. Tikhonov. "Sami" (1 hour).
B.N. Polevoy. *Povest' o nastoyashchem cheloveke* (4 hours).
S.P. Shchipachev. "Lenin" (1 hour).
A.S. Makarenko. "Chto takoe entuziazm" (a passage from *Flagi na bashnyakh*) (1 hour).
M.V. Isakovsky. "Duma o Lenine" (1 hour).

For Independent Reading

A.I. Bezymensky. "Balada ob ordene."
D. Bedny. "Snezhinki."
M.V. Isakovsky. "Russkoy zhenshchine," "Vyydi v pole," "Letyat pereletnye ptitsy."
V.P. Kataev. "Khutorok v stepi" (a passage).
Revolutionary songs: G. Machtet. "Zamuchen tyazheloy nevoley," N. Lavrov. "Kommunisticheskaya marsel'eza."
A.S. Makarenko. "Chetvertyy svodnyy" (a passage from *Pedagogicheskaya poema*).
V.V. Mayakovsky. "Poslednyaya stranichka grazhdanskoy voyny."
A.I. Panteleev. "Na yalike."
V.F. Tendryakov. "Mednyy krestik" (from the story "Chudotvornaya").

Total Hours

For the study of literary texts—47 hours.
For the development of speech—15 hours.
For the discussion of home reading—8 hours.

Grade 7 Program in
Literature (70 hours)[6]

Introduction (1 hour).

From 19th-century Literature

A.S. Pushkin. *Kapitanskaya dochka* (10 hours).
For independent reading: A.S. Pushkin. "Poltava."

M.Yu. Lermontov. "Pesnya pro kuptsa Kalashnikova," "Mtsyri" (7 hours).
Theory of literature: The notion of a theme and idea of a work of literature.

N.V. Gogol'. *Revizor* (8 hours).
Theory of literature: The notion of a plot; the notion of a comedy.

L.N. Tolstoy. "Posle bala" (3 hours).
Theory of literature: The notion of the composition of a work of literature.

From Soviet Literature

A.M. Gorky. "Pesnya o Sokole," "Pesnya o Burevestnike," "Deti Parmy" (4 hours).
For independent reading: A.M. Gorky. "Simplonskiy tunnel'."

V.V. Mayakovsky. "Neobychaynoe priklyuchenie . . . , " "Rasskaz o Kuznetskstroe i o lyudyakh Kuznetska" (3 hours).
For independent reading: V.V. Mayakovsky. "Prozasedavshiesya" (and other poems to be selected by the teacher.)

A.T. Tvardovsky. "Vasiliy Terkin" (the chapters: "Pereprava," "O nagrade," "Garmon'," "Dva soldata," "Kto strelyal?") (4 hours).
For independent reading: A. Mezhirov. "Kommunisty, vpered!"

A.A. Fadeev. *Molodaya gvardiya* (10 hours).
For independent reading: Musa Dzhalil. "Prosti Rodina," "Palachu." I. Bekher. "Dve Germanii."
Theory of literature: The artistic image and its generalizing importance. The truth and creative imagination in literature. Review and systematization of material covered in theory of literature (4 hours).

Total Hours

For the study of literary texts—50 hours.
For the development of speech—10 hours.
For the discussion of home reading—6 hours.

Grade 8 Program in Literature (105 hours)[7] (Systematic Course in Russian Literature)

Brief Survey of Russian Literature up to the 19 Century (12 hours)

Introduction.
Slovo o polku Igoreve.
From 18th century poetry: M.V. Lomonosov. "Oda na den' vosshestviya . . . " (1747), "Proslavlenie Rodiny, mira, nauki i prosveshcheniya."
G.R. Derzhavin. "Vlastitelyam i sudyam," "Pamyatnik."
D.I. Fonvizin. *Nedorosl'* (survey and reading of some scenes which are to be chosen by the teacher).
A.N. Radishchev. "Puteshestvie iz Peterburga v Moskvu" (general survey including the reading of passages selected by the teacher).

Russian Literature of the First Half of the 19th Century

Introduction (1 hour).

V.A. Zhukovsky. "Svetlana," "More" (1 hour).

K.F. Ryleev. "Grazhdanin," "Ivan Susanin," fragments from the poem "Nalivay-ko" (1 hour).
Theory of literature: Introduction of the notion of romanticism (1 hour).

A.S. Griboedov. *Gore ot uma* (9 hours).
Criticism: I.A. Goncharov. "Mil'on terzaniy" (abridged).
Theory of literature: The notion of a conflict in a work of literature.

A.S. Pushkin. "K Chadaevu," "V Sibir'," "K moryu," "Ya pomnyu chudnoe mgnovenie . . . ," "Prorok," "Anchar," "Na kholmakh Gruzii . . . ," "Ya vas lyubil," "Vnov' ya posetil . . . .," "Ya pamyatnik sebe vozdvig . . . ," *Evgeniy Onegin* (24 hours).

Criticism: V.G. Belinsky. "Sochineniya Aleksandra Pushkina" (fifth, eighth, and ninth articles; abridged).
Theory of literature: The historic and general importance of great works of literature. The notion of poetic language. The development of the notion of lyricism. Further elaboration on the notion of verse.

For independent reading:[8] *Mednyy vsadnik*; eight to ten lyrical poems to be chosen by the pupil; one from the "Southern" poems; *Boris Godunov* or *Malen'kie tragedii.*

M.Yu. Lermontov. "Smert' poeta," "Poet," "Duma," "Kak chasto, pestroyu tolpoyu okruzhen . . . ," "Iz-pod tainstvennoy, kholodnoy polumaski . . . ," "Vykhozhu ya na dorogu . . . ," "Rodina," *Geroy nashego vremeni* (14 hours).

Criticism: V.G. Belinsky. *Geroy nashego vremeni,* "Stikhotvoreniya M. Lermontova" (abridged).

Theory of literature: The development of the notion of the composition of a work of literature.

For independent reading: "Demon"; eight to ten short poems to be chosen by the pupil.

N.V. Gogol'. *Mertvye dushi* (vol. I) (12 hours).

Theory of literature: The notion of a literary type, satire, and humor.

For independent reading: "Shinel' " or "Portret."

V.G. Belinsky. Survey of literary critical activity (3 hours).

Theory of literature: The notion of critical realism.

A.I. Gertsen. Chapters from the book *Byloe i dumy* to be selected by the teacher (4 hours).

From Foreign Literature (6 hours)

J. Molière. *Le Bourgeois Gentilhomme.*

G. Byron. *Childe Harold's Pilgrimage* (fragments), and some poems in Lermontov's translation.

Theory of literature: The development of the notion of romanticism.

Total Hours:

For the study of literary texts—87 hours.

For the discussion of topics from Soviet literature—8 hours.

For the development of language skill—10 hours.

Grade 9 Program in
Literature (140 hours)[9]

Literature of the Second Half of the 19th Century (Survey—4 hours)

A.N. Ostrovsky. *Groza* (9 hours).
Theory of literature: The idea of dramatic conflict.
For independent reading: Bespridannitsa.

I.S. Turgenev. *Ottsy i deti* (12 hours).
Criticism: D.I. Pisarev. "Bazarov."
Theory of literature: The notion of a novel. The author's intention and the objective truth of a work of art.
For independent reading: One of the following novels (to be chosen by the student) *Rudin, Dvoryanskoe gnezdo, Nakanune*; one of the stories: "Asya," "Veshnie vody."

N.G. Chernyshevsky. *Chto delat'?* (8 hours).
Theory of literature: The notion about the beautiful in life and in art. The cognitive and educational importance of literature and other forms of art.

N.A. Nekrasov. "Razmyshleniya u paradnogo pod"ezda," "Zheleznaya doroga," "Puskay nam govorit izmenchivaya moda" (elegiya), "Pamyati Dobro-lyubova," "Komu na Rusi zhit' khorosho" (14 hours).
Theory of literature: The notion of *narodnost'* in literature. The idea of an author's style.
For independent reading: "Rytsar' na chas," "Rodina," "Edu li noch'yu," "V doroge," "Poet i grazhdanin," "Balet."

M.E. Saltykov-Shchedrin. *Istoriya odnogo goroda* (chapters to be selected by the teacher). Stories: "Medved' na voevodstve," "Premudryy peskar' " (6 hours).
Theory of literature: The notion of grotesque and aesopian language.
For independent reading: Gospoda Golovlevy.

F.M. Dostoevsky. *Prestuplenie i nakazanie* (12 hours).
For independent reading: Unizhennye i oskorblennye.

L.N. Tolstoy. *Voyna i mir* (22 hours).
Theory of literature: The idea of an epic novel. The world outlook and the creative activity of a writer.
For independent reading: Anna Karenina or *Voskresenie* (to be chosen by the student).

A.P. Chekhov. *Vishnevyy sad*, "Ionych" (12 hours).

Theory of literature: The development of the idea about dramatic genres.

For independent reading: One from the stories "Dom s mezoninom," "Palata No. 6," "Poprygun'ya," "Nevesta" (to be chosen by the student); plays: *Dyadya Vanya, Tri sestry.*

From Foreign Literature

W. Shakespeare. *Hamlet* (5 hours).
J. Goethe. *Faust* (4 hours).
Stendhal. *Vanina Vanini* (3 hours).
H. de Balzac. *Gobsek* (3 hours).
Theory of literature: The development of the notion of critical realism.

Total Hours

For the study of literary texts—112 hours.
For the discussion of topics from Soviet literature—12 hours.
For the development of language skill—16 hours.

Grade 10 Program in
Literature (105 hours)[10]

Soviet Literature

Introduction (3 hours).
Theory of literature: The notion of *partiynost'* in literature.

A.M. Gorky. "Starukha Izergil'," *Na dne, Mat'*, "V.I. Lenin" (16 hours).
Theory of literature: The notion of socialist realism. Socialist realism as a natural stage in the artistic development of humanity.
For independent reading (to be chosen by the student): Foma Gordeev or *Delo Artamonovykh; Vassa Zheleznova* or *Egor Bulychev i drugie.*

A.A. Blok. To be chosen by the teacher from the following: "Neznakomka," "O, vesna bez kontsa i bez krayu," "Rossiya," "O doblestyakh, o podvigakh, o slave," "Solov'inyy sad," "Na zheleznoy doroge," "Fabrika," "Dvenad-tsat' " (4 hours).

S.A. Esenin. To be chosen by the teacher from the following: "Rus' sovet-skaya," "Pis'mo materi," "Neuyutnaya zhidkaya lunnost' ...," "Kazhdyy trud blagoslavi udacha ...," "Sobake Kachalova," "Spit kovyl'. Ravnina dorogaya ...," "Ya idu dolinoy. Na zatylke kepi ...," "Ne zhaleyu, ne plachu ...," "Anna Snegina" (4 hours).

V.V. Mayakovsky. Lyrics: "Levyy marsh!," "Prozasedavshiesya," "O dryani," "Black and White," "Tovarishchu Nette ...," "Stikhi o sovetskom pas-porte," "Pis'mo t. Kostrovu o sushchnosti lyubvi." Poems: "Vladimir Il'ich Lenin," "Khorosho!" "Vo ves' golos" (15 hours).
Theory of literature: Tradition and innovation in literature. The notion of a lyric hero. Lyric-epic works. Tonic versification.
For independent reading (to be chosen by the student): "Banya" or "Klop"; eight to ten short poems.

A.A. Fadeev. *Razgrom* (5 hours).
K.A. Trenev. *Lyubov' Yarovaya* (5 hours).
Survey of Soviet poetry from the twenties and thirties (3 hours).
N.A. Ostrovsky. *Kak zakalyalas' stal'* (survey—4 hours).
A.N. Tolstoy. *Petr I* (8 hours).
M.A. Sholokhov. *Podnyataya tselina*, "Sud'ba cheloveka" (12 hours).
Theory of literature: The notion of *narodnost'* of Soviet literature.
Survey of the literature from the period of the Great Fatherland War (4 hours).

Patriotic lyrics by A. Surkov, K. Simonov, M. Isakovsky, N. Tikhonov. Poems by M. Aliger, Ya. Kolas, P. Tychina. Novels and stories. *Volokolamskoe shosse* by A. Bek; *Zvezda* by E. Kazakevich; *V okopakh Stalingrada* by V. Nekrasov; L. Leonov's play *Nashestvie.* (Several works for literary analysis to be chosen by the teacher.)

A.T. Tvardovsky. Survey of creative activity (3 hours).
Theory of literature: The diversity of styles and genres in Soviet literature.

Soviet literature of the fifties and sixties (6 hours).
Short characteristic of the creative activity of writers chosen for study in class. (To be selected from the appended list of titles recommended for home reading.)

Contemporary foreign literature (3 hours).
(To be selected from the appended list of titles recommended for home reading.)

Review and general conclusions on the course of Russian literature of the 19th and 20th centuries. The universal importance of Russian classic and Soviet literatures (10 hours).

Literature for Memorization:
Grades 5-7[1][1]

Grade 5

Riddles and proverbs (to be selected by the teacher).
I.A. Krylov. "Kvartet," "Volk na psarne."
A.S. Pushkin. "Osen' " (a fragment).
M.Yu. Lermontov. "Borodino."
F.Yu. Tyutchev. "Charodeykoyu-zimoyu," "Vesennie vody."
S.A. Esenin. "Bereza."
I.S. Nikitin. "Utro."
S.V. Mikhalkov. "V muzee Lenina" (a fragment).
K.M. Simonov. "Syn artillerista" (a fragment).
V.V. Mayakovsky. "Kem byt'?"

Grade 6

One popular song (*odna iz narodnykh pesen*).
I.A. Krylov. Dve basni.
M.Yu. Lermontov. "Parus."
N.V. Gogol'. A fragment from the description of the Ukraine steppe in *Taras Bul'ba*, "Dnepr" (one part) from the story "Strashnaya mest',"
I.S. Turgenev. A fragment from the depiction of a July day or of an early morning from the story "Bezhin lug."
N.A. Nekrasov. "Na Volge" (a fragment).
A. Tvardovsky. "Lenin i pechnik" (a fragment).
N.S. Tikhonov. "Sami" (a fragment).
S.P. Shchipachev. "Lenin."

Grade 7

M.Yu. Lermontov. "Mtsyri" (a fragment).
A.M. Gorky. "Pesnya o Sokole" (a fragment), "Pesnya o Burevestnike."
V.V. Mayakovsky. A poem to be chosen by the pupil.
A.T. Tvardovsky. "Vasiliy Terkin" (a fragment to be chosen by the pupil).

In grades 8-10 literature for memorization is selected by the teacher and in some cases by the student.

93

Literature for Home Reading: Grades 8-10[1] [2]

Russian Literature of the 19th-20th Centuries

"Povest' o Gore-Zlochastii," "Povest' o Ershe Ershoviche."

M. Lomonosov. "Oda na den' vosshestviya na prestol Elizavety Petrovny, 1747."

G. Derzhavin. "Felitsa," "Videnie murzy," "Vel'mozha," "Evgeniyu. Zhizn' zvanskaya."

D. Fonvizin. *Brigadir*, "Vseobshchaya pridvornaya grammatika."

V. Zhukovsky. *Stikhi i ballady.*

K. Ryleev. "K vremenshchiku," "Voynarovskiy," "Dumy."

A. Pushkin. *Sochineniya.*

M. Lermontov. *Sochineniya.*

N. Gogol'. *Sochineniya.*

A. Ostrovsky. *Dokhodnoe mesto, Les, Volki i ovtsy, Bez viny vinovatye.*

I. Goncharov. *Oblomov, Obryv.*

I. Turgenev. *Zapiski okhotnika, Nov'*, "Stikhotvoreniya v proze," "Gamlet i Don Kikhot."

A. Gertsen. *Kto vinovat?, Soroka vorovka, Byloe i dumy.*

N. Nekrasov. "Russkie zhenshchiny," *Stikhi.*

F. Tyutchev. *Stikhi.*

A. Fet. *Stikhi.*

Ya. Polonsky. *Stikhi.*

A.K. Tolstoy. *Stikhi, Tsar' Fedor Ioannovich.*

V. Kurochkin. *Stikhi.*

N. Pomyalovsky. *Meshchanskoe schast'e, Molotov, Ocherki bursy.*

V. Sleptsov. *Trudnoe vremya.*

F. Dostoevsky. *Brat'ya Karamazovy, Idiot.*

L. Tolstoy. *Sevastopol'skie rasskazy, Kazaki, Zhivoy trup.*

V. Garshin. "Chetyre dnya," "Krasnyy tsvetok."

G. Uspensky. *Nravy Rasteryaevoy ulitsy, Vypryamila.*

N. Leskov. "Ledi Makbet Mtsenskogo uezda," "Levsha."

V. Korolenko. "Chudnaya," "Reka igraet," "At-Davan," "Ogon'ki," "Mgnovenie," *Istoriya moego sovremennika.*

A. Chekhov. *Povesti i rasskazy, Chayka.*

A. Kuprin. *Molokh, Poedinok*, "Granatovyy braslet."

I. Bunin. "Gospodin iz San Frantsisko," *Stikhi*, "Pesn' o Gayavate" (a translation).

L. Andreev. "Dni nashey zhizni."

Soviet Literature

M. Gorky. "Chelkash," "Konovalov," *Meshchane, Vragi,* "Skazki ob Italii."

V. Mayakovsky. *Stikhi.*

V. Bryusov. *Stikhi.*

A. Blok. *Stikhi.*

S. Esenin. *Stikhi.*

D. Bedny. *Stikhi.*

E. Bagritsky. *Stikhi,* "Duma pro Opanasa."

E. Charents. *Stikhi.*

Vs. Ivanov. *Partizanskie povesti.*

A. Serafimovich. *Zheleznyy potok.*

D. Furmanov. *Chapaev.*

F. Gladkov. *Tsement.*

B. Lavrenev. *Razlom, Sorok pervyy.*

M. Bulgakov. *Dni Turbinykh.*

Vs. Vishnevsky. *Optimisticheskaya tragediya.*

M. Sholokhov. *Tikhiy Don.*

A. Tolstoy. *Khozhdenie po mukam.*

K. Fedin. *Goroda i gody, Pervye radosti, Neobyknovennoe leto.*

A. Makarenko. *Pedagogicheskaya poema, Flagi na bashnyakh.*

V. Kataev. *Vremya, vpered.*

I. Erenburg. *Den' vtoroy.*

Yu. Krymov. *Tanker 'Derbent'.*

Yu. Tynyanov. *Kyukhla.*

N. Pogodin. *Kremlevskie kuranty. Tret'ya pateticheskaya.*

A. Afinogenov. *Strakh, Mashen'ka.*

A. Korneychuk. *Platon Krechet.*

M. Ryl'sky. *Stikhi.*

M. Sholokhov. "Oni srazhalis' za rodinu."

P. Antokol'sky. "Syn," *Stikhi.*

M. Dzhalil. *Stikhi.*

S. Neris. *Stikhi.*

V. Grossman. *Narod bessmerten, Za pravoe delo.*

V. Panova. *Sputniki, Sentimental'nyy roman.*

P. Vershigora. *Lyudi s chistoy sovest'yu.*

O. Gonchar. *Znamenostsy.*

V. Latsis. *K novomu beregu.*

M. Auezov. *Abay.*

L. Leonov. *Russkiy les.*

K. Paustovsky. *Povest' o zhizni.*

P. Nilin. *Zhestokost'.*

G. Nikolaeva. *Bitva v puti.*

V. Ketlinskaya. *Inache zhit' ne stoit.*
O. Berggol'ts. "Fevral'skiy dnevnik," "Dnevnye zvezdy," *Stikhi.*
D. Kedrin. *Stikhi.*
M. Lukonin. *Stikhi.*
V. Fedorov. *Stikhi.*
S. Vurgun. *Stikhi.*
M. Tursun-zade. *Stikhi.*
K. Kuliev. *Stikhi.*
P. Brovka. *Stikhi.*
Yu. Smuul. *Ledovaya kniga.*
V. Tendryakov. "Ne ko dvoru," "Ukhaby."
E. Dorosh. *Derevenskiy dnevnik.*
V. Soloukhin. *Kaplya rosy, Stikhi.*
S. Antonov. "Alenka," *Rasskazy.*
Yu. Kazakov. *Sbornik Goluboe i zelenoe.*
Yu. Nagibin. *Sbornik Dalekoe i blizkoe.*
E. Drabkina. *Chernye sukhari.*
V. Kozhevnikov. *Zare navstrechu.*
M. Shaginyan. *Pervaya vserossiyskaya.*
M. Prilezhaeva. *Udivitel'nyy god.*
Yu. Martsinkyavichus. *Krov' i pepel.*
N. Aseev. *Stikhi.*
E. Vinokurov. *Stikhi.*
A. Voznesensky. *Stikhi.*
R. Gamzatov. *Stikhi.*
M. Dudin. *Stikhi.*
E. Evtushenko. *Stikhi.*
N. Zabolotsky. *Stikhi.*
V. Lugovskoy. *Stikhi.*
L. Martynov. *Stikhi.*
S. Marshak. *Stikhi.*
E. Mezhelaytis. *Stikhi.*
A. Mezhirov. *Stikhi.*
R. Rozhdestvensky. *Stikhi.*
Ya. Smelyakov. *Stikhi.*
B. Slutsky. *Stikhi.*
E. Isaev. *Sud pamyati.*
A. Kuznetsov. *Prodolzhenie legendy.*
A. Chakovsky. *Svet dalekoy zvezdy.*
D. Granin. *Idu na grozu.*
B. Polevoy. *Na dikom berege, Doktor Vera.*
Ch. Aytmanov. *Povesti gor i stepey, Proshchay, Gul'sary!*
A. Arbuzov. *Irkutskaya istoriya.*

A. Salynsky. *Barabanshchitsa.*

Sovetskie poety pavshie na Velikoy Otechestvennoy Voyne (sbornik, Moscow, "Sovetskiy pisatel'," 1965).

Iz dnevnikov sovremennikov (sbornik, Moscow, "Molodaya gvardiya," 1965).

I. Efremov. *Tumannost' Andromedy.*

A. i B. Strugatskie. *Dalekaya raduga, Trudno byt' bogom.*

Literature of the People of the USSR
from before the October Revolution

Firduosi. "Shakh-name."

Omar Khayyám. "Rubai."

Nizami. "Khosrov i Shirin."

Shota Rustaveli. "Vityaz' v tigrovoy shkure."

Navoi. "Leyli i Medzhnun."

K. Donelaytis. "Vremena goda."

T. Shevchenko. "Kobzar'."

I. Franko. *Stikhi.*

L. Ukrainka. *Stikhi.*

M. Kotsyubinsky. "Fata Morgana."

Ya. Kupala. *Stikhi.*

Ya. Raynis. *Stikhi.*

Sholom Aleykhem. *Bluzhdayushchie zvezdy.*

Abay Kunanbaev. *Stikhi.*

I. Chavchavadze. *Stikhi.*

M.M. Akhundov. *Komedi i povesti.*

O. Tumanyan. *Stikhi.*

Vazha Pshavela. *Stikhi, Poemy.*

K. Khetagurov. *Stikhi.*

G. Tukay. *Stikhi.*

Educational Programing in Literature on the Moscow Television Network for the Second Half of the 1969-70 School Year[1][3]

Grade 5

1. The seasons of the year. Winter. February 19, 1970.
   Lesson.
2. The seasons of the year. Spring. May 14, 1970.
   Lesson.
3. The seasons of the year. Summer. May 28, 1970.
   Lesson.

Grade 6

1. Turgenev. "Bezhin lug." February 5, 1970. Lesson.
2. Chekhov. "Khameleon." March 5, 1970. Lesson.

Grade 7

1. Bagritsky. "Smert' pionerki." March 14, 1970. Lesson.
2. From the history of the creation of the novel *Molodaya gvardiya* by Fadeev.
   April 11, 1970.
   Lesson, 35 minutes.

Grade 8

1. Pushkin. *Boris Godunov.* January 29, 1970. Evening.
2. Pushkin. Poems about Russia. January 31, 1970.
   After school.
3. Lermontov. Poems about Russia. February 14, 1970.
   After school.
4. Lermontov. *Geroy nashego vremeni.* March 12, 1970.
   Evening.
5. Critical realism. March 14, 1970. After school.
6. Preparation for examinations. March 19, 1970.
   Lesson, 35 minutes.
7. Gogol'. "Peterburgskie povesti." March 26, 1970.

Evening.
8. Commentaries to Gogol"s poem *Mertvye dushi.* April 15, 1970. Lesson, 35 minutes.

Grade 9

1. The Peterburg of Dostoevsky. February 5, 1970. Evening.
2. Moscow in Tolstoy's life. February 25, 1970. Evening.
3. Critical realism. March 14, 1970. After school.
4. Moscow in the life of Chekhov. April 2, 1970. Evening.
5. Chekhov. *Chayka.* April 16, 1970. Evening.
6. Chekhov and the *Khudozhestvennyy teatr.* April 23, 1970. Evening.
7. Chekhov the playwright. April 30, 1970. Lesson.
8. Chekhov in the reminiscences of contemporaries. April 30, 1970. Evening.

Grade 10

1. K. Trenev. *Lyubov' Yarovaya.* January 24, 1970. After School.
2. A. Tolstoy. *Khozhdenie po mukam.* February 14, 1970. Lesson, 40 minutes.
3. A. Tolstoy (a literary portrait). February 19, 1970. Evening.
4. Poetry in the years of the Fatherland War. February 28, 1970. After school.
5. Preparation for examinations. April 2, 1970. Lesson, 35 minutes.
6. Sergey Esenin. Poems about Russia. April 25, 1970. After school.
7. Drama in the years of the Fatherland War. May 7, 1970. Evening.
8. Aleksandr Blok. Poems about Russia. (Date not indicated.)
9. Socialist realism. May 23, 1970. After school.

Programs on Soviet Poetry
(Saturday, 2:25-3:05)

1. Dmitriy Kedrin. February 7, 1970.
2. Nikolay Zabolotsky. February 21, 1970.
3. Rasul Gamzatov. March 7, 1970.
4. Kaysyn Kuliev. March 21, 1970.
5. Sil'va Kaputikyan. March 28, 1970.
6. Irakliy Abashidze. April 4, 1970.
7. Olzhas Suleymenov. April 11, 1970.
8. Iustinas Martsinkyavichus. May 25, 1970.

*Department of Literature of the
teaching programs studio
of the Central Television Network*

Examination Papers in Russian Literature for Grade 10 of Secondary School for the 1968-69 School Year[14]

Paper No. 1

1. The Program of the Communist Party of the Soviet Union about the importance of Soviet literature in the communist education of the working people.
2. *Slovo o polku Igoreve*—the greatest monument of old Russian literature. The theme and idea in the *Slovo*.

Paper No. 2

1. The principle of *partiynost'* in literature. Lenin's article: "Partiynaya organizatsiya i partiynaya literatura."
2. The unmasking of the "bosses of life" in the plays of A.N. Ostrovsky.

Paper No. 3

1. The life and creative work of A.M. Gorky before the October Revolution.
2. The ideals of life and the moral face of the Famusov society (A.S. Griboedov, *Gore ot uma*).

Paper No. 4

1. Literary and social activity of A.M. Gorky after the October Revolution.
2. The power of Katerina's character and the tragic intensity of her conflict with the "dark kingdom" in the play *Groza*. The character of Katerina in the evaluation of N.A. Dobrolyubov. (The power and the contradictions of the character of Larisa in the play *Bespridanitsa*.) The notion of a conflict in a work of art.

Paper No. 5

1. The early revolutionary-romantic works of Gorky, their ideological trend and artistic peculiarity.

2. The meaning of the title and the peculiarities of composition of I.S. Turgenev's novel *Ottsy i deti*. The reflection in the novel of the socio-political struggle in the sixties of the 19th century.

Paper No. 6

1. A.M. Gorky's novel *Mat'* as a work of socialist realism. The evaluation of the novel by V.I. Lenin.
2. Evgeniy Bazarov and Pavel Petrovich Kirsanov. D.I. Pisarev about Bazarov.

Paper No. 7

1. The depiction of the growth of the revolutionary movement and of the class consciousness of the workers in the novel *Mat'* by A.M. Gorky.
2. Poems inspiring the love of freedom by A.S. Pushkin. Recite from memory one of the poems.

Paper No. 8

1. Pavel Vlasov—the first character of a worker-revolutionary in the history of world literature.
2. The life and creative work of A.S. Pushkin in exile (1820-26). Recite from memory one of Pushkin's poems.

Paper No. 9

1. The life of Nilovna. The importance of the character of Nilovna for the interpretation of the ideological conception of the novel *Mat'*.
2. A.S. Pushkin about the purpose of the poet and poetry. The *narodnost'* of Pushkin's creative work.

Paper No. 10

1. Lenin and Gorky. The character of the leader of the proletariat V.I. Lenin in Gorky's essay "V.I. Lenin." Artistic peculiarities of the essay.
2. The history of the creation and the composition of the novel *Evgeniy Onegin*. Lyrical digressions. The Onegin stanza. Recite from memory an extract from the novel.

Paper No. 11

1. The sharp criticism of the capitalistic reality in the play of A.M. Gorky, *Na dne*. The characters of the dossers.
2. The *grazhdanstvennost'* and *narodnost'* of N.A. Nekrasov's poetry. V.I. Lenin about the importance of Nekrasov's creative work for the Russian liberation movement. Recite from memory one of the poet's poems.

Paper No. 12

1. The problem of the true and the false humanism in the play *Na dne* by A.M. Gorky.
2. The depiction of the revolutionary-democrat in the works of A.N. Nekrasov.

Paper No. 13

1. The poem "Dvenadtsat' " by A.A. Blok. The idea. The composition, vocabulary, and the rhythm of the poem.
2. The civic feat of N.G. Chernyshevsky. The educational importance of the novel *Chto delat'?* V.I. Lenin about the novel.

Paper No. 14

1. The theme of the fatherland in the poetry of S.A. Esenin.
2. The depiction of the life of the "humiliated and insulted" in the novels of Dostoevsky (based on the material studied).

Paper No. 15

1. The satirical works of V.V. Mayakovsky. The Leninist evaluation of the poem "Prozasedavshiesya."
2. The problem of true and false patriotism in the novel *Voyna i mir* by L.N. Tolstoy.

Paper No. 16

1. The theme of Soviet patriotism in the poetry of V.V. Mayakovsky. Recite from memory one of the poet's poems.
2. *Voyna i mir* by L.N. Tolstoy as a heroic epic.

Paper No. 17

1. The character of Lenin in the poem "Vladimir Il'ich Lenin" by V.V. Mayakovsky.
2. The nature of the social protest and the problem of transformation of life in the works of F.M. Dostoevsky (on the example of one of his novels).

Paper No. 18

1. The poem "Khorosho!" by V.V. Mayakovsky. Its problems, ideological depth, and artistic peculiarities.
2. V.I. Lenin about L.N. Tolstoy.

Paper No. 19

1. The artistic peculiarities of V.V. Mayakovsky's lyrics and their political actuality.
2. The typical characters in the poem *Mertvye dushi* by N.V. Gogol' (based on the example of one chapter).

Paper No. 20

1. The basic problems and the artistic peculiarities of the novel *Razgrom* by A.A. Fadeev.
2. The theme of love and friendship in the poetry of A.S. Pushkin. The notion about a lyrical work.

Paper No. 21

1. The heroic characters in the play *Lyubov' Yarovaya* by K.A. Trenev.
2. The problem of happiness in N.A. Nekrasov's poem "Komu na Rusi zhit' khorosho."

Paper No. 22

1. The life and creative activity of N.A. Ostrovsky as an example of selfless service to the socialist fatherland and to the Soviet people.
2. The lyrical digressions in the poem *Mertvye dushi.* The belief of N.V. Gogol' in a bright future for Russia.

Paper No. 23

1. The problems in the novel *Kak zakalyalas' stal'* by N.A. Ostrovsky and their educational importance.
2. The main motives of M.Yu. Lermontov's lyrics. Recite from memory one of the poet's poems.

Paper No. 24

1. The depth of depiction of the contradictions of the epoch in A.N. Tolstoy's novel *Petr I.*
2. A.S. Pushkin's novel *Evgeniy Onegin* in the evaluation of V.G. Belinsky.

Paper No. 25

1. The depiction of the beauty of the soul and the character strength of the Soviet man, the fighter and toiler, in the story "Sud'ba cheloveka" by M.A. Sholokhov.
2. The ideological direction and artistic peculiarities of M.E. Saltykov-Shchedrin's satire. Characters by Saltykov-Shchedrin in the works of V.I. Lenin.

Paper No. 26

1. The leading role of the party in the socialist transformation of the countryside according to the novel *Podnyataya tselina* by M.A. Sholokhov. The depiction of the heroic feats of the communists in the novel.
2. The creative activity of A.S. Pushkin in the thirties. The increasing contradictions with the autocracy and the death of the poet.

Paper No. 27

1. The mass scenes in the novel *Podnyataya tselina* by M.A. Sholokhov and their meaning.
2. Pechorin—a hero of his time. V.G. Belinsky about the character of Pechorin.

Paper No. 28

1. V.V. Mayakovsky about the role of the poet and the purpose of poetry. Recite by memory a fragment from the introduction to the poem "Vo ves' golos."

2. "The particular man" Rakhmetov in the novel *Chto delat'?* by N.G. Chernyshevsky. The society of the future in the novel.

Paper No. 29

1. The theme of the Great Fatherland War in Soviet poetry. Recite by memory one poem on this topic.
2. Chatskiy and Molchalin.

Paper No. 30

1. The theme of heroism of the toilers in Soviet literature of the fifties and sixties (based on the example of two or three works).
2. The people and the individual in the understanding of L.N. Tolstoy (according to the novel *Voyna i mir*). The character of the people's general Kutuzov in the novel.

Paper No. 31

1. The Leninist theme in Soviet literature of the fifties and sixties.
2. The paths in the search for the meaning of life by the progressive upper class intelligentsia in the novel *Voyna i mir* by L.N. Tolstoy (based on the example of one hero).

Paper No. 32

1. The complicated path of the formation of socialist consciousness of the working peasantry in the novel *Podnyataya tselina* by M.A. Sholokhov.
2. The problems and the heroes of one of A.P. Chekhov's plays. The innovations in the plays of Chekhov.

Paper No. 33

1. The contemporary hero in Soviet literature of the fifties and sixties (based on the example of two or three works).
2. The exposure of *poshlost'* and philistinism in the works of A.P. Chekhov. The characters of Chekhov in the works of V.I. Lenin.

Secondary School Examination Papers in Russian Literature for the 1967-68 School Year[1] [5]

Paper No. 1

1. The breadth of the depiction of Russian life in the novel *Evgeniy Onegin* by A.S. Pushkin.
2. The success of the Soviet Union in the conquest of the cosmos.

Paper No. 2

1. The love of freedom and patriotism in the creative work of M.Yu. Lermontov.
2. The most interesting event in my life.

Paper No. 3

1. *Mertvye dushi* by N.V. Gogol'—a satire on serfdom in Russia.
2. Recite from memory your favorite poem (or prose fragment).

Paper No. 4

1. Your attitude to Bazarov (according to I.S. Turgenev's novel *Ottsy i deti.*).
2. On the building projects of the five-year plan (cities, districts, *kolkhoz*).

Paper No. 5

1. The depiction of the gloomy life and excessive toil of the people in the poem "Moroz, krasnyy nos" by N.A. Nekrasov.
2. My favorite contemporary writer (poet).

Paper No. 6

1. The heroism and patriotism of the Russian people in the novel *Voyna i mir* by L.N. Tolstoy.
2. The Soviet Union on guard of peace.

Paper No. 7

1. What attracts me in Natasha Rostov (according to the novel *Voyna i mir* by L.N. Tolstoy).
2. My native city (*kolkhoz*) changes with every day.

Paper No. 8

1. The basic theme and idea of *Vishnevyy sad* by A.P. Chekhov.
2. The accomplishments of science in Soviet Lithuania.

Paper No. 9

1. A.M. Gorky—the founder of Soviet literature.
2. My thoughts on the screen version of the novel *Voyna i mir* by L.N. Tolstoy (or any other literary work).

Paper No. 10

1. Recite from memory a fragment from "Starukha Izergil' " by A.M. Gorky (the legend about Danko). In what manifests itself the heroism of Danko?
2. A movie which impressed me most of all.

Paper No. 11

1. The path of Pavel Vlasov from a town fellow to a revolutionary leader of the workers (according to the novel *Mat'* by A.M. Gorky).
2. Recite from memory a poem by a contemporary Soviet poet.

Paper No. 12

1. The place of the character Palageya Nilovna in the novel *Mat'* by A.M. Gorky.
2. There is always room in life for great deeds.

Paper No. 13

1. The essay "V.I. Lenin" by A.M. Gorky—a characteristic of the greatest man of our epoch.
2. A play about which I want to tell.

Paper No. 14

1. V.V. Mayakovsky—the poet of revolution.
2. My thoughts about a future profession.

Paper No. 15

1. Recite from memory a fragment of V.V. Mayakovsky's poem "Vladimir Il'ich Lenin." To what thoughts and feelings does this poem give rise?
2. My favorite painter.

Paper No. 16

1. The immortality of man is in his deeds (according to V.V. Mayakovsky's poem "Tovarishchu Nette—parokhodu i cheloveku").
2. My favorite composer.

Paper No. 17

1. Read expressively a fragment from the poem "Rus' sovetskaya" by S. Esenin (as indicated by the teacher). To what thoughts does this poem give rise?
2. A memorable school evening.

Paper No. 18

1. A.M. Sholokhov—an outstanding contemporary writer.
2. My impressions of a trip to the city (countryside).

Paper No. 19

1. The struggle in the countryside according to M.A. Sholokhov's novel *Podnyataya tselina.*
2. Recite from memory a poem by a contemporary Soviet poet.

Paper No. 20

1. The complexity of the characters of the heroes in the novel *Podnyataya tselina* by M.A. Sholokhov.
2. How does the Komsomol live and work (possibly on the example of your own Komsomol organization)?

Paper No. 21

1. The novel *Molodaya gvardiya* by A.A. Fadeev as an optimistic tragedy.
2. My impressions from an excursion.

Paper No. 22

1. Who did you like most from the heroes of Krasnodon, and why? (According to the novel *Molodaya gvardiya* by A.A. Fadeev.)
2. Sportsmen's achievements in our republic.

Paper No. 23

1. The poem "Vasiliy Terkin" by A.T. Tvardovsky—a truthful depiction of the severe war life conditions of Soviet soldiers.
2. What did school give me?

Paper No. 24

1. The path along which contemporary Soviet literature develops.
2. My thoughts about a book read.

Paper No. 25

1. The universal importance of Russian classic and Soviet literatures.
2. Read expressively a fragment from a work of prose by a contemporary Soviet writer (indicated by the teacher).

Program for the Entrance Examinations into Institutions of Higher Learning in Russian Literature for the Year 1972[16]

Those entering institutions of higher learning must demonstrate at their examination: (a) a knowledge of Russian prerevolutionary and Soviet works of literature enumerated below; the comprehension of their ideological content, and artistic peculiarities; (b) an understanding of the artistic, historic, and social significance of the literary work in conjunction with the sociopolitical conditions of the given time; (c) a knowledge of the basic notions contained in the articles "Partiynaya organizatsiya i partiynaya literatura" and "Lev Tolstoy, kak zerkalo russkoy revolyutsii"; in the Program of the Communist Party of the Soviet Union (Part II, Section V, points 1 and 4); in the materials of the Twenty-fourth Congress of the Communist Party of the Soviet Union about the development of literature and art (report of the Central Committee of the Communist Party of the Soviet Union to the Twenty-fourth Congress, Section III); (d) a comprehension of the ideological wealth and high artistic qualities of Russian nineteenth-century literature and of its universal significance; (e) an understanding of the ideological and artistic essence of Soviet literature; of its creative development of the best traditions of Russian classical literature; and its innovatory character and universal importance; (f) a comprehension of the general laws of the historical and literary process (to know the basic periods in the development of Russian nineteenth-century and Soviet literature).

In the theory of literature the examinee is required to know the following:

1. The connection between the *Weltanschauung* and the creative work of a writer; the notions of *klassovost'*, *narodnost'*, and *partiynost'* of literature.
2. The notions of classicism, romanticism, critical realism, social realism.
3. Artistic image, literary type, lyrical hero.
4. Theme, idea, composition, conflict, plot.
5. Basic types of artistic works—epic, lyric, drama—and their major genres.
6. Satire, humor, irony, grotesque.
7. Epithet, metaphor, comparison, antithesis, hyperbole, "aesopic language."
8. Basic meters.

Works of Literature

A.S. Griboedov. *Gore ot uma*. A.I. Goncharov. "Mil'on terzaniy" (in abbreviation).

111

A.S. Pushkin. *Evgeniy Onegin, Dubrovskiy, Kapitanskaya dochka, Mednyy vsadnik*; poems: "K Chadaevu," "K moryu," "Ya pomnyu chudnoe mgnovenie . . . ," "Prorok," "V Sibir'," "Na Kholmakh Gruzii . . . ," "Vnov' ya posetil . . . ," "Ya pamyatnik sebe vozdvig nerukotvornyy . . ."

M.Yu. Lermontov. *Geroy nashego vremeni,* "Mtsyri," "Pesnya pro kuptsa Kalashnikova," poems: "Parus," "Borodino," "Smert' poeta," "Duma," "Kak chasto pestroyu tolpoyu okruzhen . . . ," "Is-pod tainstvennoy kholodnoy polumaski . . ."

N.V. Gogol'. *Revizor, Mertvye Dushi.*

V.G. Belinsky. "Eighth and ninth articles on Pushkin" (in abbreviation), "Geroy nashego vremeni" and "Stikhotvoreniya Lermontova" (in abbreviation).

A.N. Ostrovsky. *Groza.*

N.A. Dobrolyubov. "Luch sveta v temnon tsarstve" (in abbreviation).

I.S. Turgenev. *Ottsy i deti,* "Russkiy yazyk." D.I. Pisarev. "Bazarov" (in abbreviation).

N.G. Chernyshevsky. *Chto delat'?* (A general characteristic).

N.A. Nekrasov. "Komu na Rusi zhit' khorosho," "Zheleznaya doroga," "Razmyshleniya u paradnogo pod"ezda," "Pamyati Dobrolyubova," "Puskay im govorit izmenchivaya moda."

M.E. Saltykov-Shchedrin. *Gospoda Golovlevy* (chapters: "Semeynyy sud," and "Po-rodstvennomu"), two or three fables (to be chosen by examiner).

L.N. Tolstoy. *Voyna i mir,* "Posle bala."

F.M. Dostoevsky. *Prestuplenie i nakazanie.*

A.P. Chekhov. "Ionych," *Vishnevyy sad.*

A.M. Gorky. "Starukha Izergil'," "Pesnya o Sokole," "Pesnya o Burevestnike," *Na dne, Mat',* "V.I. Lenin" (in abbreviation).

A.A. Blok. "Dvenadtsat'," "Neznakomka," "O, vesna bez kontsa i krayu . . . ," "Solov'inyy sad," "Na zheleznoy doroge," "Fabrika."

S.A. Esenin. "Rus' sovetskaya," "Pis'mo materi," "Neuyutnaya zhidkaya lunnost' . . . ," "Kazhdyy trud blagoslovi, udacha!" "Spit kovyl'. Ravnina dorogaya . . . ," "Ya idu dolinoy. Na zatylke kepi . . . ," "Ne zhaleyu, ne zovu, ne plachu . . . ," "Anna Snegina."

V.V. Mayakovsky. "Vladimir Il'ich Lenin," "Khorosho!" "Vo ves' golos," poems: "Levyy marsh," "Neobychaynoe priklyuchenie . . . ," "O dryani," "Prozasedavshiesya," "Black and white," "Tovarishchu Nette—parokhodu i cheloveku," "Pis'mo tovarishchu Kostrovu iz Parizha o sushchnosti lyubvi," "Stikhi o sovetskom pasporte," "Rasskaz o Kuznetskstroe i o lyudyakh Kuznetska."

A.A. Fadeev. *Razgrom. Molodaya gvardiya.*

K.A. Trenev. *Lyubov' Yarovaya.*

N.A. Ostrovsky. *Kak zakalyalas' stal'.*

A.N. Tolstoy. *Petr Pervyy.*

M.A. Sholokhov. *Podnyataya tselina.* "Sud'ba cheloveka."

Two or three other works from contemporary Soviet literature (to be chosen by examiner).

For students who graduate from non-Russian schools:

A.S. Griboedov. *Gore ot uma.*

A.S. Pushkin. "K Chadaevu," "Ya pamyatnik sebe vozdvig nerukotvornyy . . .," *Kapitanskaya dochka, Evgeniy Onegin* (in abbreviation).

M.Yu. Lermontov. "Smert' poeta," "Duma," "Rodina," *Geroy nashego vremeni* (stories: "Bela," "Maksim Maksimych," "Taman' ").

N.V. Gogol'. *Revizor. Mertvye dushi* (chapters 1, 2, 6, 11).

A.N. Ostrovsky. *Groza.*

I.S. Turgenev. *Ottsy i deti* (in abbreviation).

N.G. Chernyshevsky. *Chto delat'?* (general characteristic).

N.A. Nekrasov. "Razmyshleniya u paradnogo pod"ezda," "Komu na Rusi zhit' khorosho" (in abbreviation).

L.N. Tolstoy. *Voyna i mir* (in abbreviation).

A.P. Chekhov. *Vishnevyy sad.*

A.M. Gorky. *Na dne, Mat',* "V.I. Lenin."

V.V. Mayakovsky. "Stikhi o sovetskom pasporte," "Tovarishchu Nette—parokhodu i cheloveku," "V.I. Lenin" (in abbreviation), "Khorosho!" (in abbreviation).

A.A. Fadeev. *Razgrom.*

M.A. Sholokhov. *Podnyataya tselina* (in abbreviation), "Sud'ba cheloveka."

**Ministry of Higher and
Secondary Specialized
Education of the USSR**

Table A-2

Approved:

Deputy Minister of Higher and
Secondary Specialized Education
of the USSR

INDIVIDUAL

MOSCOW STATE UNIVERSITY

CURRICULUM (*UCHEBNYY PLAN*)[1][7]

SPECIALTY 2001/V-1

RUSSIAN LANGUAGE AND LITERATURE

QUALIFICATION OF SPECIALIST: PHILOLOGIST. RUSSIAN LANGUAGE
AND LITERATURE SECONDARY SCHOOL TEACHER

PERIOD OF STUDY: FIVE YEARS

MOSCOW, 1964

Table A-3

Subjects of Instruction	Exams	Tests	Course Projects Essays
1. History of the CPSU	2	2	
2. Marxist-Leninist philosophy	2	1	
3. Marxist-Leninist aesthetics	1	–	
4. Political economy	2	1	
5. Foundations of scientific communism	1	1	
6. Logic	1	–	
7. Psychology	–	1	
8. Pedagogy and history of pedagogy	1	–	
9. Methodology of teaching Russian language	–	1	
10. Methodology of teaching Russian literature	–	1	
11. Latin	1	2	
12. Foreign language	3	4	
13. Introductory linguistic	1	–	
14. Modern Russian language	3	4	1
15. Applied stylistics of Russian language	–	1	
16. Old Church Slavonic	1	2	
17. History of Russian language and Russian dialectology	2	3	
18. Introduction to literary theory	1	–	
19. Russian folklore	1	–	
20. History of Russian literature	6	1	
21. History of foreign literature (including ancient literature)	2	5	
22. History of literature of the peoples of the USSR	–	2	
23. Elective courses, special courses, special seminars	–	12	3
24. Physical education	–	4	
Total	31	48	4

Table A-4

Subjects of Instruction[a]	Total Hours	Lectures	Practical Training Seminars	Hours of Study per Week. Five Years. Two Semesters Each Year. 38 Weeks a Year.									
				1	2	3	4	5	6	7	8	9	10
1. History of the CPSU	160	80	80	2	2	3	2						
2. Marxist-Leninist philosophy	120	60	60					2	2	3			
3. Marxist-Leninist aesthetics	32	32	–								2		
4. Political economy	100	50	50							2	2	2	
5. Foundations of scientific communism	70	35	35								2	2	
6. Logic	36	36	–	2									
7. Psychology	36	36	–							2			
8. Pedagogy and history of pedagogy	32	32	–								2		
9. Methodology of teaching Russian language	32	16	16								2		
10. Methodology of teaching Russian literature	32	16	16										
11. Latin	208	–	208	4	4	4							
12. Foreign language	544	–	544	4	4	4	4	4	4	4	4	4	
13. Introductory linguistic	68	36	32	2	2								
14. Modern Russian language	340	136	204	4	4	4	4	4					
15. Applied stylistics of Russian language	64	28	36						4				
16. Old Church Slavonic	102	34	68			3	3						
17. History of Russian language and Russian dialectology	204	104	100				3	4	3	2			
													Preparation of Diploma Work

Table A-4 (cont.)

18. Introduction to literary theory, theory	84	56	28	2	3							
19. Russian folklore	72	36	36	4								
20. History of Russian literature	426	408	18		2	3	2	4	4	2	4	4
21. History of foreign literature	304	304	–		2	2	2	4	4	2	2	
22. History of literature of the peoples of the USSR	136	136	–								4	4
23. Elective courses, special courses, special seminars	644	408	236		2	2	4	6	6	8	6	4
24. Physical education	136	–	136	2	2	2	2					
Total	3982	2079	1903	32	31	27	28	28	25	25	26	12
Course projects	4			–	1	1	1	–	–	1	–	–
Examinations	31			3	5	2	5	3	4	4	2	3
Tests	48			6	6	5	6	6	5	5	5	4

aThe errors in addition in this table are reproduced from the original.

Table A-5

Courses Required for Specialization	One Test in Following Semester	Total Hours
In Literature		
Compulsory:		
1. Theory and history of Russian verse	4	30
2. History of literatures of South and West Slavs	5	30
3. History of Russian and Soviet poetry	6	60
4. History of the Russian novel	7	30
5. Theory of literature	8	60
6. History of Russian and Soviet criticism	9	60
7. History of the Russian and Soviet novel	8	30
Elective courses, to be selected from:		
1. History of Russian drama	9	60
2. Russian heroic epos	9	30
3. Folklore of South and West Slavs	8	30
4. Literary trends in Russian poetry and prose	9	60
5. History of the Russian poem	6	30
6. Satire in Russian literature	6	30
7. Foundations of textology	6	30
8. Special courses and special seminars	–	254
In Linguistics		
Compulsory:		
1. Comparative grammar of Slavic languages	8	60
2. General linguistics	8	30
3. History of linguistic sciences	9	30
4. One South Slavic language	5	60
5. One West Slavic language	7	60
6. Foundations of culture of speech	5	30
7. Theory of literary styles	8	30
Elective courses, to be selected from:		
1. Comparative grammar of Indo-European languages	9	60
2. History of styles of Russian artistic prose	9	60
3. Principles and methods of literary stylistic analysis	6	30
4. Contemporary methods of language teaching	6	30
5. History of the study of styles of Russian language	6	30
6. The basic trends in contemporary linguistics	9	30
7. History of linguistics	8	30
8. Special courses and special seminars	–	254

Table A-6

Practical training (folklore, dialectology, lexicography, textology, archaives, bibliography, museums) to be taken in the following periods:

Second semester:	four weeks	July 1 to July 30
Fourth semester:	four weeks	July 1 to July 30
Sixth semester:	four weeks	July 1 to July 30
Eighth semester:	four weeks	July 1 to July 30
Ninth semester:	eighteen weeks	September 1 to December 31

State examinations period: June 1 to July 30.

Diploma works to be submitted and defended in the period between February 7 and June 30.

State examinations include:

1. The defence of the diploma work.
2. Foundations of scientific communism.
3. Foreign language (to be taken in the eighth semester).

Notes:

1. The council of the philological faculty can change the number of hours assigned to separate subjects and the sequence in which they are studied, except for the subjects in the social sciences, under the condition that the students will acquire the scientific knowledge as determined by the curriculum, without increasing the maximum of the approved weekly study load.

2. In the ninth semester the students combine study with practice teaching at a secondary school (no more than twelve study hours per week).

3. The Department in which the student specializes determines the nature of practical training in the second, fourth, sixth, and eighth semesters.

4. In the fourth, fifth, sixth, seventh, eighth, and ninth semesters the student is required to take compulsory special courses and to pass the required tests in literature or linguistics, depending on the chosen specialty. In the sixth, eighth, and ninth semesters the student is required to take not less than two elective special courses and to pass the required tests.

5. The departments of History of Russian Literature and History of Soviet Literature can introduce in the lecture courses compulsory written assignments (no more than two in one semester) in order to examine the level of students' proficiency in the general courses.

6. The number and the sizes of special courses and special seminars is each year determined by the council of the faculty. The programs of the special courses are approved by the appropriate departments. The students are required to take one special course in the sixth and seventh semesters and to pass the

required tests. Besides, students are required to participate in the work of the yearly seminars in the second-third, fourth-fifth, and sixth-seventh semesters and to complete not less than four course works (essays).

History of Russian Literature Program: Old Russian Literature[18]

Textbook

N.K. Gudzy. *Khrestomatiya po drevney russkoy literature XI-XVII yekov*. Sixth edition. 1955.

Texts

Povest vremennykh let. Parts I and II in the series *Literaturnye pamyatniki*. A.n. SSSR edition. 1950.

Slovo o polku Igoreve. In the series *Literaturnye pamyatniki*. 1950.

Voinskie povesti drevney Rusi. In the series *Literaturnye pamyatniki*. 1948.

"Khozhdenie za tri morya" Afanasiya Nikitina. In the series *Literaturnye pamyatniki*. Second edition. 1958. "Poslaniya Ivana Groznogo" in the series *Literaturnye pamyatniki*. 1951

"Russkaya dramaticheskaya satira XVII veka" in the series *Literaturnye pamyatniki*. 1954.

Simeon Polotsky. *Izbrannye sochineniya*. In the series *Literaturnye pamyatniki*. 1953.

Khudozhestvennaya proza Kievskoy Rusi XI-XIII vekov. Compiled by I.P. Eremin and D.S. Likhachev. 1957.

Russkie povesti XV-XVI vekov. Compiled by M.O. Skripil'. Moscow-Leningrad, 1958.

G.N. Moyseeva. *Kazanskaya istoriya*. 1954.

V.I. Malyshev. *Povest' o Sukhane*. 1956.

Russkaya povest' XVII veka. Compiled by M.O. Skripil'. 1954.

Virshi. Sillabicheskaya poeziya XVII-XVIII vv. Ed. P.N. Berkov. (Biblioteka poeta, malaya seriya). 1935.

Zhitie protopopa Avvakuma, im samim napisannoe, i drugie ego sochineniya. Ed. N.K. Gudzy. Moscow, 1960.

General Courses

N.K. Gudzy. *Istoriya drevney russkoy literatury*. Sixth edition. 1956.

A.S. Orlov. *Drevnyaya russkaya literatura XI-XVII vekov*. 1945.

Institut russkoy literatury Akademii nauk SSSR. *Istoriya russkoy literatury*. Vol. I, 1941; vol. II, part 1, 1945; vol. II, part 2, 1948.

Istoriya russkoy literatury . Vol. I (literatura X-XVIII vekov). A.n. SSSR. Moscow-Leningrad, 1958.

G.V. Plekhanov. *Istoriya russkoy obshchestvennoy mysli*. Vol. I Second edition. 1925.

Separate Research Publications

A.A. Shakhmatov. "Russkie letopisi i ikh kul'turnoistoricheskoe znachenie." 1947.

E.V. Barsov. *"Slovo o polku Igoreve" kak khudozhestvennyy pamyatnik Kievskoy druzhinnoy Rusi*. Vols. I-III. 1887-1889.

A.S. Orlov. *Slovo o polku Igoreve*. Second edition. 1946.

Slovo o polku Igoreve. Sbornik issledovaniy i statey. Ed. V.P. Andrianova-Peretts. 1950.

N.P. Piksanov. *Starorusskaya povest'*. 1923.

V.P. Andrianova-Peretts. *Ocherki po istorii russkoy satiricheskoy literatury XVII v*. 1937.

Literature for the Whole Course

K. Marks i F. Engel's. *Ob iskusstve*. Sbornik. 1938.

V.I. Lenin. "Kriticheskie zametki po natsional'nomu voprosu," *Sochineniya*. Vol. XX.

V.I. Lenin. *O literature. Sbornik statey i otryvkov*. 1941.

N.S. Khrushchev. "Vysokoe prizvanie literatury i iskusstva." 1963.

G.V. Plekhanov. *Istoriya russkoy obshchestvennoy mysli*. Vols. II-III. Second edition. 1925.

D.D. Blagoy. *Istoriya russkoy literatury XVIII v*. Fourth edition. 1961.

Istoriya russkoy literatury. A.n. SSSR. Vols. III, V, 1941; Vol. IV, 1947.

Ocherki po istorii russkoy zhurnalistiki i kritiki. Vol. I, XVIII Century and First Half of XIX Century. 1950.

Russkie pisateli XVIII veka. Rekomendatel'nyy spisok literatury. 1954.

P.N. Berkov. *Istoriya russkoy zhurnalistiki XVIII veka*. 1952.

Textbooks

Khrestomatiya po russkoy literature XVIII v. Compiled by A.V. Kokorev. Third edition. 1961.

Russkaya proza XVIII veka. Vols. I-II. 1950.

Russkaya komediya i komicheskaya opera XVIII veka. Ed. and introduction by P.N. Berkov. 1950

Literature for Section I (1800-30)

Texts

Virshi. Sillabicheskaya poeziya XVII-XVIII vv., sbornik. 1935.

N.E. Onchukov. *Severnye narodnye dramy*. 1911 (tekst "Tsarya Maksimil'yana"); there are also available separate editions of "Tsar' Maksimil'yan."

Literature for Section II (1830-50)

Texts

F. Engel's. "Zametki o Lomonosove." *Lomonosov. Sbornik statey i materialov*. Vol. III. 1951.

Feofan Prokopovich. *Sochineniya.* Ed. by I.P. Eremin. Moscow-Leningrad, 1961.
Antiokh Kantemir.*Sobranie stikhotvoreniy.* Second edition. Leningrad, 1956.
M.V. Lomonosov. *Polnoe sobranie sochineniy.* Vol. VII. "Trudy po filologii."
1952.
Tredyakovsky, Lomonosov i Sumarokov. V serii "Biblioteka poeta," 1935.
Lomonosov. *Stikhotvoreniya.* 1948.
Sumarokov. *Stikhotvoreniya.* 1953.

Textbooks

V.G. Belinsky. *Kantemir.*
G.V. Plekhanov. *Istoriya russkoy obshchestvennoy mysli.* Vol. II (chapters on
Kantemir, Lomonosov, Sumarokov).
A.A. Morozov. *M. V. Lomonosov.* Second edition. 1952.
P.N. Berkov. *A.P. Sumarokov.* 1949 (V serii *Russkie dramaturgi*).

Additional Material
N.L. Brodsky. "Istoriya stilya russkoy komedii XVIII v.," *Iskusstvo*, No. 1,
1923.
G.N. Pospelov. "Sumarokov i problemy russkogo klassitsizma," *Uchenye zapiski
MGU. Trudy kafedry russkoy literatury*. Vol. III. 1948.
A.V. Kokorev. "Sumarokov i russkie narodnye kartinki," *Uchenye zapiski MGU,
Trudy Kafedry russkoy literatury.* Vol. III. 1948.
Literaturnoe tvorchestvo M.V. Lomonosova. Issledovaniya i materialy. Izdatel'
stvo A.n. SSSR. Moscow-Leningrad, 1962.
Problemy russkogo prosveshcheniya v literature XVIII veka. Izdatel'stvo A.n.
SSSR. Moscow-Leningrad, 1961.
A.V. Kokorev. "Lomonosov-velikiy russkiy natsional'nyy poet," *Vestnik MGU.*
Seriya III, No. 5, 1961.

Literature for Section III
(Last third of the eighteenth century)

Texts

Russkie satiricheskie zhurnaly XVIII veka. Ed. by N.K. Gudzy. 1940.
Satiricheskie zhurnaly N.I. Novikova. Ed. with introduction and comments by
P.N. Berkov. 1951.
D.I. Fonvizin. *Sobranie sochineniy v dvukh tomakh.* Moscow-Leningrad, 1959.
N.F. Bogdanovich. *Stikhotvoreniya i poemy.* Second edition. Leningrad, 1957.
G.R. Derzhavin. *Stikhotvoreniya.* Introduction by D.D. Blagoy. 1957.

I.A. Krylov. *Sochineniya*. Vols. I-III. 1944-46.

A.N. Radishchev. *Polnoe sobranie sochineniy*. Vol. I-III. Isdatel'stvo A.n. SSSR. 1938-52.

A.N. Radishchev. *Puteshestvie iz Peterburga v Moskvu*. Fotograficheskoe vosproizvedenie izdaniya 1790 g. "Akademiya." 1935.

N.M. Karamzin. *Sochineniya*

Textbooks

N.A. Dobrolyubov. "Russkaya satira i vek Ekateriny."

G. Makogonenko. *Nikolay Novikov i russkoe prosveshchenie XVIII v*. 1951.

D.D. Blagoy. "D.I. Fonvizin." V sbornike *Klassiki russkoy literatury*. 1953.

G. Makogonenko. *D.I. Fonvizin*. 1950.

P.N. Berkov. *V.V. Kapnist*. 1950.

L.I. Kulakova. *Ya.B. Knyazhnin*. Second edition. 1961.

A.V. Zapadov. *I.A. Krylov*.

V.G. Belinsky. "Sochineniya Derzhavina."

Vl. Orlov. *Radishchev i russkaya literatura*. 1949.

G.N. Makogonenko. *Radishchev i ego vremya*. Moscow, 1956.

Additional Material

I.A. Krylov. *Issledovaniya i materialy*. Ed. by D.D. Blagoy and N.L. Brodsky. 1947.

N.L. Stepanov. *Krylov*. 1951.

K.V. Pigarev. *Tvorchestvo Fonvizina*. 1954.

History of Russian Literature Program: Nineteenth Century[20]

Texts Which the Student Must Know

Zhukovsky. *Stikhotvoreniya.*

Batyushkov. *Stikhotvoreniya.*

Krylov. *Basni.*

Griboedov. *Gore ot uma,* "1812 god."

Ryleev. *Stikhotvoreniya,* "Dumy," "Voynarovskiy," "Nalivayko."

Pushkin. *Sobranie sochineniy.*

Baratynsky. *Stikhotvoreniya.*

Polezhaev. *Stikhotvoreniya.*

Lermontov. *Sobranie sochineniy.*

Kol'tsov. *Stikhotvoreniya.*

Gogol'. *Sobranie sochineniy.*

Gertsen. *Kto vinovat? Doktor Krupov, Soroka vorovka, S togo berega, Byloe i dumy,* "O razvitii revolyutsionnykh idey v Rossii."

Ogarev. *Stikhotvoreniya.*

Grigorovich. *Derevnya, Anton Goremyka.*

Turgenev. *Zapiski okhotnika, Mesyats v derevne, Dnevnik lishnego cheloveka,* "Asya," "Mumu," "Faust," *Rudin, Dvoryanskoe gnezdo, Nakanune, Ottsy i deti, Dym, Nov',* "Stikhotvoreniya v proze."

Goncharov. *Obyknovennaya istoriya, Oblomov, Obryv,* "Mil'on terzaniy."

Ostrovsky. *Svoi lyudi-sochtemsya, Bednost'-ne porok, Dokhodnoe mesto, Groza, Goryachee serdtse, Beshenye den'gi, Les, Snegurochka, Volki i ovtsy, Bespridanitsa, Bez viny vinovatye.*

Nikitin. *Stikhotvoreniya.*

A.K. Tolstoy. *Stikhotvoreniya.*

Tyutchev. *Stikhotyoreniya.*

Fet. *Stikhotvoreniya.*

Nekrasov. *Sobranie sochineniy.*

Kurochkin. *Stikhotvoreniya.*

Pomyalovsky. *Meshchanskoe schast'e, Molotov.*

Reshetnikov. *Podlipovtsy.*

Sleptsov. *Trudnoe vremya.*

Chernyshevsky. *Chto delat'?* "Prolog."

Saltykov-Shchedrin. *Gubernskie ocherki, Pompadury i pompadurshi, Istoriya odnogo goroda, Blagonamerennye rechi, Gospoda Golovlevy, Ubezhishche Monrepo, Za rubezhom,* "Skazki," *Poshekhonskaya starina.*

Dostoevsky. *Bednye lyudi, Zapiski iz mertvogo doma, Unizhennye i oskorblennye, Zapiski iz podpol'ya, Prestuplenie i nakazanie, Idiot, Brat'ya Karamazovy.*
Gl. Uspensky. *Nravy Rasteryaevoy ulitsy, Razoren'e, Vlast' zemli, Krest'yanin i krest'yanskiy trud, Vypryamila.*
Tolstoy. *Detstvo, Otrochestvo, Yunost', Sevastopol'skie rasskazy,* "Utro pomeshchika," "Lyutsern," *Kazaki, Voyna i mir, Anna Karenina, Ispoved',* "Smert' Ivana Il'icha," *Voskresenie,* "Posle bala," *Khadzhi Murat, Vlast' t'my, Zhivoy trup,* "Ne mogu molchat'."
Korolenko. *Rasskazy, povesti, ocherki, Istoriya moego sovremennika.*
Chekhov. *Rasskazy i povesti, Chayka, Dyadya Vanya, Tri sestry, Vishnevyy sad.*

Basic Reference Literature
(Rukovodyashchaya literatura)

K. Marks i F. Engel's ob iskusstve. Vols. I and II. Moscow-Leningrad, 1958.
V.I. Lenin o literature i iskusstve. Moscow, 1957.
N.S. Khrushchev. "Vysokoe prizvanie literatury i iskusstva." Moscow, 1963.

Textbooks

A.N. Sokolov. *Istoriya russkoy literatury XIX veka.* Vol. I. Moscow, 1960.
G.N. Pospelov. *Istoriya russkoy literatury XIX veka.* Vol. II, part I. Moscow, 1962.

General Courses, Monographs, Articles

Istoriya russkoy literatury. A.n. SSSR. Vols. V, VI, VII, VIII, IX.
G.V. Plekhanov. *Literatura i estetika.* Vols. I and II. Moscow, 1958.
A.M. Gorky. *Istoriya russkoy literatury.* Moscow, 1939.
B. Meylakh. *Lenin i problemy russkoy literatury kontsa XIX-nachala XX vv.* Third edition. Moscow, 1956.
Istoriya russkoy kritiki v dvukh tomakh. Moscow-Leningrad, 1958.

Krylov

V.G. Belinsky. "Ivan Andreevich Krylov."
N.I. Stepanov. *I.A. Krylov. Zhizn' i tvorchestvo.* Second edition, 1959.

Griboedov

I.A. Goncharov. "Mil'on terzaniy."
A.V. Lunacharsky. "A.S. Grioedov," in A.V. Lunacharsky, *Klassiki russkoy literatury.* Moscow, 1937.
N. Piksanov. *Tvorcheskaya istoriya "Gorya ot uma."* Moscow-Leningrad, 1928.

The Decembrist Poets

A.G. Tseytlin. *Tvorchestvo Ryleeva.* 1955.
V.G. Bazanov. *Ocherki dekabristskoy literatury. Poeziya.* Moscow-Leningrad, 1961.

Pushkin

V.G. Belinsky. "Stat'i o Pushkine."
N.G. Chernyshevsky. "Aleksandr Sergeevich Pushkin, ego zhizn' i sochineniya."
D.I. Pisarev. "Pushkin i Belinsky."
N.L. Brodsky. *A.S. Pushkin. Biografiya.* Moscow, 1937.
D. Blagoy. *Masterstvo Pushkina.* Moscow, 1955.
B. Tomashevsky. *Pushkin. Kniga pervaya (1813-1824).* Moscow-Leningrad, 1956.
G.A. Gukovsky. *Pushkin i problemy realisticheskogo stilya.* Moscow, 1957.
N.L. Stepanov. *Lirika Pushkina.* Moscow, 1961.
B. Meylakh. *Pushkin i ego epokha.* Moscow, 1958.
Leonid Grossman. *Pushkin.* Moscow, 1958.
A. Slonimsky. *Masterstvo Pushkina.* Moscow, 1959.

Lermontov

V.G. Belinsky. " 'Geroy nashego vremeni,' sochinenie M. Lermontova."
V.G. Belinsky. "Stikhotvoreniya M. Lermontova."
N.L. Brodsky. *M.Yu. Lermontov, biografiya.* Vol. I. 1945.
A.N. Sokolov. *Mikhail Yur'evich Lermontov.* Second edition. Moscow, 1957.
E. Mikhaylov. *Proza Lermontova.* Moscow, 1957.
D. Maksimov. *Poeziya Lermontova.* Leningrad, 1959.

Kol'tsov

V.G. Belinsky. "Stikhotvoreniya Kol'tsova."
N.A. Dobrolyubov. "A.V.Kol'tsov."

Gogol'

V.G. Belinsky. "O russkoy povesti i povestyakh Gogolya."
V.G. Belinsky. "Stat'i o 'Mertvykh dushakh.' "
V.G. Belinsky. "Pis'mo k Gogolyu."
N.G. Chernyshevsky. "Ocherki gogolevskogo perioda russkoy literatury."
M.B. Khrapchenko. *Tvorchestvo Gogolya.* Second edition. Moscow, 1956.
G.A. Gukovsky. *Realizm Gogolya.* Moscow-Leningrad, 1959.
N.I. Stepanov. *N.V. Gogol'. Tvorcheskiy put'.* Second edition. Moscow, 1959.
V.V. Ermilov. *Geniy Gogolya.* Moscow, 1959.
M.S. Gus. *Gogol' i nikolaevskaya Rossiya.* Moscow, 1957.

Belinsky

"V.I. Lenin o Belinskom." Sbornik *V.I. Lenin o literature i iskusstve.* Moscow, 1957.
N. Mordovchenko. *Belinsky i russkaya literatura ego vremeni.* Moscow-Leningrad, 1950.
V.S. Nechaev. *V.G. Belinsky. Nachalo zhiznenogo puti i literaturnoy deyatel'nosti.* Moscow, 1949.
A. Lavretsky. *Estetika Belinskogo.* Moscow, 1959.

Gertsen

V.I. Lenin. "Pamyati Gertsena."
G.V. Plekhanov. "Filosofskie vzglyady A.I. Gertsena."
Ya.E. El'sberg. *Gertsen. Zhizn' i tvorchestvo.* Third edition. Moscow, 1956.

Turgenev

V.G. Belinsky. "Vzglyad na russkuyu literaturu 1847 goda."
N.G. Chernyshevsky. "Russkiy chelovek na rendez-vus."
N.A. Dobrolyubov. "Kogda zhe pridet nastoyashchiy den'?"
D.I. Pisarev. " 'Dvoryanskoe gnezdo,' roman I.S. Turgeneva."
D.I. Pisarev. "Bazarov."
D.I. Pisarev. "Realisty."
V.V. Vorovsky. "Bazarov i Sanin."
P.G. Pustovoyt. *Ivan Sergeevich Turgenev.* Moscow, 1957.
S. Petrov. *I.S. Turgenev.* Moscow, 1961.
A.G. Tseytlin. *Masterstvo Turgeneva-romanista.* Moscow, 1958.

N. Bogoslovsky. *Turgenev*. Moscow, 1959.
Tvorchestvo I.S. Turgeneva. Sbornik statey. Moscow, 1959.

Goncharov

V.G. Belinsky. "Vzglyad na russkuyu literaturu 1847 goda."
N.A. Dobrolyubov. "Chto takoe oblomovshchina?"
D.I. Pisarev. "Pisemsky, Turgenev i Goncharov."
A.G. Tseytlin. *Ivan Aleksandrovich Goncharov*. Moscow, 1952.
A. Rybasov. *I.A. Goncharov*. Moscow, 1962.

Ostrovsky

N.A. Dobrolyubov. "Temnoe tsarstvo."
N.A. Dobrolyubov. "Luch sveta v temnom tsarstve."
D.I. Pisarev. "Motivy russkoy dramy."
G.V. Plekhanov. "Dobrolyubov i Ostrovsky."
A.I. Revyakin. *A.N. Ostrovsky. Zhizn' i tvorchestvo.* Moscow, 1949.

Tyutchev

K.V. Pigarev. "F.I. Tyutchev" (vstupitel'naya stat'ya), *F.I. Tyutchev. Stikhot-voreniya. Pis'ma.* Moscow, 1957.
K.V. Pigarev. *F.I. Tyutchev. Zhizn' i tvorchestvo.* Moscow, 1962.

Fet

B.Ya. Bukhshtab. "Fet" (vstupitel'naya stat'ya), *A.A. Fet. Stikhotvoreniya.* Biblioteka poeta, 1959.

Nekrasov

Korney Chukovsky. *Masterstvo Nekrasova.* Third edition. Moscow, 1962.

Chernyshevsky

"V.I. Lenin o Chernyshevskom." Sbornik: *Lenin o literature i iskusstve.* Moscow, 1957.

134

D.I. Pisarev. "Myslyashchiy proletariat."
A.V. Lunacharsky. "N.G. Chernyshevsky kak pisatel'," in A.V. Lunacharsky. *Stat'i o literature.* Moscow, 1957.
B. Bursov. *Masterstvo Chernyshevskogo-kritika.* Second edition. Moscow, 1959.
N.V. Bogoslovsky. *Chernyshevsky.* Second edition. Moscow, 1957.

Dobrolyubov

V. Zhdanov. *Nikolay Aleksandrovich Dobrolyubov.* Moscow, 1961.

Democratic Fiction of the Sixties

N.G. Chernyshevsky. "Ne nachalo li peremeny?"
Korney Chukovsky. *Lyudi i knigi.* Moscow, 1958. (Stat'i o N. Uspenskom i V. Sleptsove).
I.G. Yampol'sky. "Pomyalovsky" (vstupitel'naya stat'ya), in *N.G. Pomyalovsky. Sochineniya.* Moscow-Leningrad, 1951.

Saltykov-Shchedrin

N.G. Chernyshevsky. " 'Gubernskie ocherki' Shchedrina."
N.A. Dobrolyubov. " 'Gubernskie ocherki' M.E. Saltykova-Shchedrina."
M. Ol'minsky. *Stat'i o Saltykove-Shchedrine.* Moscow, 1958.
A. Bushlin. *Satira Shchedrina.* A.n. SSSR, 1959.

Dostoevsky

V.G. Belinsky. "Vzglyad na russkuyu literaturu 1846 g."
V.G. Belinsky. "Vzglyad na russkuyu literaturu 1847 g."
N.A. Dobrolyubov. "Zabitye lyudi."
D.I. Pisarev. "Bor'ba za zhizn'."
A.M. Gorky. "Zametki o meshchanstve."
A.M. Gorky. "O 'Karamazovshchine.' "
A.V. Lunacharsky. "Dostoevsky kak myslitel' i khudozhnik," in A.V. Lunacharsky. *Russkaya literatura. Izbrannye stat'i.* Moscow, 1947.
M.S. Gus. *Idei i obrazy Dostoevskogo.* Moscow, 1962.
V.V. Ermilov. *Dostoevsky.* Moscow, 1956.
Tvorchestvo Dostoevskogo. A.n. SSSR. Institut mirovoy literatury im. A.M. Gorkogo. Moscow, 1959.

Uspensky

G.V. Plekhanov. "G.I. Uspensky."
N.I. Sokolov. *Masterstvo G.I. Uspenskogo.* Leningrad, 1958.

Tolstoy

V.I. Lenin, "Stat'i o Tolstom."
N.G. Chernyshevsky. " 'Detstvo i otrochestvo.' Sochineniya grafa L.N. Tolstogo." "Voennye rasskazy grafa L.N. Tolstogo."
D.I. Pisarev. "Promakhi nezreloy mysli."
N.K. Gudzy. *Lev Nikolaevich Tolstoy.* Moscow, 1960.
A.A. Saburov. *"Voyna i mir" L.N. Tolstogo. Problematika i poetika.* Moscow, 1959.

Korolenko

A.M. Gorky. "V.G. Korolenko."
G.A. Byaly. *V.G. Korolenko.* Moscow, 1949.
A.K. Kotov. *V.G. Korolenko.* Moscow, 1957.

Chekhov

V.V. Vorovsky. "A.P. Chekhov."
V.V. Vorovsky. "Lishnie lyudi."
A. Derman. *O masterstve Chekhova.* Moscow, 1959.
G.A. Berdnikov. *Chekhov.* Moscow, 1961.

History of Russian Literature Program: Twentieth Century[2][1] (up to 1917)

Works of Literature

A.M. Gorky. "Makar Chudra," "Devushka i smert'," "Ded Arkhip i Len'ka," "O chizhe, kotoryy lgal, i o dyatle-lyubitele istiny," "Moy sputnik," "Starukha Izergil'," "Chelkash," "Pesnya o Sokole," "Konovalov," "Mal'va," "Suprugi Orlovy," "Byvshie lyudi," "Ozornik," "Dvadtsat' shest' i odna," "Kirilka," *Foma Gordeev*, "Troe," "Pesnya o Burevestnike," "O pisatele, kotoryy zaznalsya," *Meshchane, Na dne*, "Chelovek," "Dachniki," "Deti solntsa," "Varvary," *Vragi, Mat'*, "V Amerike," "Moi interv'yu," "9 yanvarya," "Poslednie," "Leto," "Gorod Okurov," "Zhizn' Matveya Kozhemyakina," *Vassa Zheleznova* (first edition), "Russkie skazki," "Skazki ob Italii," *Detstvo, V lyudyakh,* "Khozyain," stories from the collection *Po Rusi*, "Rozhdenie cheloveka," "Strasti-mordasti," "Pokoynik," "Zhenshchina," "Ledokhod."

V.V. Mayakovsky. "Vladimir Mayakovsky," "Oblako v shtanakh," "Voyna i mir," "Fleyta-pozvonochnik," "Chelovek," poems from vol. I of *Collected Works*, "Ya sam" (autobiography).

D. Bedny. Fables, lyrical poems, "Pro zemlyu, pro volyu, pro rabochuyu dolyu."

A.S. Serafimovich. "Na l'dine," "Pod zemley," "Pokhoronnyy marsh," "Sredi nochi," "U obryva," "Peski," "Gorod v stepi."

A.I. Kuprin. *Molokh*, "Olesya," "Nochnaya smena," *Poedinok*, "Gambrinus," "Belyy pudel'," "Ispoliny," "Izumrud," "Granatovyy braslet."

S.P. Pod"yachev. "Semeynoe torzhestvo," "Razlad," "Kar'era Drykalina," "Zabytye," "Za yazyk propadayu."

I.A. Bunin. "Tank'ka," "Antonovskie yabloki," "Derevnya," "Sukhodol'," "Gospodin iz San-Frantsisko," "Brat'ya."

V. Veresaev. "Bez dorogi," "Povetrie," "Na povorote," "K zhizni," "Zapiski o voyne."

I.S. Shmelev. "Chelovek iz restorana."

A.N. Tolstoy. "Priklyucheniya Rastegina," "Mishuka Nalymov."

L.N. Andreev. "Bargamot i Garas'ka," "Pet'ka na dache," "Angelochek," "Zhizn' cheloveka," "T'ma," "Tsar'-gorod."

V.Ya. Bryusov. Selected poems (from the 1955 two-volume edition).

A.A. Blok. Lyrical poems (from the 1955 two-volume edition of Blok's *Collected Works*). Plays: "Balaganchik," "Neznakomka," "Pesnya sud'by." Poems: "Vozmezdie," "Solov'inyy sad."

F. Sologub. *Melkiy bes.*[2][2]

Sbornik: Revolyutsionnaya poeziya. Sovetskiy pisatel'. Bol'shaya seriya biblioteki poeta, 1954.

Scholarly and Critical Literature

Compulsory

V.I. Lenin. "Partiynaya organizatsiya i partiynaya literatura," "O 'Vekhakh,' " "Iz proshlogo rabochey pechati v Rossii," "Pis'ma k Gor'komu."
Istoriya Kommunisticheskoy partii Sovetskogo Soyuza. 1959. (Chapters I-VII).
N.S. Khrushchev. "Vysokoe prizvanie literatury i iskusstva," Izdatel'stvo "Pravda." 1963.

Optional (as recommended by instructor)

G.V. Plekhanov. "K psikhologii rabochego dvizheniya," "Iskusstvo i obshchestvennaya zhizn'." Preface to the third edition of the collection: *Za dvadtsat' let.* A letter to Gorky: "O zhizni Matveya Kozhemyakina."
V.V. Vorovsky. "Raskol v temnom tsarstve," "V noch' posle bitvy," "Bazarov i Sanin," "Stat'i o Gor'kom, Andreeve, Kuprine, Bunine."
A.M. Gorky. "Pol' Verlen i dekadenty," "Zametki o meshchanstve," "Razrushenie lichnosti." Preface to the first collection of proletarian writers. "O tom kak ya uchilsya pisat'," "Besedy o remesle."
A.V. Lunacharsky. "Stat'i o Gor'kom," 1938 ("Gorky-khudozhnik," "Predislovie k sobraniyu sochineniy," "Dachniki," "Varvary").
V. Afanas'ev. *Kuprin.* 1960.
A.A. Volkov. *A.S. Serafimovich.* 1960.
A.A. Volkov. *Russkaya literatura XX veka.* 1960.
A.M. Gorky. *Materialy i issledovaniya.* Vol. IV. Sbornik IMLI, A.n. SSSR, 1951.
M. Gorky v epokhu revolyutsii 1905-1907 gg. Sbornik IMLI. Moscow, 1957.
Gor'kovskie chteniya. Sbornik IMLI. Moscow, 1959, 1961.
O khudozhestvennom masterstve Gor'kogo. Sbornik IMLI. Moscow, 1960.
Gorky i zarubezhnaya literatura. Sbornik IMLI. Moscow, 1961.
Tvorchestvo Gor'kogo i voprosy sotsialisticheskogo realizma. Sbornik IMLI. Moscow, 1958.
I.A. Gruzdev. *Gorky. Biografiya.* 1959.
V.A. Desnitsky. *Gorky.* 1959.
S.V. Kastorsky. *Povesti Gor'kogo "Gorodok Okurov," "Zhizn' Matveya Kozhemyakina."* 1960.
S.V. Kastorsky. *Povest' Gor'kogo "Mat'."* Uchpedgiz, 1954.
A.S. Myasnikov. The Introductory Article to the *Collected Works* of V.V. Veresaev in four volumes. GIKHL, 1948.

139

Vl. Orlov. *Aleksandr Blok.* Moscow, 1956.

A.S. Serafimovich. *Sbornik statey, vospominaniy, materialov, pisem.* A.n. SSSR, 1950.

L. Timofeev. *Aleksandr Blok.* Moscow, 1957.

History of Russian Literature
Program: Soviet Literature[2][3]

Literature

A.M. Gorky. "V.I. Lenin," "Lev Tolstoy," *Moi universitety, Delo Artamono-vykh, Zhizn' Klima Samgina, Egor Bulychev i drugie*, "Dostigaev i drugie," *Vassa Zheleznova* (second edition), "Po Soyuzu Sovetov," "Doklad na I Vsesoyuznom s"ezde pisateley." Articles: "O p'esakh," "O sotsialis-ticheskom realizme," "O 'malen'kikh lyudyakh,' o velikoy ikh rabote," "Istoriya molodogo cheloveka," "O formalizme," "Otkrytoe pis'mo Serafim-ovichu," "Esli vrag ne sdaetsya-ego unichtozhayut," "S kem vy, mastera kul'tury?" "O starom i novom cheloveke."

V. Mayakovsky. Lirika ("Oda revolyutsii," "Levyy marsh," "Khoroshee ot-noshenie k loshadyam," "Neobychaynoe priklyuchenie," "Prikaz po armii iskusstv," "Yubileynoe," "Tamara i demon," "Komsomol'skaya," tsikly parizhskikh i amerikanskikh stikhov, "Tovarishchu Nette," "Razgovor s finin-spektorom o poezii," "Sergeyu Eseninu," "Poslanie proletarskim poetam," Stikhi o sovetskom pasporte," i drugie). Satira ("O dryani," "Prozasedav-shiesya," "Byurokratiada," "Pompadur," "Plyushkin." "Spletnik," "Khan-zha," i drugie). Poemy ("150 000 000," "Pro eto," "Vladimir Il'ich Lenin," "Khorosho!," "Vo ves' golos"). Plays ("Klop," "Banya"). Stat'i ("Kak delat' stikhi?" i drugie). Ocherki ("Moe otkrytie Ameriki").

D. Bedny. "Provody," "Manifest barona fon Vrangelya," "Glavnaya ulitsa," "Snezhinki," "Nikto ne znal," "Moy stikh," "O solov'e," "O pisatel'skom trude," "Nesokrushimaya uverennost'," i drugie.

A. Blok. "Dvenadtsat'," "Inteligentsiya i revolyutsiya."

V. Bryusov. *V takie dni. (Sbornik).*

S. Esenin. "Vozvrashchenie na rodinu," "Rus' sovetskaya," "Pesn' o velikom pokhode," "Ballada o dvadtsati shesti," "Kapitan zemli," "Anna Snegina," "Persidskie motivy" i drugie.

A. Serafimovich. *Zheleznyy potok.*

D. Furmanov. *Chapaev, Myatezh.*

A.K. Tolstoy. *Khozhdenie po mudam, Petr I, Rodina. Sbornik statey.*

M. Sholokhov. *Tikhiy Don, Podnyataya tselina,* "Nauka nenavisti," "Sud'ba cheloveka."

A. Fadeev. *Razgrom, Molodaya gvardiya.*

Vs. Ivanov. *Bronepoezd 14-69.*

A. Malyshkin. "Lyudi iz zakholust'ya."

F. Panferov. *Bruski.*

K. Fedin. *Goroda i gody, Pervye radosti, Neobyknovennoe leto.*

F. Gladkov. *Tsement.*

L. Leonov. *Barsuki, Sot', Nashestvie, Russkiy les.*

K. Trenev. *Lyubov' Yarovaya.*

N. Tikhonov. "Sami," "Kirov s nami," "Dva potoka," "Na Vsemirnom kongresse."

E. Bagritsky. "Duma pro Opanasa," "Pobediteli" (a cycle of poems).

N. Ostrovsky. *Kak zakalyalas' stal'.*

A. Makarenko. *Pedagogicheskaya poema.*

P. Bazhov. *Malakhitovaya shkatulka.*

M. Prishvin. *Korabel'naya chaschcha.*

I. Il'f. i E. Petrov. "Dvenadtsat' stul'ev," "Zolotoy telenok."

A. Gaydar. *Timur i ego komanda.*

Vs. Vishnevsky. *Optimisticheskaya tragediya.*

V. Kataev. "Beleet parus odinokiy," *Vremya vpered!*

A. Tvardovsky. "Strana muraviya," "Vasiliy Terkin," "Za dal'yu-dal'."

M. Isakovsky. "Vdol' derevni," "Provozhan'e," "Katyusha," "V prifrontovom lesu," "Russkoy zhenshchine" i drugie.

A. Prokof'ev. "Priglashenie k puteshestviyu" i drugie.

V. Lugovskoy. "Seredina veka."

A. Novikov-Priboy. *Tsusima.*

Yu. Krymov. *Tanker "Derbent."*

K. Paustovsky. *Kara-Bugaz.*

A. Afinogenov. *Mashen'ka.*

A. Arbuzov. *Tanya, Irkutskaya istoriya.*

N. Pogodin. *Chelovek s ruzh'em, Kremlevskie kuranty.*

M. Aliger. "Zoya."

B. Gorbatov. *Nepokorennye.*

K. Simonov. *Russkie lyudi, Druz'ya i vragi, Zhivye i mertvye.*

A. Korneychuk. *Front.*

B. Lavrenev. *Razlom, Za tekh kto v more!*

P. Pavlenko. *Schast'e.*

B. Polevoy. *Povest' o nastoyashchem cheloveke.*

V. Azhaev. *Daleko ot Moskvy.*

V. Panova. *Sputniki, Valya, Volodya.*

E. Kazakevich. *Zvezda, Pri svete dnya.*

V. Kochetov. *Zhurbiny.*

G. Nikolaeva. *Bitva v puti.*

V. Ovechkin. *Rayonnye budni.*

D. Granin. "Iskateli."

V. Kozhevnikov. *Znakomtes', Baluev.*

P. Nilin. *Zhestokost'.*

V. Tendryakov.

V. Soloukhin. "Kaplya rosy."

V. Fomenko. "Pamyat' zemli."

A. Solzhenitsyn. *Odin den' Ivana Denisovicha*.

Beside the indicated titles it is recommended to include into the reading list the most important new works of literature which are just appearing.

Scholarly and Critical Literature

V.I. Lenin. "Partiynaya organizatsiya i partiynaya literatura," *Sochineniya*. Vol. X.

V.I. Lenin. "O proletarskoy kul'ture," *Sochineniya*. Vol. XXXI.

V.I. Lenin. "Zadachi soyuzov molodezhi" (speech delivered at the Third All Russian Congress of the Russian Communist Youth League, October 4, 1920). *Sochineniya*. Vol. XXXI.

Lenin o kul'ture i iskusstve. Moscow, 1956.

Lenin, V.I. i Gorky, A.M. Pis'ma, vospominaniya, dokumenty. Moscow, 1958.

Programma KPSS. Moscow, 1962.

Materialy iyun'skogo Plenuma (1963 g.) Ts.K. KPSS po ideologicheskim voprosam.

Postanovleniya Ts.K. KPSS o literature i iskusstve (Pis'mo Ts.K. o problematike i o politike partii v oblasti khudozhestvennoy literatury. O perestroyke literaturno-khudozhestvennykh organizatsiy. O zhurnalakh *Zvezda* i *Leningrad*. O repertuare dramaticheskikh teatrov.); ob ispravlenii oshibok v otsenke oper "Velikaya druzhba," "Bogdan Khmel'nitskiy" i "Ot vsego serdtsa." Postanovlenie Ts.K. KPSS ot 28 maya 1958 g.

L.F. Il'ichev. "Tvorit' dlya naroda, vo imya kommunizma."

A.M. Gorky, *O literature*. Moscow, 1953.

A. Lunacharsky. *Stat'i o Gor'kom*. Moscow, 1938.

A. Lunacharsky. "Vl. Mayakovsky-novator," in the collection *Klassiki russkoy literatury*. Goslitizdat, 1947.

A. Lunacharsky. *Stat'i o sovetskoy literature*. Moscow, 1958.

A. Fadeev. *Za tridtsat' let*. Moscow, 1957.

Sovetskie pisateli. Avtobiografii v dvukh tomakh. Moscow, 1959.

Istoriya russkoy sovetskoy lirertury. Vol. I. MGU edition, 1958. Vol. II. MGU edition, 1963.

Istoriya russkoy sovetskoy literatury (v trekh tomakh). A.n. SSSR, 1958-1961.

B. Mikhaylovsky i E. Tager. *Tvorchestvo A.M. Gor'kogo*. Uchpedgiz, 1956.

K.M. Muratova. *Gorky v bor'be za razvitie sovetskoy literatury*. Moscow-Leningrad, 1958.

B. Byalik. *M. Gorky-dramaturg*. Moscow, 1962.

A. Ovcharenko. *Publitsistika M. Gor'kogo*. Moscow, 1961.

V. Pertsov. *V. Mayakovsky. Zhizn' i tvorchestvo*. Vols. I-II. Moscow, 1957.

A. Metchenko. *Tvorchestvo Mayakovskogo 1925-1930 gg*. Moscow, 1961.

Mayakovsky v shkole. Sbornik statey. Moscow, 1961.

Z. Paperny. *Poeticheskiy obraz u Mayakovskogo*. A.n. SSSR, 1961.

L. Timofeev. *Aleksandr Blok*. Moscow, 1957.

A. Serafimovich. *Issledovaniya, vospominaniya, materialy, pis'ma*. Moscow-Leningrad, 1950.

A.A. Volkov. *Tvorcheskiy put' A.S. Serafimovicha*. Moscow, 1960.

B.R. Shcherbina. *A.N. Tolstoy*. Moscow, 1956.

Yu.A. Krestinsky. *A.N. Tolstoy. Zhizn' i tvorchestvo (kratkiy ocherk)*. Moscow, 1960.

A.V. Alpatov. *Aleksey Tolstoy-master istoricheskogo romana*. Moscow, 1958.

B.Ya. Braynina. *Fedor Gladkov*. Goslitizdat, 1957.

K.A. Zelinsky. *A. Fadeev*. Moscow, 1956.

A. Bushmin. *Roman A. Fadeeva "Razgrom."* Leningrad, 1954.

Yu.A. Lukin. *S. Makarenko*. Moscow, 1954.

E. Naumov. *Furmanov*. Moscow, 1954.

B. Braynina. *Konstantin Fedin*. Moscow, 1956.

I. Lezhnev. *Put' Sholokhova*. Moscow, 1958.

L. Yakimenko. *"Tikhiy Don" M. Sholokhova. O masterstve pisatelya*. Moscow, 1958.

L. Yakimenko. *O "Podnyatoy tseline" M. Sholokhova*. Moscow, 1960.

V. Gura. *Zhizn' i tvorchestvo M. Sholokhova*. Moscow, 1960.

Yu.B. Lukin. *Mikhail Sholokhov. Kritiko-biograficheskiy ocherk*. Moscow, 1962.

E. Surkov. *K.A. Trenev*. Moscow, 1953.

P. Vykhodtsev. *Aleksandr Tvardovsky*. Moscow, 1958.

E. Lyubareva. *A.T. Tvardovsky*. Moscow, 1958.

L.P. Levin. *P.A. Pavlenko*. Moscow, 1953.

V. Kovalev. *Tvorchestvo L. Leonova. K kharakteristike tvorcheskoy individual'nosti pisatelya*. Moscow-Leningrad, 1962.

A. Khvatov. *Aleksandr Malyshkin*. Moscow-Leningrad, 1959.

A. Ershov. *Sovetskaya satiricheskaya proza 20-kh godov*. Moscow-Leningrad, 1960.

V. Shcherbina. *Epokha i chelovek*. Moscow, 1960.

Russian Folklore (Russkoe narodnoe tvorchestvo) Program for Philological Faculties of State Universities[2 4]

Leading Literature

K. Marks. "K kritike politicheskoy ekonomii." Vvedenie. *Sobranie sochineniy* K. Marksa i F. Engel'sa, vol. XII, Part I, Partizdat, 1935.

F. Engel's. *Nemetskie narodnye knigi. Stat'i, pis'ma 1838-1845 gg.* Goslitizdat, 1940, pp. 26-34.

F. Engel's. "Proiskhozhedenie sem'i, chastnoy sobstvennosti i gosudarstva." K. Marks, F. Engel's. *Izbrannye proizvedeniya v dvukh tomakh*, vol. II. Moscow, 1948, pp. 160-310.

V.I. Lenin. "Evgeniy Pott'e." *Sbornik Lenin o kul'ture i iskusstve.* Moscow, Izdatel'stvo "Iskusstvo," 1956, pp. 129-130.

V.I. Lenin. "Razvitie rabochikh khorov v Germanii." *Lenin o kul'ture i iskusstve*, pp. 131-132.

Textbooks

Compulsory Literature

Russkoe narodnoe poeticheskoe tvorchestvo. Posobie dlya vuzov. Ed. by Professor P.G. Bogatyrev. Second edition. Moscow, Uchpedgiz, 1956.

Ustnoe poeticheskoe tvorchestvo naroda. Khrestomatiya. Compiled by S.I. Vasilenok and V.M. Sidel'nikov. Moscow, MGU, 1954.

Russkiy folklor. Khrestomatiya. Compiled by Professor N.P. Andreev. Moscow, Uchpegiz, 1938.

E.V. Pomerantseva. *Russkie narodnye skazki (antologiya).* MGU, 1957.

P.D. Ukhov. *Bylina (antologiya).* MGU, 1957.

V.I. Chicherov. *Russkoe narodnoe tvorchestvo.* MGU, 1959.

Additional Literature

Russkoe narodnoe poeticheskoe tvorchestvo. Moscow-Leningrad, Izdanie A.n. institut russkoy literatury, vol. I (11th-13th cent.), 1953; vol. II, book 1 (from middle eighteenth cent. to the first half of the 19th cent.), 1955; vol. II, book 2, (from the second half or the 19th cent. to the beginning of the 20th cent.), 1956.

146

Yu.M. Sokolov. *Russkiy folklor*. Moscow, Uchpedgiz, 1938, 1940.
T.M. Animova. *Seminariy po poeticheskomu tvorchestvu*. Saratov, 1959.

Articles and Research

Compulsory Literature

A.N. Afanas'ev. *Poeticheskie vozreniya slavyan na prirodu*, vol. I. Moscow, 1965, Introduction, chapter one.

V.G. Belinsky. "Drevnie rossiyskie stikhotvoreniya, sobrannye Kirsheyu Danilovym i vtorichno izdannye. Drevnie russkie stikhotvoreniya, sobrannye M. Sukhanovym. Skazaniya russkogo naroda, sobrannye I. Sakharovym, vol. I, books 1, 2, 3, 4, third edition. Russkie narodnye skazki, part one," *Polnoe sobranie sochineniy,* vol. V. Moscow, 1954, pp. 289-450.

V.G. Belinsky. (O narodnykh skazkakh) *Polnoe sobranie sochineniy*, vol. 5, pp. 660-76.

V.G. Belinsky. "Pis'mo Gogolyu," *Polnoe sobranie sochineniy v trekh tomakh*, vol. III. Moscow, 1958, pp. 707-15.

V.D. Bonch-Bruevich. "Lenin ob ustnom narodnom tvorchestve," *Sovetskaya etnografiya*, 1954, No. 4.

F.I. Buslaev. "Epicheskaya poeziya," in *Istoricheskie ocherki russkoy narodnoy slovesnosti i "iskusstva,"* vol. I, "russkaya narodnaya poeziya," St. Petersburg, 1861.

F.I. Buslaev. "Perekhozhie povesti," in the collection *Moi dosugi*, part II, 1884.

A.N. Veselovsky. "Psikhologicheskiy parallelizm i ego formy v otrazheniyakh poeticheskogo stilya," three chapters on historic poetics, *Sobranie sochineniy*, vol. I, St. Petersburg, 1913.

A.M. Gorky. "Razrushenie lichnosti," in the collection *M. Gorky o literature*. Sovetskiy pisatel', 1953, pp. 48-91.

A.M. Gorky. "Sovetskaya literatura," doklad na Pervom vsesoyuznom s"ezde pisateley 17 avgusta 1934 g. *M. Gorky o literature*, pp. 690-739.

A.M. Gorky. "O skazkakh," *M. Gorky o literature*, pp. 760-67.

A.M. Gorky. ("O skazkakh"), *Sobranie sochineniy v 30 tomakh*, vol. 25. Moscow, 1953, pp. 86-89.

A.M. Gorky. "O religiozno-mifologicheskom momente v epose drevnikh," *Polnoe sobranie sochineniy v 30 tomakh*, vol. 27. Moscow, 1953, pp. 496-97.

N.A. Dobrolyubov. "Narodnye russkie skazki" A. Afanas'eva i "Yuzhno russkie pesni." Kiev, 1857 (Review), *Polnoe sobranie sochineniy v 6 tomakh*, vol. I. GIKhL, 1934, pp. 429-34.

N.A. Dobrolyubov. "O poetichnykh osobennostyakh velikorusskoy narodnoy poezii v vyrazheniyakh i oborotakh," *Polnoe sobranie sochineniy v 6 tomakh*, vol. I pp. 522-24.

N.A. Dobrolyubov. "Zamechaniya o sloge i mernosti narodnogo yazyka," *Polnoe sobranie sochineniy v 6 tomakh*, vol. I, pp. 525-57.

N.A. Dobrolyubov. "O stepeni uchastiya narodnosti v razvitii russkoy literatury," *Polnoe sobranie sochineniy v 6 tomakh*, vol. I, pp. 203-45.

Lafarg Pol'. "Narodnye svadebnye pesni i obryady," in the collection *Ocherki po istorii pervobytnoy kul'tury*, vol. II. Moscow, 1926.

V.F. Miller. *Ocherki russkoy narodnoy slovesnosti*, vol. I, Ocherki 1, 2, 3. St. Petersburg, 1897. Vol. II, ocherki o Sadko i o Dobryne i Aleshe. Moscow, 1910. Vol III, ocherk 1. Moscow, 1924.

G.V. Plekhanov. "Pis'ma bez adresa," in the collection *Iskusstvo i literatura*. Moscow, 1948, pp. 42-164.

N.G. Chernyshevsky. "Pesni raznykh narodov. Translated by N. Berg," (Review). *Polnoe sobranie sochineniy*, vol. II. GIKhL, 1949, pp. 291-317, 362-68.

N.G. Chernyshevsky. "Esteticheskie otnosheniya iskusstva k deystvitel'nosti," *Polnoe sobranie sochineniy*, vol. II, pp. 5-15 (a passage).

N.G. Chernyshevsky. "Polemicheskie krasoty," *Polnoe sobranie sochineniy*, vol. VII, Moscow, 1950, pp. 740-58 (a passage).

N.G. Chernyshevsky. "Arkhiv istoriko-yuridicheskikh svedeniy, otnosyashchikhsya do Rosii, izdavaemoy N. Kalachevym," (Review). *Polnoe sobranie sochineniy*, vol. II, pp. 369-81, 735-39.

V.I. Chicherov. "Literatura i ustnoe narodnoe tvorchestvo," *Kommunist*, 1955, No. 14.

Additional Literature

M.K. Azadovsky. *Istoriya folkloristiki*. Leningrad, 1959.

E.V. Anichkov. "Vesennyaya obryadovaya poeziya na Zapade i u slavyan," part one. St. Petersburg, 1903; part two, 1905.

P.V. Vladimirov. *Vvedenie v istoriyu russkoy slovesnosti*. Kiev, 1896.

A.M. Gorky. "Voplenitsa," *M. Gorky o literature*. Sovetskiy pisatel', 1953, pp. 15-18.

V.E. Gusev. *Russkie revolyutsionnye demokraty o narodnoy poezii*. Uchpedgiz, 1955.

N.A. Dobrolyubov. "O nekotorykh mestnykh poslovitsakh i pogovorkakh Nizhnegorodskoy gubernii," *Polnoe sobranie sochineniy v 6 tomakh*, vol. I, pp. 493-95.

N.A. Dobrolyubov. "Zametki i dopolneniya k sborniku russkikh poslovits g. Buslaeva," *Polnoe sobranie sochineniy v 6 tomakh*, vol. I, pp. 495-521.

S.F. Eleonsky. *Literatura i narodnoe tvorchestvo*. Moscow, 1956.

O.I. Kapitsa. *Detskiy folklor*. Leningrad, 1928.

V.Ya. Propp. *Russkiy geroicheskiy epos.* Leningrad, 1955.

Russkoe narodnopoeticheskoe tvorchestvo (materialy dlya izucheniya obshchestvenno-politicheskikh vozzreniy naroda). *Trudy Instituta etnografii Akademii nauk SSSR*, vol. XX, 1953.

K.V. Chistov. *Narodnaya poetessa Irina Fedosova.* Petrozavodsk, 1956.

M.P. Shtokmar. *Issledovaniya v oblasti russkogo narodnogo stikhoslozheniya.* Moscow, 1952.

Collections of Texts

A.N. Afanas'ev. *Narodnye russkie skazki*, vol. I, 1936; vol. II, 1938; vol. III, 1940.

E.V. Barsov. *Prichitaniya Severnogo kraya*, vol. I, 1872; vol. II, 1882; vol. III, 1886.

A.F. Gil'ferding. *Onezhskie byliny*, vols. I-III. Fourth edition, 1949-51.

V.I. Dal'. *Poslovitsy russkogo naroda.* Moscow, 1861. Second edition, Moscow, 1879. Third edition, Moscow, 1957.

Drevnie rossiyskie stikhotvoreniya, sobrannye Kirshey Danilovym. Ed. by S.K. Shambinago. Moscow, 1938.

E.N. Eleonskaya. *Sbornik velikorusskikh chastushek.* Moscow, 1914.

P.V. Kireevsky. *Pesni, sobrannye P.V. Kireevskim.* Editor M.N. Speransky. First edition, Moscow, 1911. Second edition, part one, Moscow, 1918; part two, Moscow, 1929.

A.N. Lozanova. *Pesni i predaniya o Stepane Razine i Pugacheve.* Moscow, 1935.

V.F. Miller. *Istoricheskie pesni russkogo naroda XVI-XVII vv.* Peterburg, 1915.

N.N. Rozhdestvenskaya and S.S. Zhislina. *Russkie chastushki.* Moscow, 1956.

I.N. Rozanov. *Pesni russkikh poetov.* Sovetskiy pisatel', 1936.

P.N. Rybnikov. *Pesni sobrannye P.N. Rybnikovym v 4 tomakh*, 1861-67. Second edition; ed. A.E. Gruzinsky. Vols. I-III, 1909-10.

D. Sadovnikov. *Zagadki russkogo naroda*, 1876. St. Petersburg, 1901. Moscow, 1959.

A.I. Sobolevsky. *Velikorusskie narodnye pesni.* Vols. I-VII. St. Petersburg, 1895-1902.

Tvorchestvo narodov SSSR. Pravda, 1937.

P.V. Sheyn. *Velikoruss v svoikh pesnyakh, obryadakh, verovaniyakh, skazkakh, legendakh i t.p.*, vol. I. First edition, 1898; second edition, St. Petersburg, 1900.

Folklore

Folklore as an expression of the working people's creative activity. The peculiarities of folklore and its importance in the development of Russian literature. The classics of Marxism-Leninism and A.M. Gorky on folklore.

The epic genres in Russian folklore. The ideological and artistic characteristics of the *bylina* epos (civilization, themes, images, poetics).

Different varieties of lyric folk songs, their ideological and thematic contents and artistic peculiarities.

The classification of the Russian national tales. The analysis of the ideological and thematic contents of the tales and their artistic peculiarities.

The distinctive features of the folklore of the Soviet period. Its connection with the main periods in the life of the Soviet people.

Old Russian Literature

General characteristic of old Russian literature. Its importance and distinctive features.

Slovo o polku Igoreve as a work of genius of old Russian literature. The ideological meaning, the images, and the artistic peculiarities of the *Slovo*.

Old Russian patriotic tales about the Tartar invasion and about the struggle against the Tartar yoke.

Zhitie protopopa Avvakuma on the background of the traditional "Life" literature. The ideological and artistic contradictions of this monument.

Original Russian eighteenth-century tales (tales from everyday life, parody and satirical tales, etc.) and their ideological and class meaning; the growth of realistic tendencies.

Eighteenth-century Literature

Classicism as a literary trend. The development of classicism in Russia. Its place and meaning in the history of Russian literature.

The satires of A.D. Kantemir. The subsequent development of the satire in eighteenth-century literature.

149

M.V. Lomonosov. The ideological and artistic direction of his creative activity. The importance of his theoretical works for the development of Russian literature.

G.R. Derzhavin. The main themes of his poetry. The peculiarities of Derzhavin's odes.

D.I. Fonvizin and his role in the development of the Russian drama. The analysis of the comedy *Nedorosl'*.

A.N. Radischev and his book *Puteshestvie iz Peterburga v Moskvu*. The style of this work. The importance of Radishchev in the history of the Russian liberation movement.

A characteristic of sentimentalism. The literary and artistic activity of N.M. Karamzin.

Nineteenth-century Literature

The characteristic peculiarities of Russian nineteenth-century classical literature and its universal importance.

I.A. Krylov, the fable writer. The realism and *narodnost'* of his fables. The mastery of Krylov.

Romanticism in Russian literature of the first quarter of the nineteenth century. The Decembrist poets. A characteristic of Ryleev's creative activity.

Gore ot uma, by A.S. Griboedov. The style of the comedy. The innovations of Gribiedov, the playwright.

The lyrics of A.S. Pushkin; their evolution and ideological and artistic contents.

A.S. Pushkin's romantic poems. "Tsygany" (Pushkin's shift towards realism and *narodnost'*).

The tragedy *Boris Godunov*, by A.S. Pushkin. The national, historical, social, and political problems in the tragedy and their artistic peculiarities.

Evgeniy Onegin, by A.S. Pushkin—the first example of a Russian realistic novel, "an encyclopedia of Russian life." The main characters in the novel *Evgeniy Onegin*.

The poems *Poltava* and *Mednyy vsadnik*, by A.S. Pushkin. The main problems dealt with in these poems and the artistic solutions offered to these problems.

A.S. Pushkin's prose and its importance for the development of Russian literature. The novelette *Kapitanskaya dochka*.

The main motives, the character and importance of M.Yu. Lermontov's lyrics.

M.Yu. Lermontov's poems ("Pesnya pro kuptsa Kalashnikova," "Mtsyry," and "Demon"). The peculiarities of their style.

Geory nashego vremeni, by M.Yu. Lermontov, as a social and psychological novel.

The *narodnost'* of A.V. Kol'tsov's poetry.

Vechera na khutore bliz Dikan'ki and *Mirgorod* by N.V. Gogol'. The romanticism and realism in these works.

N.V. Gogol's Peterburg tales. The depiction of social contradictions in these tales.

Revizor by N.V. Gogol'. The social, political, artistic, and literary importance of the comedy.

N.V. Gogol's poem *Mertvye dushi*. The problems, ideas, and images. The peculiarities of Gogol's satire.

V.G. Belinsky. His aesthetic principles and literary and critical activity.

"The natural school" of the forties of the nineteenth century. Belinsky's role in the formation of the school.

A general characteristic of A.I. Gertsen's creative activity. The novel *Kto vinovat?* V.I. Lenin about Gertsen.

The literary movements of the fifties and sixties of the nineteenth century. The journal *Sovremennik*—the fighting center of the revolutionary-democratic camp.

N.G. Chernyshevsky—the leader of the revolutionary democrats. V.I. Lenin about Chernyshevsky. Chernyshevsky's views on literature and art. Chernyshevsky the critic.

N.G. Chernyshevsky's novel *Chto delat'?* and its importance. The problem of the positive hero in the novel.

The critic N.A. Dobrolyubov, a most prominent representative of the revolutionary democrats.

The peculiarity of D.I. Pisarev's literary and aesthetic position.

N.A. Nekrasov's poems about peasant life. The analysis of the poem "Komu na Rusi zhit' khorosho."

The problem of the revolutionary feat in the lyrics of N.A. Nekrasov and in the poems of the Decembrists ("Dedushka," "Russkie zhenshchiny").

The revolutionary-democratic character of N.A. Nekrasov's lyrics. The peculiarity of his realism.

The development of A.N. Ostrovsky the artist in the forties and fifties.

A.N. Ostrovsky's play *Groza*. The character of Katerina. The ideological and aesthetic importance of the play.

The social drama and comedy of A.N. Ostrovsky in the seventies and eighties. The importance of Ostrovsky for the development of Russian drama and theater.

Zapiski okhotnika, by I.S. Turgenev. The themes, their ideological meaning and artistic peculiarity.

The reflection of social and intellectual life of the forties and fifties in I.S. Turgenev's novels *Rudin, Dvoryanskoe gnezdo, Nakanune*.

Ottsy i deti. I.S. Turgenev's depiction of a *raznochinets*—democrat. Turgenev a master of the realistic novel.

The creative path of I.A. Goncharov. The analysis of the novel *Oblomov*. N.A. Dobrolyubov about Oblomov and Oblomovism. V.I. Lenin about Oblomovism.

The nature and the development of the characters in M.E. Saltykov-Shchedrin's satire. *Istoriya odnogo goroda, Skazki.*

Gospoda Golovlevy, by M.E. Saltykov-Shchedrin, as a new type of a social novel.

The novel *Prestuplenie i nakazanie*, by F.M. Dostoevsky. The character of Raskol'nikov. The strong and weak points in Dostoevsky's creative work.

V.I. Lenin about L.N. Tolstoy, the thinker and the artist of genius.

L.N. Tolstoy's creative work in the fifties.

Voyna i mir by L.N. Tolstoy—a heroic and patriotic epic. Andrey Bolkonsky and Pierre Bezukhov in their search for a socially useful meaning of life.

L.N. Tolstoy's novel *Anna Karenina*. The reflection in the novel of Tolstoy's mood and views before the decisive break in his *Weltanschauung*.

The novel *Voskresenie* as L.N. Tolstoy's highest achievement in critical realism.

The basic stages in G.I. Uspensky's creative path. Uspensky a master of the sketch.

The ideological motives and the artistic images in the creative work of V.G. Korolenko.

A.P. Chekhov, the great master of the realistic story.

The innovations of A.P. Chekhov the playwright. *Vishnevyy sad.*

**Twentieth-century Literature
(Before the October Revolution)**

The critical realism of the period of the end of the nineteenth century—beginning of the twentieth century and its representatives.

The creative path of A.I. Kuprin. The novels *Molokh* and *Poedinok*.

The prose of I.A. Bunin. The stories and tales about the countryside. "Gospodin iz San-Frantsisko," "Brat'ya."

A characteristic of the decadent trends.

The peculiarity of V.Ya. Bryusov's creative path.

The themes of the "terrible world," of the motherland and of the revolution in the poetry of A.A. Blok.

A.M. Gorky and his revolutionary-romantic works in the nineties and the beginning of the twentieth century. The connection of these works with the liberation movement of that period. The themes and characters of these works.

The ideological and artistic innovations of A.M. Gorky in his solution to the "vagabond theme" (the stories of the nineties, the play *Na dne*). The unmasking of capitalism and the pathos of the struggle with false humanism.

The theme of the intelligentsia in A.M. Gorky's plays of the beginning of the twentieth century.

A.M. Gorky's novel *Mat'*—a classic of socialist realism. V.I. Lenin about the novel.

The image of the revolutionary proletariat in the works of A.M. Gorky (*Meshchane, Vragi, Mat'*).

A.M. Gorky's autobiographical trilogy. The generalizing force of the character of the autobiographical hero and his path in life.

The creative work of A.S. Serafimovich before the October Revolution. His path towards socialist realism.

The pre-October creative work of V.V. Mayakovsky. "Oblako v shtanakh"—a reflection of Mayakovsky's program of that period.

Soviet Literature

V.I. Lenin about the *partiynost'* of literature.

The role of the Communist party in the development of Soviet literature.

Socialist realism—the creative method of Soviet literature.

The basic traits of Soviet literature and its universal importance.

The characteristic peculiarities of the development of literature and literary movements in the period of the revolution and the civil war.

A.M. Gorky's sketch "V.I. Lenin." The mastery of a writer in the creation of a literary portrait.

The theme of capitalism in A.M. Gorky's post-October works (*Delo Artamonovykh, Egor Bulychov i drugie*).

Zhizn' Klima Samgina, by A.M. Gorky, as a moving panorama of decades. The unmasking of Samginovism.

A.M. Gorky the journalist. The struggle of Gorky with the reactionary bourgeois ideology. The notions of Soviet patriotism and humanism in Gorky's articles.

The themes and the ideological direction of Soviet literature of the twenties. The image of a communist in the works of that period.

The Soviet heroic drama of the twenties. *Lyubov' Yarovaya* by K.A. Trenev. *Razlom* by B.A. Lavrenev.

Socialist lyrics by V.V. Mayakovsky. Verses about the poet and about poetry.

The image of V.I. Lenin in V.V. Mayakovsky's poem "V.I. Lenin." The artistic peculiarities of this poem.

V.V. Mayakovsky's poem "Khorosho!" an outstanding achievement of socialist realism.

V.V. Mayakovsky's satiric verses and plays of the twenties.

The poetic innovations of V.V. Mayakovsky.

The satiric creative activity of D. Bedny. The importance of the poet for the development of Soviet agitational poetry.

The patriotic character of S.A. Esenin's poetry. The theme of Soviet reality in his verses. The ideological contradictions in the poet.

The traits of the Soviet heroic epos in *Zheleznyy potok* by A.S. Serafimovich. The depiction of the hero and of the people's masses in the novel.

D.A. Furmanov and his work *Chapaev*. The role of Furmanov in the creation of the image of a positive hero.

The works of the thirties about socialist construction. The theme of the upbringing of a new man in A.S. Makarenko's *Pedagogicheskaya poema*.

The birth and the formation of a socialist individual the main theme of N.A. Ostrovsky's creative work. The educational importance of *Kak zakalyalas' stal'.*

Tikhiy Don—an epic novel by M.A. Sholokhov. The character of Grigory Melekhov, its typicalness and artistic peculiarity.

M.A. Sholokhov's novel *Podnyataya tselina*, the best work about the period of collectivization. The mastery of Sholokhov the artist.

A.N. Tolstoy's novel *Petr I* and its importance in the development of the Soviet historical novel.

A.N. Tolstoy's trilogy *Khozhdenie po mukam*. The themes and the main characters.

The poetry of M.V. Isakovsky and its main peculiarities.

The development and the importance of Soviet literature in the years of the Great Fatherland War. The heroic and patriotic themes in poetry, journalism, drama, and prose.

A.A. Fadeev's novel *Razgrom* and its place among the works of the twenties about the civil war.

A.A. Fadeev's novel *Molodaya gvardiya*. The unity of realistic and romantic elements in the depiction of the positive heroes.

The creative path of A.T. Tvardovsky. The poems "Vasiliy Terkin" and "Za dal'yu—dal,'" The generalizing power of the character of the main hero.

The stages in the creative path of L.M. Leonov. The artistic embodiment of the patriotic pathos in the novel *Russkiy les*.

K.A. Fedin's trilogy *Pervye radosti, Neobyknovennoe leto, Koster*. The innovative approach to traditional, for the author, themes and problems.

The depiction of the historic exploits of the Soviet people in the tales and novels about the Great Fatherland War (*Povest' o nastoyashchem cheloveke*, by B.N. Polevoy, *Burya*, by I.G. Erenburg, and others).

The theme of socialist labor and the country's movement toward communism in Soviet literature of the postwar period. The place and the importance of the novels by V.A. Kochetov (*Zhurbiny*) and G.E. Nikolaeva (*Bitva v puti*).

The image of V.I. Lenin in the dramatic trilogy by N.F. Pogodin (*Chelovek s ruzh'em, Kremlevskie kuranty, Tret'ya pateticheskaya*).

The peculiarities of the development of the literary process after the Twentieth Congress of the CPSU. The achievements of Soviet literature in this period.

The tasks of Soviet literature in the present period.

Moscow State University[2][6]

Department of Russian Folklore
(Kafedra russkogo narodnogo tvorchestva)

Special Seminars Offered in the Second
Semester of the 1969-70 Academic Year

1. Russian literature of the nineteenth century and folklore (N.I. Kravtsov).
2. The poetics of Russian folklore (P.G. Bogatyrev).
3. The poetics of folklore (the lyrical origins in the folklore genres) (V.P. Anikin).
4. The people's prose (*narodnaya proza*) (N.I. Savushkina).
5. The poetics of the *bylina* (F.M. Selivanov).

Special Courses Offered in the Second
Semester of the 1969-70 Academic Year

1. The poetics of Russian folklore (P.G. Bogatyrev).
2. Folklore as a result of the people's collective creation (*tvorchestvo*) (V.P. Anikin).
3. The people's theater (*narodnyy teatr*) (N.I. Savushkina).
4. The history of collecting and studying of the people's prose (Staff).

Department (*Kafedra*) of History
of Russian Literature

Special Courses Offered to Third- and
Fourth-year Students in the 1969-70
Academic Year

1. Literary and critical activity of V.G. Belinsky (S.N. Limantseva).
2. Dramatic works by A. Pushkin (S.M. Bondy).
3. The realism of Chekhov (M.P. Gromov).
4. A.I. Gertsen (L.I. Matyushenko).
5. Gogol' in Russian criticism (N.I. Gerasimov).
6. The Russian historic novel of the nineteenth and the beginning of the twentieth centuries (A.V. Alpatov).
7. I.S. Turgenev (P.G. Pustovoyt).
8. F.I. Tyutchev (O.V. Orlov).

155

Special Seminars Offered to Second-year
Students in the 1969-70 Academic Year

1. M.Yu. Lermontov.
2. N.V. Gogol'.
3. A.P. Chekhov.
4. L.N. Tolstoy.

Special Seminars Offered to Third- and
Fourth-year Students in the 1969-70
Academic Year

1. A seminar in old Russian literature (V.V. Kuskov).
2. Pushkin and nineteenth-century Russian lyrics (S.N. Limantseva).
3. N.V. Gogol' (P.A. Orlov).
4. *Byloe i dumy* by Gertsen and the memoir-autobiographical literature (L.I. Matyushenko).
5. F.M. Dostoevsky (K.I. Tyun'kin).
6. Chekhov's prose of the nineties and 1900s (V.B. Kataev).
7. The style of L.N. Tolstoy (N.V. Nikolaeva).
8. Tyutchev and Russian romanticism (O.V. Orlov).
9. Artistic trends in Russian literature of the end of the nineteenth century (Palievsky).
10. The Russian historic novel of the nineteenth and the beginning of the twentieth centuries (A.V. Alpatov).
11. Experimental poetics in Russian literature of the nineteenth century (V.N. Turbin).
12. L.N. Tolstoy (M.N. Zozulya).
13. The traditions of the revolutionary-democratic criticism (N.A. Glagolev).
14. The satire of Gogol' and Shchedrin (V.F. Mochul'sky).
15. The novelists of the seventies of the nineteenth century (N.I. Liban).
16. Russian-Polish literary connections (N.I. Gerasimov).

Department of Soviet Literature

Special Courses Offered in the 1969-70 Academic Year

1. Soviet poetry of the fifties and sixties (V.A. Zaytsev).
2. Romantic trends in the poetry of the twenties (E.P. Lyubareva).
3. Ideological and stylistic trends in Russian Soviet prose of the twenties (E.B. Skorospelova).

4. Sergey Esenin and the literary movement of the period of 1910-20 (P.F. Yushin).
5. Kuprin and Russian critical realism of the end of the nineteenth and the beginning of the twentieth centuries (I.V. Karetskaya).
6. The image of Lenin in the literatures of the peoples of the USSR (A.A. Sharif).

Special Seminars Offered to Second-year Students in the 1969-70 Academic Year

1. Contemporary Soviet poetry (V.A. Zaytsev).
2. Contemporary Soviet prose (V.V. Petelin).

Special Seminars Offered to Third- and Fourth-year Students in the 1969-70 Academic Year

1. Problems of Russian prose of the sixties (V.A. Apukhtin).
2. The development of prose in the literatures of the peoples of the USSR. The importance of artistic cooperation (R.G. Bikmukhametov).
3. Revolutionary romanticism in the works of Soviet literature (I.M. Dubrovina).
4. The lyrics and the poem of the fifties and sixties (V.A. Zaytsev).
5. Contemporary prose (L.A. Kolobaev).
6. Contemporary dramatic works and the theater (E.P. Lyubareva).
7. Mayakovsky and the poetic trends of the twentieth century (A.I. Metchenko).
8. Gorky and the literary trends of the twentieth century (A.I. Ovcharenko).
9. A. Tolstoy and the writers of the historic theme (A.I. Pautkin).
10. The diversity of artistic form in the literature of socialist realism (S.M. Petrov).
11. Soviet children's literature (F.I. Setin).
12. M. Gorky and the realistic prose of the end of the nineteenth and the beginning of the twentieth centuries (A.G. Sokolov).
13. Artistic prose of the twenties (M.N. Sotskova).
14. Genre and style diversity in the poetry of the twenties (V.I. Fatyushchenko).
15. The Azerbaydzhan novel (A.A. Sharif).
16. Sergey Esenin and Soviet poetry (P.F. Yushin).
17. Genres and styles of Soviet prose (L.G. Yakimenko).

Department of Theory of Literature

*Diploma Works by Graduating Students to be
Defended in the Spring of 1970*

1. The problem of the positive hero in the novel *Idiot* by F.M. Dostoevsky.
2. The principles of the depiction of life in the novel *Besy* by F.M. Dostoevsky.
3. The originality of the characters in the works of A.P. Chekhov.
4. The epilogues and their importance in the plot structure of Chekhov's stories of the nineties.
5. The system of images in Chekhov's stories (of the nineties).
6. The peculiarities of Chekhov's drama style.
7. The interdependence of the evolution of artistic form and aesthetic perception.
8. The method, style, and genre of Dostoevsky's novels in the criticism of the Russian symbolists.

Department of Soviet Literature

*Diploma Works by Graduating Students to be
Defended in the Spring of 1970*

1. The problem of character in the dramatic works of A. Arbuzov.
2. The dramatic works of M. Gorky and their staging in the sixties.
3. The theme of the city in the lyrics of V. Bryusov.
4. Peterburg in the creative work of A. Blok.
5. A.M. Gorky and L.N. Andreev.
6. *Zametki iz dnevnika. Vospominaniya* by A.M. Gorky.
7. Actual reality in the creative work of A. Blok (1907-17).
8. The romanticism of A. Grin.
9. The theme of Russia in the works of I. Bunin.
10. The stylistic atmosphere surrounding the hero as a means of the historic-psychological characteristic in the novel *Pushkin* by Yu. Tynyanov.
11. The landscape in the novel *Petr Pervyy* by A. Tolstoy. (Peculiarities of style, ideologic and aesthetic functions of landscape in a historic narrative.)

Department of History of Russian Literature

*Diploma Works by Graduating Students to
be Defended in the Spring of 1970*

1. Artistic forms of the secret psychology in the creative work of I.S. Turgenev.
2. *Sentimental'naya povest'* by Karamzin and *Povesti Belkina*.

3. Elements of Pushkin's influence in the creative work of I.S. Turgenev.
4. Satire and humor in *Zhitie Avvakuma*.
5. The problem of character in *Brat'ya Karamazovy* by Dostoevsky.
6. The problem of the typological in the realism of Chekhov.
7. Composition as a means of creating artistic unity in the novel *Brat'ya Karamazovy* by Dostoevsky.
8. Confession as a characterization device in the works of Dostoevsky.
9. Fabulousness (*fantastika*) in Turgenev's creative work of the seventies and eighties.

Along with these topics there were four others dealing with different aspects of Nakrasov's creative work.

**Suggested Topics for Class
Reports (Term Papers) in the
Seminar on L.N. Tolstoy
given at the Moscow State
University in the 1969-70
Academic Year
Instructor N.V. Nikolaeva**[2][7]

1. L.N. Tolstoy in Literary Criticism

   a. L.N. Tolstoy and the democratic-revolutionary critics of the fifties.

   b. L.N. Tolstoy and the liberal critics of the fifties (Druzhinin, Annenkov).

   c. *Voyna i mir* in Russian literary criticism of the sixties and seventies.

   d. B. Eykhenbaum on Tolstoy.

   e. The psychological school on Tolstoy (Ovsyanik-Kulikovsky).

   f. The methodological importance of Lenin's articles on Tolstoy.

*2. The Chronological Study of the Works
of L. Tolstoy*

   a. The problem of the people in the early works of L. Tolstoy.

   b. Man at war in the early Tolstoy.

   c. The genre of Tolstoy's stories of the fifties.

   d. The principles of Tolstoy's work on his language (style) in the fifties.

   e. The evolution of the forms of psychological analysis in Tolstoy's work of the fifties.

   f. Tolstoy and Gertsen at the end of the fifties and the beginning of the sixties.

   g. War in the early works of Tolstoy and in *Voyna i mir*.

   h. The philosophy of nature in *Voyna i mir*.

   i. The composition of the novel *Voyna i mir*.

   j. The problems of the psychological analysis in *Voyna i mir*.

   k. P. Bezukhov and A. Bolkonsky.

   1. *Anna Karenina* as a sociophilosophical novel.

   m. The evolution of the forms and methods of portrayal in *Anna Karenina*.

   n. The style of the inner monologues in *Anna Karenina*.

   o. *Anna Karenina* and *Gospoga Golovlevy*.

   p. Tolstoy and Turgenev in the seventies.

   q. Tolstoy and Dostoevsky in the seventies (the type of novel and hero; methods of narration and portrayal).

r. *Voskresenie* as a social novel.

s. The peculiarities of narration in *Voskresenie*.

t. The detail and its function in the later works of Tolstoy.

u. Tolstoy the satirist in *Voskresenie*.

v. The traditions of Lermontov in the works of Tolstoy.

w. Tolstoy and Korolenko.

x. Tolstoy the writer and man in the evaluation of Romain Rolland.

Notes

Notes

Preface

1. James S. Coleman, Introduction to Part Two, *Education and Political Development*, ed. by James S. Coleman (Princeton, N.J., 1965), p. 225.

2. The only article, dealing in some detail with the teaching of Russian literature in Soviet education, which has ever to my knowledge appeared in North America is that of Professor F. Lilge, "The Study of Literature in the Soviet School," in U.S. Office of Education, *Studies in Comparative Education*, XI (1959), pp. 30-40. This article contains many valuable remarks concerning the teaching of Russian literature in Soviet schools. It deals, however, only with the secondary school, and due to numerous changes in Soviet education since 1959 it could be regarded as partially outdated.

3. Rima Drell Reck, "The Politics of Literature," *Publications of the Modern Language Association of America*, LXXXV (1970), No. 3, p. 431. (An address read to Forum One at the 84th Annual Meeting of the Modern Language Association of America in Denver, Colorado.)

4. Henry Nash Smith, "Something Is Happening But You Don't Know What It Is, Do You, Mr. Jones?" *Publications of the Modern Language Association of America*, LXXXV (1970), No. 3, p. 419. (The presidential address delivered at the 84th Annual Meeting of the Modern Language Association of America in Denver, Colorado, December 27, 1969.)

Chapter 1
Ideology–The Essence of Soviet Education

1. A. Kosygin, *Direktivy XXIII s"ezda KPSS* (Moscow, 1966).

2. V. Lenin, *Sochineniya*, XXVIII, 4th edition (n.p., 1950), p. 68.

3. F. Lilge, "Lenin and the Politics of Education," *Slavic Review*, XXVII (June 1968), p. 233.

4. L. Brezhnev, "Rech' na Vsesoyuznom s"ezde uchiteley," *Uchitel'skaya gazeta*, July 5, 1968, p. 1.

5. M. Prokof'ev, "O sostoyanii i merakh dal'neyshego uluchsheniya raboty sredney obshcheobrazovatel'noy shkoly," *Uchitel'skaya gazeta*, July 3, 1968, p. 2.

6. *24th Congress of the Communist Party of the Soviet Union. March 30-April 9, 1971. Documents* (Moscow, 1971), p. 111.

7. M.A. Prokof'ev, "Shkola i ee problemy," *Sovetskaya pedagogika*, March 1971, No. 3, pp. 14-15.

8. V.P. Eliutin, "Successfully Fulfill the Party's Designs," *Soviet Education*, XIV, No. 5 (March 1972), p. 37.

165

166

9. *24th Congress of the CPSU*, pp. 237-38.
10. I.T. Ogorodnikov, *Pedagogika* (Moscow, 1968), pp. 13-14.
11. Ibid., p. 8.
12. Ibid., p. 92.
13. Ibid., p. 52.
14. I.A. Kairov, and others, eds., *Pedagogicheskaya entsiklopediya,* III (Moscow, 1966), p. 122.
15. M.N. Parkhomenko, "Nasushchnye problemy esteticheskogo vospitaniya naroda," in G.E. Glezerman and M.N. Parkhomenko, eds., *Voprosy teorii i praktiki kommunisticheskogo vospitaniya* (Moscow, 1962), p. 280, quoting A.P. Fomichev and V.I. Shatskaya, *Proekt glavy dlya uchebnika pedagogiki* (Moscow, 1954).
16. O.V. Larmin, "Rol' iskusstva v esteticheskom vospitanii trudyashchikhsya," *Voprosy kommunisticheskogo vospitaniya. Sbornik statey* (Moscow, 1961), p. 112.
17. Ibid., p. 118.
18. L.I. Timofeev, *Osnovy teorii literatury* (Moscow, 1966), p. 57.
19. Ibid.
20. Ibid.
21. N.I. Kudryashev, "Analiz literaturnogo proizvedeniya i zadachi razvitiya uchashchikhsya," in N.I. Kudryashev, ed., *Za tvorcheskoe izuchenie literatury v shkole* (Moscow, 1968), pp. 7-33.
22. V.P. Turgarinov, "Nekotorye gnoseologicheskie problemy izobrazitel'nogo iskusstva," *Leninskaya teoriya otrazheniya i sovremennaya nauka* (Moscow, 1966), p. 147.
23. Ibid., p. 143.
24. L.V. Shchepilova, *Vvedenie v literaturovedenie*, 2nd edition, (Moscow, 1968), p. 20.
25. L.I. Timofeev, *Osnovy teorii literatury*, p. 426.
26. George Z.F. Bereday and Bonnie B. Stretch, "Political Education in the USA and the USSR," *Comparative Education Review*, VII (1963), No. 1, p. 9.
27. A. Arsen'ev, F. Korolev, "Metodologicheskie problemy marksistsko-leninskoy pedagogiki," *Narodnoe obrazovanie*, 1972, No. 4, p. 6.
28. I.T. Ogorodnikov, *Pedagogika*, p. 94.
29. V. Odintsov, "Voennaya podgotovka uchashchikhsya," *Narodnoe obrazovanie*, 1969, No. 6, p. 45.
30. L. Voskovtsova and N. Biryukova, "Desyat' vzvolnovannykh let," *Uchitel'skaya gazeta*, June 21, 1969, p. 2.
31. P. Belov, "Tol'ko pri sochetanii," *Uchitel'skaya gazeta*, June 20, 1968, p. 2.
32. James S. Coleman, ed., *Education and Political Development*, (Princeton, N.J., 1965), Introduction, p. 11.
33. George S. Counts, *Khrushchev and the Central Committee Speak on Education* (Pittsburgh, 1959), p. 64.

Chapter 2
Literature in the Soviet School

1. N.I. Kudryashev, "The Literary Course in the Secondary School," *Soviet Education*, VII (1965), No. 7, p. 36.

2. Ministerstvo prosveshcheniya RSFSR. *Programmy vos'miletney i sredney shkoly na 1969/70 uchebnyy god. Russkiy yazyk i literatura* (Moscow, 1969), p. 24.

3. *24th Congress of the Communist Party of the Soviet Union. Documents* (Moscow, 1971), p. 106.

4. G.I. Belen'kii, "The Program of the Communist Party of the Soviet Union and Some Problems in the Teaching of Literature," *Soviet Education*, IV (1962), No. 5, p. 22.

5. The discussion of the literature curriculum is based on the programs approved and presently in use. It is necessary to bear in mind that the transition from the old to the new programs began in the subject of literature in the 1966-67 school year and proceeds according to the following schedule: 1966-67, grades seven and eight; 1967-68, grade nine; 1968-69, grade ten; 1970-71, grade four; 1971-72, grade five; 1972-73, grade six. Quoted from *Narodnoe obrazovanie*, 1969, No. 6, p. 91. The changes in the literature programs are connected with the shortening of elementary school from four years to three, and secondary school from eleven to ten.

6. "Konkurs, student, ball," *Uchitel'skaya gazeta*, March 16, 1972, p. 2.

7. These figures are arrived at by comparing the 1959 and 1966 school curricula. The Kosygin educational reforms introduced in 1966 make provision for a shortening of the secondary school course from eleven to ten years.

8. See Bibliography (p. 185) for readers and Russian literature textbooks used on the elementary and secondary school levels.

9. See Appendix (p. 77) for an outline of the required study material for grades four to ten.

10. "Analiz ekzamenatsionnogo sochineniya v VIII klasse," *Literatura v shkole*, 1968, No. 5, pp. 73-83, and No. 6, pp. 57-60.

11. *Literatura v shkole*, 1968, No. 6, pp. 57 and 59.

12. S. Trembitskaya, "Vernemsya k Pushkinu," and O. El'tseva, "Shablon," *Uchitel'skaya gazeta*, June 22, 1972, p. 3.

13. B.I. Bursov, ed., *Russkaya literatura: uchebnoe posobie dlya IX klassa sredney shkoly* (Moscow, 1969).

14. S.N. Gromtseva, "K ustnomu ekzamenu v X klasse," *Literatura v shkole*, 1969, No. 1, p. 76.

15. I. Kaplan, Ya. Nesturkh, "Zametki s ustnykh ekzamenov," *Literatura v shkole*, 1969, No. 5, pp. 48-58.

16. A. Korchagin, "Obuchat' po novomu," *Novy mir*, 1963, No. 9, p. 274.

17. Ibid., p. 275.

18. V. Semenikhin, "Uchit' i uchit'sya razumno," *Novy mir* 1962, No. 11, p. 206. See Appendix (p. 101) for a Sample List of Examination Papers.

19. L. Ayzerman, "K miru prekrasnogo," *Novy mir*, 1962, No. 11, p. 211.

20. Ibid., p. 213.

21. Nigel Grant, *Soviet education* (Middlesex, Eng., 1964), pp. 146 and 171, quoting *Uchitel'skaya gazeta*, November 22, 1962 and January 10, 1963.

22. L.S. Ayzerman, "Contemporary Literature Through the Eyes of Upper-Grade Pupils," *Soviet Education*, VII (1965), No. 3, p. 7.

23. Ibid., p. 10.

24. Ibid., p. 11.

25. V. Strezikozin, "Uchitel' i novaya programma," *Narodnoe obrazovanie*, 1969, No. 8, p. 129.

26. V. Stakhov, "Esli ne zabyvat' o psikhologii uchenika (O problemakh prepodavaniya literatury v shkole)," *Zvezda*, 1968, No. 3, p. 141.

27. Ibid.

28. R. Rivina, "A chto za slovom?" *Uchitel'skaya gazeta*, June 25, 1968, p. 3.

29. Ibid.

30. A. Solzhenitsyn, *Cancer Ward* (New York, 1969), pp. 128-29.

31. L.N. Lesokhin, "O problemnosti uroka literatury," *Literatura v shkole*, 1965, No. 6, p. 32.

32. G. Andrianov, "Tsel' nashikh urokov," *Uchitel'skaya gazeta*, December 2, 1969, p. 3.

33. N.I. Kudryashev, "Ob effektivnosti zanyatiy po literature," *Literatura v shkole*, 1970, No. 4, p. 17.

34. Ibid.

35. A.M. Matyushkin, "Teoreticheskie osnovy problemnogo obucheniya," *Sovetskaya pedagogika*, 1971, No. 7, p. 38.

36. G.I. Belen'kii, "The CPSU and . . . the Teaching of Literature," p. 22.

37. B. Glebov, "A Letter to the Editor," *Literatura v shkole*, 1970, No. 4, p. 92.

38. V. Stakhov, "Esli ne zabyvat' o psikhologii uchenika," p. 145.

39. "S pervykh dney," editorial, *Uchitel'skaya gazeta*, September 4, 1969, p. 1.

40. N.E. Kydryashev, "Literature in the New School," *Soviet Education*, I (1959), No. 7, p. 26; also in B. Glebov, "A Letter to the Editor," *Literatura v shkole*, 1970, No. 4, pp. 91-93.

Chapter 3
Literature in Higher Education

1. In the beginning of the 1969-70 school year there were in the USSR, in grades five to eleven, 194,000 teachers of Russian language and literature in schools where Russian was the language of instruction, 76.8 percent of whom had completed higher education. There were 83,000 Russian language and

literature teachers in schools where a native tongue, other than Russian, was the language of instruction. Of these, 68.5 percent had completed higher education; see, *Narodnoe khozyaystvo SSSR v 1969 godu* (Moscow, 1970), p. 670.

2. V.I. Tropin, ed., *Spravochnik dlya postpupayushchikh v moskovskiy universitet* (Moscow, 1969), pp. 77-82.

3. Leningradskiy universitet. *Spravochnik dlya postupayushchikh v 1965 godu* (Leningrad, 1965), pp. 106-11.

4. N. Gudzy, "Kak prepodavat' literaturu v shkole," *Voprosy literatury*, 1961, No. 12, p. 119.

5. Ibid.

6. *Voprosy literatury*, 1963, No. 1, pp. 159-82.

7. N. Gulyaev, "Literatura i vospitanie novogo cheloveka," *Voprosy literatury*, 1963, No. 8, p. 160.

8. A. Tatuyko, "Za realisticheskiy podkhod," *Voprosy literatury*, 1963, No. 8, p. 162.

9. E. Moss, "The Changes in Soviet Schools in September 1964," *Comparative Education Review*, VIII (December 1964), No. 3, p. 267.

10. A. Boborykin, S. Il'enko, E. Lyapin, V. Izvozchikov, "Vremya eksperimentov," *Uchitel'skaya gazeta*, May 16, 1968, p. 2.

11. See Appendix (p. 111) for the program for entrance examinations into institutions of higher learning in Russian literature.

12. P. Pustovoyt, "O nashem filologicheskom obrazovanii," *Voprosy literatury*, 1962, No. 3, p. 179.

13. "Postanovlenie Ts.K. KPSS i Sm SSSR ob organizatsii podgotovitel'nykh otdeleniy pri vysshikh uchebnykh zavedeniyakh," *Byulleten' Ministerstva vysshego i srednego spetsial'nogo obrazovaniya SSSR*, 1969, No. 10, pp. 1-4.

14. *Voprosy literatury*, 1963, No. 1, p. 179. From a speech by L.G. Andreev delivered at a conference at the Moscow State University, discussing the teaching of literature in institutions of higher learning.

15. A. Bogomolov, "Poleznaya diskussiya," *Voprosy literatury*, 1964, No. 4, p. 188.

16. *Voprosy literatury*, 1963, No. 1, p. 177. From a speech by L.G. Andreev.

17. See Appendix (p. 115) for the Moscow State University Curriculum (*Uchebnyy plan*) for the specialty: philologist, teacher of Russian language and literature.

18. L.V. Shchepilova, *Vvedenie v literaturovedenie*, 2nd edition (Moscow, 1968), and L.I. Timofeev, *Osnovy teorii literatury* (Moscow, 1966).

19. A.I. Revyakin, *O prepodavanii khudozhestvennoy literatury* (Moscow, 1968), p. 61.

20. Ibid., p. 62.

21. S. Vayman, "A kto u nikh vel teoriyu?" *Voprosy literatury*, 1964, No. 4, p. 169.

22. A.I. Revyakin, *O prepodavanii khudozhestvennoy literatury*, p. 161.

23. V.I. Kuleshov, "Printsipy postroeniya obshchego kursa russkoy literatury XIX veka," in V.I. Kuleshov, ed., *Sovetskoe literaturovedenie za pyat'desyat let* (Moscow, 1967), p. 406.

24. A.I. Revyakin, *O prepodavanii khudozhestvennoy literatury*, p. 169.

25. B.G. Reizov, "Istoriya literatury i ee rol' v universitetskom obrazovanii," in D.A. Kerimov, ed., *Voprosy vospitaniya i prepodavaniya v universitete*, II (Leningrad, 1967), p. 37.

26. Ibid., p. 38.

27. Ibid.

28. B. Ryurikov, "V.I. Lenin i voprosy literatury," *V.I. Lenin o literature i iskusstve* (Moscow, 1957), p. 20.

29. V.I. Kuleshov, "Printsipy postroeniya obshchego kursa," p. 400.

30. B.G. Reizov, "Istoriya literatury," p. 49.

31. N.K. Gudzy, "Nuzhny li obshchie kursy?" *Literaturnaya gazeta*, June 11, 1959, p. 3.

32. N.K. Gudzy, from a speech delivered at a conference on teaching literature. Stenographic report: *Voprosy literatury*, 1963, No. 1, p. 161.

33. A.I. Revyakin, *O prepodavanii khudozhestvennoy literatury*, p. 164.

34. Ibid., p. 219.

35. From a questionnaire distributed among American and Canadian exchange students who have studied and done literary research in the USSR.

36. In some seminars there is no oral test and the final mark is made up by combining the mark for an essay, which is read in class, and the mark for participation in class discussions. The lists of special courses and special seminars to be given each year are approved by the council of a philological faculty of a university or institute. The programs and reading lists for these courses and seminars are suggested by individual instructors and submitted to the faculty after approval by the appropriate department.

37. B.S. Meylakh, *A.S. Pushkin. Seminariy* (Leningrad, 1959), p. 246. See Appendix (p. 161) for a list of topics suggested in the seminar on L.Tolstoy at the Moscow State University.

38. A.I. Revyakin, *O prepodavanii khudozhestvennoy literatury*, p. 262.

39. In some institutions of higher learning a copy of the report is placed in the library's reading room where the students can become acquainted with the contents of the report.

40. A.I. Revyakin, *O prepodavanii khudozhestvennoy literatury*, p. 261.

41. Ibid.

42. A.I. Barsuk, *Pechatnye seminarii po russkoy literature (1904-1963)* (Moscow, 1964).

43. S. Reyser, "Evolutsiya zhanra," *Voprosy literatury*, 1964, No. 4, p. 183.

44. Ibid.

45. A.I. Revyakin, *O prepodavanii khudozhestvennoy literatury*, p. 260.

46. N.K. Gudzy, *Lev Tolstoy* (Moscow, 1960).

47. M.B. Khrapchenko, *Lev Tolstoy kak khudozhnik* (Moscow, 1963).

48. B.I. Bursov, *Lev Tolstoy. Ideynye iskaniya i tvorcheskiy metod. 1847-1862* (Moscow, 1960).

49. E.N. Kupreyanova, *Estetika L.N. Tolstogo* (Moscow-Leningrad, 1966).

50. V.F. Asmus, "Mirovozzrenie Tolstogo," *Literaturnoe nasledstvo*, LXIX, Book I (1961), pp. 35-105.

51. B.M. Eykhenbaum, *Lev Tolstoy. Semidesyatye gody* (Leningrad, 1960).

52. B.I. Bursov, *L.N. Tolstoy. Seminariy* (Leningrad, 1963); A.A. Tikhovodov, *Spetsseminariy po tvorchestvu L.N. Tolstogo* (Moscow, 1961).

53. K.N. Leont'ev, *Analiz, stil' i veyanie. O romanakh gr. L.N. Tolstogo* (Moscow, 1911); D.S. Merezhkovsky, *L. Tolstoy i Dostoevsky* (Peterburg, 1909).

54. B.I. Bursov, *L.N. Tolstoy. Seminariy*, pp. 25-27.

55. A. Kurbanov, "Vsem li pisat' diplomy," *Uchitel'skaya gazeta*, July 4, 1972, p. 3.

56. *Narodnoe khozyaystvo SSSR v 1969 godu* (Moscow, 1970), p. 700.

57. *Uchitel'skaya gazeta*, June 20, 1972, p. 4.

58. *Vestnik vysshey shkoly*, March 1960, p. 3, quoted in I.N. Shumilin, *Soviet Higher Education* (Munich, 1961), p. 63.

59. A. Bogomolov, "Poleznaya diskussiya," p. 186.

Chapter 4
The Russian Classical Literary Heritage
and the Basic Concepts of Soviet
Literary Education

1. B. Meylakh, "Novye materialy o vzglyadakh Lenina na literaturu i iskusstvo," *Zvezda*, 1961, No. 4, p. 187.

2. T.P. Golovanov, "Turgenev i sovetskaya literatura," *Russkaya literatura*, 1968, No. 4, p. 25.

3. A. Shishkin, "Podstupy k resheniyu vazhnoy zadachi," *Zvezda*, 1950, No. 4, pp. 167-73.

4. From a speech by L. Timofeev delivered at a conference discussing the three-volume *Istoriya russkoy sovetskoy literatury*, at the Institute of World Literature named after A.M. Gorky. See *Voprosy literatury*, 1962, No. 3, pp. 59-60.

5. From a speech by P. Kraevsky at the same conference. Ibid., p. 65.

6. M.T. Iovchuk, "O meste gumanitarnykh nauk v sisteme formirovaniya kommunisticheskogo mirovozzreniya molodezhi," *Voprosy filosofii*, 1959, No. 6, p. 21.

7. A.I. Revyakin, *Problema tipicheskogo v khudozhestvennoy literature. Posobie dlya uchitelya* (Moscow, 1959), p. 28.

8. L. Plotkin, *Partiya i literatura* (Leningrad, 1960), p. 18.

9. A.I. Revyakin, *Problema tipicheskogo*, p. 28.

10. G. Kunitsyn, "Klassovost' v literature," *Znamya*, 1968, No. 1, p. 226.

11. A.I. Revyakin, *Problema tipicheskogo*, p. 32.

12. MGU, Kafedra russkoy literatury, *Proekt programma po kursu "Vvedenie v literaturovedenie (dlya filologicheskikh fakul'tetov gosudarstvennykh universitetov)"* (Moscow, 1960), p. 77. The difficulty in understanding by secondary school graduates certain notions of Soviet literary theory, and, in particular, of the principles of *klassovost', ideynost', narodnost'*, and *partiynost'*, prompted the publication of a special aid in the theory of literature intended for those who apply for admittance to philological faculties of institutions of higher learning. (M.A. Palkin, *Voprosy teorii literatury. Posobie dlya postupayushchikh v vysshie uchebnye zavedeniya* [Minsk, 1971]). The author of this book makes an effort to clarify and to define the notions discussed but he often contradicts himself, and it seems that nothing is left to the student but to memorize the definitions suggested, without being able to apply them creatively to a prerevolutionary work of literature.

13. *Khrestomatiya po dialekticheskomu i istoricheskomu materializmu*, 2nd edition (Moscow, 1970), p. 333.

14. L. Plotkin, *Partiya i literatura*, p. 13.

15. V. Kaminsky, "Problema khudozhestvennoy pravdy v otsenkakh V.I. Lenina," *Neva*, 1964, No. 4, p. 164.

16. A.J. Revyakin, *Problema tipicheskogo*, p. 325.

17. O.G. Drobnitsky and I.S. Kon, eds., *Slovar' po etike*, 2nd edition (Moscow, 1970), pp. 92-93.

18. E.N. Kupreyanova, *Estetika L.N. Tolstogo* (Moscow-Leningrad, 1966), p. 13.

19. M.G. Zel'dovich, L.Ya. Livshits, *Russkaya literatura XIX v. Khrestomatiya kriticheskikh materialov* (Moscow, 1964), pp. 110-11. An. Dremov claims that "the first thorough attempt to define the principle of *narodnost'* of art was made in Russia by the Decembrist O. Somov, in his monograph *O romanticheskoy poezii* (1823). (See "Iskusstva vysshiy kriteriy," *Literaturnaya gazeta*, June 23, 1971, p. 4.)

20. A. Pushkin, *Polnoe sobranie sochineniy*, XI (Leningrad, 1949), p. 40.

21. N.V. Gogol', *Sobranie sochineniy v semi tomakh* VI (Moscow, 1967), pp. 69-70.

22. V.G. Belinsky, *Polnoe sobranie sochineniy*, I (Moscow, 1953), p. 295.

23. Ibid., p. 151.

24. L.I. Timofeev, *Osnovy teorii literatury* (Moscow, 1966), p. 124.

25. Ibid., p. 121.

26. G. Makogonenko, "Russkaya klassicheskaya literatura v svete leninskoy kontseptsii osvoboditel'nogo dvizheniya," *Voprosy literatury*, 1968, No. 4, p. 10.

27. A. Solodovnikov, "Ob otnoshenii k klassicheskomu naslediyu," *Kommunist*, 1968, No. 13, p. 103.

28. Maurice Friedberg writes in the preface to *Russian Classics in Soviet Jackets* (New York and London, 1962): "So far as we know, the texts of literary works by the nineteenth-century Russian masters have not been tampered with by Soviet editors; in any case, no evidence to the contrary has been discovered to date by Western scholars, with the exception of some liberties that were taken in the selection and abridgment of the correspondence of Chekhov and Dostoevsky" (pp. XII-XIII). In a later study, however, Friedberg expresses doubts about the conclusions quoted above. In his article "Keeping up with the Censor," *Problems of Communism*, November-December 1964, pp. 23-31, he writes: "As to the occurrence of censorship changes in classical Russian literature, recent evidence seems to contradict this author's earlier conclusion that such texts do not appear to be tampered with by Soviet censors. Serious doubts in this matter have been raised recently by V.N. Orlov in an introduction to a book on the problems of publishing prerevolutionary Russian poetry" (p. 26). Friedberg quotes Orlov, who writes, "Not infrequently it turns out that—as a result of any number of accidental circumstances—the author's final version is *less valuable ideologically and artistically* [italics added] than earlier versions, and to give preference to this version only because of formal adherence to the principle of following [the poet's] 'last will' is definitely incorrect." See *Izdanie klassicheskoy literatury: Iz opyta "Biblioteki poeta"* (Moscow, 1963), p. 12.

Examples of changes introduced by editors in the works of Russian classics are reported by Gleb Struve in his article "Chekhov in Communist Censorship," *Slavonic and East European Review*, XXXIII (1955), No. 1, pp. 327-41. Struve analyzes in this article A.P. Chekhov's *Polnoe sobranie sochineniy i pisem*, 20 vols. (Moscow, 1944-51), and he points out that there are some omissions in the letters marked by ellipses within brackets. Though in some places these omissions are for the sake of propriety, in others they are for political reasons. For example, Chekhov's praise of the West, his praise of Vsevolod Meyerhold, and his criticism of the Russian theater are left out of the text. In some instances even the ellipses are omitted. Meyerhold's name is omitted from the indexes.

29. F.M. Golovenchenko, *Vvedenie v literaturovedenie* (Moscow, 1964), pp. 54.

30. L.V. Shchepilova, *Vvedenie v literaturovedenie*, 2nd edition (Moscow, 1968), pp. 78-91.

31. Ibid., p. 81.

32. N. Vorob'eva, S. Khitarova, "Nazad, k 'istokam' ili ot 'istokov'—v budushchee?", *Literaturnaya gazeta*, December 10, 1969, p. 4.

33. A.I. Iezuitov, "V.I. Lenin o partiynosti literatury," in Akademiya nauk SSSR, Institut russkoy literatury, *V.I. Lenin i voprosy literaturovedeniya* (Moscow-Leningrad, 1961), pp. 60-117.

174

34. Ibid., p. 75.

35. V.I. Lenin, "Partiynaya organizatsiya i partiynaya literatura," *Sochineniya*, X (n.p., 1947), pp. 26-31.

36. G.I. Kunitsyn, *V.I. Lenin o klassovosti i partiynosti literatury* (Moscow, 1960), pp. 20-21.

37. A. Belik, "O nekotorykh oshibkakh v literaturovedenii," *Oktyabr'*, 1950, No. 2, p. 160.

38. L. Plotkin, *Partiya i literatura*, p. 57.

39. Ya. Strochkov, *Literaturnaya gazeta*, January 10, 1957, quoted in G.I. Kunitsyn, *V.I. Lenin o klassovosti i partiynosti literatury*, p. 72.

40. I. Dzeverin, "Znamya revolyutsionnogo iskusstva," *Literaturnaya gazeta*, January 21, 1970, p. 5.

41. G.I. Belen'ky, "Stat'i V.I. Lenina na urokakh literatury," *Literatura v shkole*, 1969, No. 4, p. 24. Also in "Nekotorye voprosy podgotovki shkol k 100-letiyu so dnya rozhdeniya Vladimira Il'icha Lenina," *Narodnoe obrazovanie*, 1969, No. 9, p. 138.

42. M. Suslov, "Obshchestvennye nauki—b evoe oruzhie partii v stroitel'stve kommunizma," *Kommunist*, 1972, No. 1, p. 27.

43. G.I. Kunitsyn, *V.I. Lenin o klassovosti i partiynosti literatury*, p. 56.

44. L.V. Shchepilova, *Vvedenie v literaturovedenie*, p. 89. This view was until recently also held by one of the leading authorities in the area of Soviet literary theory dealing with problems of *partiynost'* of literature, G. Kunitsyn. As of late, however, in an article "Partiynost' i narodnost' sovetskoy literatury," which appeared in the April 17, 1968 issue of *Literaturnaya gazeta*, Kunitsyn introduced a notion that *narodnost'* is to be, in turn, regarded as a criterion of *partiynost'*. This statement drew sharp criticism from I. Dzeverin in the article "Znamya revolyutsionnogo iskusstva," in *Literaturnaya gazeta*, January 21, 1970, p. 5.

45. L.V. Shchepilova, *Vvedenie v literaturovedenie*, p. 89.

46. A.I. Metchenko, "Formirovanie teorii sotsialisticheskogo realizma," in V.I. Kuleshov, ed., *Sovetskoe literaturovedenie za pyat'desyat let* (Moscow, 1967), p. 132.

47. A.I. Revyakin, *O prepodavanii khudozhestvennoy literatury* (Moscow, 1968), p. 74. It seems that Soviet literary theoreticians have difficulties in specifying clearly what is the relationship between *partiynost'* and *narodnost'*, and while trying to define these notions and their relationship they make often contradictory statements. For example, An. Dremov writes in *Literaturnaya gazeta*: "*partiynost'* and *narodnost'* do not concur, they do not 'merge' despite the fact that these notions are close and organically corelated." Several lines further we read, however, that "the *narodnost'* of our art is a communist *narodnost'* which is inseparably linked with communist *partiynost'*. *Partiynost'* and *narodnost'* merge in one only in the creative work of progressive writers who have artistic talent and a clear and distinct class world outlook." ("Iskusstva vysshiy kriteriy," June 23, 1971, p. 4.)

175

48. V.I. Lenin, *What Is To Be Done?* (Moscow, n.d.), p. 133.

49. Ibid., p. 67.

50. A.I. Revyakin, *O prepodavanii khudozhestvennoy literatury*, p. 74.

51. A.I. Smirnov, "O partiynosti literatury i iskusstva," *Uchenye zapiski Volgogradskogo pedagogicheskogo instituta imeni A.S. Serafimovicha*, kafedra literatury, vupusk 15 (Volgograd, 1961), pp. 22-23, quoted in A.I. Revyakin, *O prepodavanii khudozhestvennoy literatury*, p. 74.

52. S. Mikhalkov, "Tvorchestvo eto bor'ba," *Literaturnaya Rossiya*, December 19, 1969, No. 5, p. 4.

Chapter 5
Lenin's Articles on Tolstoy and the Development
of the Approach to Russian Classics in Soviet
Education

1. B.I. Bursov, *L.N. Tolstoy. Seminariy* (Leningrad, 1963), p. 33.

2. Plekhanov's articles on Tolstoy "Simptomaticheskaya oshibka" (1907), "Tolstoy i priroda" (1908), "Zametki publitsista" (Otsyuda i dosyuda) (1910), "Smeshenie predstavleniy" (1910-11), "Karl Marks i Lev Tolstoy" (1911), "Eshche o Tolstom" (1911), are published in S.P. Bychkov, ed., *L.N. Tolstoy v russkoy kritike. Sbornik statey* (n.p., 1949).

3. G.V. Plekhanov, "Zametki publitsista" (Otsyuda i dosyuda), in S.P. Bychkov, ed., *L.N. Tolstoy v russkoy kritike*, p. 315.

4. A.V. Lunacharsky, "Tolstoy i Marks," in V.M. Friche, ed., *O Tolstom. Literaturno-kriticheskiy sbornik* (Moscow-Leningrad, 1928), p. 331.

5. M. Ol'minsky, "O L.N. Tolstom," *Pravda*, January 31, 1928 and "Tov. Lenin ili Lev Tolstoy?" *Pravda*, February 4, 1928, quoted in O. Semenovsky, *Marksistskaya kritika o Chekhove i Tolstom* (Kishinev, 1968), pp. 299-300.

6. An interesting article about the sociological analysis of a work of art by E. Safronova, "O sotsiologicheskom analize v literaturnoy kritike," appears in Vil'nyuskiy gosudarstvennyy universitet im. V. Kapsukasa, *Uchenye zapiski*, XXXI, Literatura II (Vilnius, 1960), pp. 77-97. The author makes an effort to demonstrate that it is a big mistake to contrapose sociological and aesthetic analysis, since while one extreme would lead to vulgar sociologism the other one would lead to formalism and aestheticism. The author claims that aesthetic analysis must be sociological and that a work of art should be studied and analyzed in the unity of content and form; of sociological and aesthetic analysis.

7. V.A. Kovalev and E.A. Maymin, "50-letie so dnya smerti L.N. Tolstogo. Tolstovedenie v vysshey shkole," *Vestnik vysshey shkoly*, VII (November, 1960), p. 80.

8. I. Nusinov, "Predislovie," in L.N. Tolstoy, *Neizdannye teksty* (Academia–GIKhL, 1933), p. VII.

9. Ibid., p. IX.

10. Ibid., p. X.

11. Ibid., p. XV.

12. O. Semenovsky, *Marksistskaya kritika o Chekhove i Tolstom*, p. 238.

13. V.I. Lenin, *Collected Works*, XV (Moscow, 1963), pp. 202-09.

14. Ibid., p. 202.

15. Ibid., p. 207.

16. *V.I. Lenin o L.N. Tolstom* (Moscow, 1969), p. 6.

17. V.I. Lenin, *Collected Works*, XVI (Moscow, 1963), pp. 331-32.

18. Ibid., pp. 353-54.

19. Ibid., XVII (Moscow, 1963), p. 49.

20. Ibid., p. 52.

21. S. Breytburg, "Tolstoy–chitatel' Lenina," in *V.I. Lenin o L.N. Tolstom* (Moscow, 1969), pp. 114-17.

22. Harold Swayze, *Political Control of Literature in the USSR, 1946-1959* (Cambridge, Mass., 1962), p. 8.

23. V.A. Kovalev and E.A. Maymin, "50-letie so dnya smerti L.N. Tolstogo," p. 80.

24. M.B. Khrapchenko, *Lev Tolstoy kak khudozhnik* (Moscow, 1963), p. 659.

25. Ibid., pp. 659-60.

26. E.L. Lozovskaya, "Nravstvennyy ideal i khudozhestvennyy metod L.N. Tolstogo. Tolstoy i Shchedrin," *Uchenye zapiski magnitogorskogo pedagogicheskogo instituta*, vypusk XV (II) 1963, p. 181, quoted in A.A. Nesterenko, "Ob izuchenii pozitsii pisatelya v khudozhestvennom proizvedenii (na primere tvorchestva L.N. Tolstogo)," *Vestnik moskovskogo universiteta*, seriya X, filologiya 2 (1966), pp. 53-57.

27. N.V. Chistyakova, "Roman 'Voyna i mir' i desyatiklassniki," *Literatura v shkole*, 1966, No. 4, p. 48.

28. I. Vidmar, "Iz dnevnika," *Delo*, 1956, quoted in L. Plotkin, *Partiya i literatura* (Leningrad, 1960), p. 51. It is important to remember that the period after the Twentieth Party Congress was a period of a "thaw" in literature, when liberal ideas connected with art developed in the Soviet Union and penetrated from abroad. Of particular importance in this case was the influence of some unorthodox East European Marxist literary scholars whose articles were appearing in publications distributed in the Soviet Union.

29. "Tolstoy segodnya," editorial, *Voprosy literatury*, 1960, No. 11, p. 9.

30. M.B. Khrapchenko, *Tolstoy kak khudozhnik*, p. 654.

31. B.I. Bursov, *L.N. Tolstoy. Seminariy*, p. 33.

32. "Tolstoy segodnya," p. 13.

33. A.I. Revyakin, *O prepodavanii khudozhestvennoy literatury* (Moscow, 1968), p. 244.

34. V.I. Arkhipovsky, "Lev Tolstoy i nasha sovremennost'," M.V. i S.S.O. U.R.S.R. Uzhhorods'kyy derzhavnyy universytet. *Dopovydy ta povydomlennya.* Seryya fylolohychna, VII (Uzhhorod, 1961), p. 9.

35. K. Leont'ev, *Analiz, stil' i veyanie. O romanakh gr. L.N. Tolstogo* (Moscow, 1911), Brown University Slavic Reprint III (Providence, 1965).

36. D. Merezhkovsky, *L. Tolstoy i Dostoevsky* (Peterburg, 1909).

37. V. Shklovsky, *Mater'yal i stil' v romane L'va Tolstogo "Voyna i mir"* (Moscow, 1926).

38. B. Eykhenbaum, *Molodoy Tolstoy* (Peterburg-Berlin, 1922); *Lev Tolstoy. 50-ye gody* (Leningrad, 1928); *Lev Tolstoy. 60-ye gody* (Leningrad-Moscow, 1931).

39. For a detailed examination of the teaching of Tolstoy's works in Soviet education see N.N. Shneidman, "Soviet Approaches to the Teaching of Literature. A Case Study: L. Tolstoy in Soviet Education," *Canadian Slavonic Papers*, Vol. XV, No. 3 (fall 1973).

Chapter 6
The Basic Principles and Literary Practice

1. F. Lilge, "The Study of Literature in the Soviet School," U.S. Office of Education. *Studies in Comparative Education*, XI (1959), p. 35, quoting G. Abramovich and F. Golovchenko, *Russkaia literatura*, 2nd edition (Moscow, 1935), pp. 107-16.

2. D. Tamarchenko, *Literatura i estetika* (Leningrad, 1936), p. 212.

3. Ibid., p. 222.

4. F. Lilge, "Literature in the Soviet School," pp. 35-36, summarizing S.M. Florinskii, *Russkaia literatura* (Moscow, 1957), pp. 245-82.

5. A.M. Dokusov and V.G. Marantsman, *Izuchenie komedii N. V. Gogolya "Revizor" v shkole* (Moscow-Leningrad, 1967).

6. Gogol' himself formulated the purpose of *Revizor* in the following manner: "In the comedy are accumulated exceptions of the truth, faults and abuse from all over Russia with the purpose of serving one ideal, namely: to create in the spectator a bright and noble aversion of much that is base" (D. Tamarchenko, *Literatura i estetika*, p. 213).

7. A Slonimsky, Introduction to *Izbrannye proizvedeniya* (Moscow, 1963), by N.V. Gogol', p. 27.

8. A.M. Dokusov and V.G. Marantsman, *Izuchenie komedii N.V. Gogolya "Revizor,"* p. 5.

9. S.M. Florinsky, *Russkaya literatura* (Moscow, 1967), p. 226.

10. Ibid., p. 213.

11. Ibid., p. 221.

12. R.Z. Kanunova, *Nekotorye osobennosti realizma N.V. Gogolya* (Tomsk, 1962), pp. 110-11.

13. G.A. Gukovsky, *Realizm Gogolya* (Moscow-Leningrad, 1959), p. 357.

14. Glavnoe upravlenie vysshikh i srednikh pedagogicheskikh uchebnykh zavedeniy ministerstva prosveshcheniya RSFSR, *Programmy pedagogicheskikh institutov. Russkaya literatura XIX veka* (Moscow, 1959), p. 31.

15. Ministerstvo vysshego i srednego spetsial'nogo obrazovaniya SSSR, *Programma po istorii russkoy literatury. Chast' 3-ya. XIX v.* (Moscow, 1964), p. 15.

16. Ibid., p. 16.

17. F. Lilge, "Literature in the Soviet School," p. 36.

18. A few serious monographs published on Dostoevsky in the Soviet Union in the last decade: M. Bakhtin, *Problemy poetiki Dostoevskogo* (2nd edition, revised, Moscow, 1963, and 3rd edition, Moscow, 1972); G.M. Fridlender, *Realizm Dostoevskogo* (Moscow-Leningrad, 1964); V.Ya. Kirpotin, *F.M. Dostoevsky* (Moscow, 1960); L. Grossman, *Dostoevsky* (Moscow, 1962); L. Grossman, *Dostoevsky* (2nd edition, Moscow, 1965); V.Ya. Kirpotin, *Razocharovanie i krushenie Rodiona Raskol'nikova* (Moscow, 1970); M. Gus, *Idei i obrazy F.M. Dostoevskogo* (Moscow, 1971). In connection with the one hundred and fiftieth anniversary of Dostoevsky's birth, which was celebrated in 1971, many monographs and articles were published. A decision has been also reached to publish a thirty-volume edition of Dostoevsky's collected works.

19. B.I. Bursov, ed., *Russkaya literatura: uchebnoe posobie dlya 9 klassa sredney schkoly* (Moscow, 1968), p. 250.

20. E. Trushchenko, "Kakim zhe on dolzhen byt', uchebnik po russkoy literature," *Voprosy literatury*, 1967, No. 4, p. 248.

21. N.I. Kravtsov, ed., *Istoriya russkoy literatury vtoroy poloviny XIX veka* (Moscow, 1966), p. 437.

22. Ibid., p. 458.

23. Ibid., p. 462.

24. *Programmy pedagogicheskikh institutov. Russkaya literatura XIX veka* (Moscow, 1959), p. 69.

25. N.I. Kravtsov, ed., *Istoriya russkoy literatury*, p. 438.

26. M.M. Bakhtin's book *Problems of the Works of Dostoevsky* is thoroughly discussed and analyzed in an article by A. Lunacharsky, "Dostoevsky's 'Plurality of Voices' " in his *On Literature and Art* (Moscow, 1965), pp. 101-35.

27. M. Bakhtin, *Problemy poetiki Dostoevskogo*, 2nd edition, revised (Moscow, 1963).

28. Ibid., p. 4.

29. A.I. Revyakin, *O prepodavanii khudozhestvennoy literatury* (Moscow, 1968), p. 210.

30. L. Grossman, *Dostoevsky* (Moscow, 1962 and 1965 editions).

31. Ibid., (1965 edition), p. 532.

32. Such an accusation is directed at S. Karlinsky for his article "Dostoevsky as Rorschach Test," *The New York Times Book Review*, June 13, 1971. (Ya. El'sberg, "Oblachivshis' v togu uchenogo," *Literaturnaya gazeta*, September 22, 1971, p. 2.)

33. *F. Dostoevsky v russkoy kritike. Sbornik statey* (Moscow, 1956), pp. 387 and 401.

34. B. Suchkov, *Voprosy literatury*, 1971, No. 4, p. 224, and Yu.G. Kudryavtsev, *Bunt ili religiya* (Moscow, 1969), p. 92.

179

35. Yu.G. Kudryavtsev, *Bunt ili religiya*, p. 36.

36. A.G. Dostoevskaya, *Vospominaniya* (Moscow, 1971), pp. 259-61.

37. B. Suchkov, *Voprosy literatury*, 1971, No. 4, p. 224.

38. B. Meylakh, "O khudozhestvennom myshlenii Dostoevskogo," *Voprosy literatury*, 1972, No. 1, p. 89.

39. U. Gural'nik, "Dostoevsky i sovremennost'," *Novy mir*, 1971, No. 8, p. 247.

40. *Voprosy literatury*, 1971, No. 4, p. 233.

41. F.M. Dostoevsky, *The Diary of a Writer*, translated and annotated by Boris Brasol, vol. 2 (New York, 1949), p. 787.

42. Glavnoe upravlenie vysshikh i srednikh pedagogicheskikh uchebnykh zavedeniy ministerstva prosveshcheniya RSFSR, *Programmy pedagogicheskikh institutov. Russkaya literatura predoktyabr'skogo perioda (1890-1917 gg.)* (Moscow, 1958), p. 10.

43. Ministrestvo vysshego i srednego spetsial'nogo obrazovaniya SSSR. Ministerstvo prosveshcheniya RSFSR, *Programmy pedagogicheskikh institutov. Russkaya literatura predoktyabr'skogo perioda* (1890-1917) (Moscow, 1964), p. 13.

44. L. Timofeev, "O poezii Aleksandra Bloka," *Literatura v shkole*, 1968, No. 5, p. 26.

45. A. Dement'ev, E. Naumov, L. Plotkin, *Russkaya sovetskaya literatura* (Moscow, 1968), p. 89.

46. Ibid., p. 90.

47. P.K. Serbin, "Izuchenie poemy V.V. Mayakovskogo 'Khorosho!,' " in Ministerstvo prosveshcheniya USSR [Ukraine], *Metodika prepodavaniya russkogo yazyka i literatury*, Respublikanskiy nauchno-metodicheskiy sbornik, II (Kiev, 1966), p. 140.

48. A.A. Volkov, *Russkaya literatura XX veka. Dooktyabr'skiy period* (Moscow, 1966), p. 489.

49. L. Trotsky, *Literature and Revolution* (New York, 1957), pp. 120-25.

50. V. Erlich, *The Double Image* (Baltimore, 1964), p. 116.

51. V.I. Lenin, *Collected Works*, V (Moscow, 1961), pp. 375-85.

52. A. Blok, *Sobranie sochineniy*, VII (Moscow-Leningrad, 1963), p. 474.

53. A. Lunacharsky, "Alexander Blok" in A. Lunacharsky, *On Literature and Art* (Moscow, 1965), p. 205.

54. Ibid., p. 202.

55. Ibid., p. 160.

56. Ibid., p. 212.

57. B.I. Bursov, ed., *Russkaya literatura*, p. 402.

58. M. Semanova, *Chekhov v shkole* (Leningrad, 1949), p. 127.

59. B.I. Bursov, ed., *Russkaya literatura*, p. 404.

60. Ronald Hingley, *Chekhov* (New York-London, 1966), pp. 92-95.

61. Ministerstvo vysshego i srednego spetsial'nogo obrazovaniya SSSR, *Programma po istorii russkoy literatury. Chast' 3-ya. XIX v.* (Moscow, 1964), p. 35.

62. Ibid., p. 36.

63. D.S. Mirsky, *A History of Russian Literature from Its Beginnings to 1900* (New York, 1958), pp. 373 and 377.

64. A.F. Britikov, "Iz nablyudeniy nad psikhologicheskim analizom v 'Tikhom Done,' " in V.A. Kovalev and A.I. Pavlovsky, eds., *Vorprosy sovetskoy literatury*, VII (Moscow-Leningrad, 1958), p. 449.

65. A.O. Boguslavsky and L.I. Timofeev, eds., *Russkaya sovetskaya literatura. Ocherki istorii* (Moscow, 1963), p. 428.

66. E.J. Brown, *Russian Literature Since the Revolution* (New York, 1963), p. 188.

67. Ministerstvo vysshego i srednego spetsial'nogo obrazovaniya SSSR, *Programma po istorii russkoy literatury. Chast' 5-ya. Sovetskaya literatura* (Moscow, 1964), p. 37.

68. Ibid., p. 40.

69. Ministerstvo vysshego i srednego spetsial'nogo obrazovaniya SSSR, Ministerstvo prosveshcheniya RSFSR, *Programmy pedagogicheskikh institutov. Russkaya sovetskaya literatura* (Moscow, 1967), pp. 53-55.

70. In 1956 the American literary scholar Professor George Gibian visited university literature classes in the Soviet Union and related the following: "At the University of Odessa I attended classes in Russian literature of the nineteenth and twentieth centuries. The woman professor spoke without notes; her delivery was excellent and the lectures were packed with material. The emphasis, however, fell heavily on the sociological and political implications of literature. On which side of the political struggle was Nekrasov engaged? What are the political views implicit in his poems? What did Gorky say was the social role of a revolutionary author's work at a certain period of history? Such were the questions with which the professor was most concerned." (George Gibian, "Literature and Universities in Soviet Russia: Impressions of an American Visitor," Institute of International Education *News Bulletin*, New York, May 1957, vol. 32, p. 10.)

71. I. Prussakova, "Vsegda v nastuplenii," *Uchitel'skaya gazeta*, September 20, 1969, p. 3.

72. An interesting story, "Obedennyy pereryv," by A. Kurlyandsky and A. Khayt, illustrating the extent to which Soviet citizens are hesitant to speak in public, or to complain about anything relevant, appeared in *Literaturnaya gazeta*, February 25, 1970, p. 16.

Conclusion

1. A. Nuykin, "Iskusstvo—ne arifmetika," *Voprosy literatury*, 1970, No. 3, p. 42.

Appendix

1. M.A. Prokof'ev and others, eds., *Narodnoe obrazovanie v SSSR. 1917-1967* (Moscow, 1967), p. 91.

2. *Literatura v shkole*, 1970, No. 1, pp. 29-30.

3. The works for independent reading are to be found in the appendix of the textbook (*khrestomatiya*).

4. Ministerstvo prosveshcheniya RSFSR. *Programmy vos'miletney i i sredney shkoly na 1969/70 uchebnyy god. Russkiy yazyk i literatura* (Moscow, 1969), pp. 36-40.

5. Ibid., pp. 40-45.

6. Ibid., pp. 45-48.

7. Ibid., pp. 48-53.

8. The reading of the works included in the section for independent reading is not compulsory.

9. Ibid., pp. 53-58.

10. Ibid., pp. 59-64.

11. Ibid., pp. 69-70. The teacher can supplement this list as well as change it at his own discretion.

12. Ibid., pp. 64-68.

13. *Literatura v shkole*, 1970, No. 1, pp. 95-96. Class programs are 25-35 minutes long; after-class programs are 40-60 minutes long.

14. *Literatura v shkole*, 1969, No. 1, pp. 77-80.

15. "Ekzaminatsionnye bilety po russkomu yazyku i literature," in Lietuvos TSR, Švietimo Ministerija. *Vidurinio Mokslo Egzaminu Bilietai 1967-1968 m.m.* (Kaunas, 1968), pp. 6-11. Each paper contains three questions; the third, in Russian, is here omitted. These examination papers are intended for those studying Russian at schools where the language of instruction is Lithuanian.

16. *Spravochnik dlya postupayushchikh v moskovskiy universitet* (Moscow, 1972), pp. 107-110.

17. Ministerstvo vysshego i srednego spetsial'nogo obrazovaniya SSSR. *Uchebnyy plan: Spetsial'nosti 2001/V-1. Russkiy yazyk i literatura* (Moscow, 1964).

18. Ministerstvo vysshego i srednego spetsial'nogo obrazovaniya SSSR. *Programma po istorii russkoy literatury. Chast' 1-ya. Drevnyaya russkaya literatura* (Moscow, 1963), pp. 10-11.

19. *Programma po istorii russkoy literatury. Chast' 2-ya. XVIII v.* (Moscow, 1963), pp. 16-18.

20. *Programma po istorii russkoy literatury. Chast' 3-ya. XIX v.* (Moscow, 1964), pp. 36-41.

21. *Programma po istorii russkoy literatury. Chast' 4-ya. XX vek (do 1917 g.)* (Moscow, 1964), pp. 20-22.

22. Recommended for noncompulsory elective reading (*fakul'tativno*).

23. *Programma po istorii russkoy literatury. Chast' 5-ya. Sovetskaya literatura* (Moscow, 1964), pp. 38-41.

24. Ministerstvo vysshego i srednego spetsial'nogo obrazovaniya RSFSR. *Programma po russkomu narodnomu tvorchestvu* (Moscow, 1960), pp. 18-20.

25. *Programmy pedagogicheskikh institutov. Russkaya literatura* (dlya gosudarstvennykh ekzamenov po spetsial'nosti "Russkiy yazyk i literatura")

(Moscow, 1967). Each paragraph is a question in the examination paper. Each paper contains three questions.

26. The lists of special courses and special seminars, as well as the titles of diploma works to be defended, were taken from bulletin boards at the Moscow State University, where they were posted for the students' information.

27. From an interview with the instructor in the seminar N.V. Nikolaeva conducted in the city of Moscow, May 13, 1970. The seminar was originally intended to be given under the title *"Stil' Tolstogo"* (The Style of Tolstoy), but was later changed into *"Tvorchestvo Tolstogo"* (The Creative Work of Tolstoy).

Bibliography

Bibliography

Books and Articles

Akademiya nauk SSSR. Institut mirovoy literatury. Gosudarstvennyy muzey L.N. Tolstogo. *Lev Nikolaevich Tolstoy: sbornik statey i materialov*. Moscow, 1951.

Akademiya nauk SSSR. Institut mirovoy literatury. *Istoriya russkoy sovetskoy literatury. 1917-1929*. Vol. I. Moscow, 1958.

Akademiya nauk SSSR. Institut russkoy literatury. B. Meylakh, *V.I. Lenin i voprosy literaturovedeniya*. Moscow, 1961.

Akademiya nauk SSSR. Institut russkoy literatury. *Voprosy izucheniya russkoy literatury XI-XX vekov*. Moscow, 1958.

Akademiya nauk SSSR. *Nauchnye kadry v SSSR*. Ed. by A.V. Topchiev. Moscow, 1959.

Aktivizatsiya metodov prepodavaniya russkogo yazyka i literatury: sbornik statey. Leningrad, 1960.

"Analiz ekzamenatsionnogo sochineniya v VIII klasse," *Literatura v shkole*, 1968, No. 5, pp. 73-83.

"Analiz ekzamenatsionnogo sochineiya v VIII klasse," *Literatura v shkole*, 1968, No. 6, pp. 57-60.

Arkhipovsky, V.I. "Lev Tolstoy i nasha sovremennost'," M.V. i S.S.O. USSR Ushhorods'kyy derzhavnyy universytet. *Dopovydy ta povydomlennya. Seryya fylolohychna*, VII (Uzhhorod, 1961), pp. 8-11.

Arsen'ev, A.M. "Basic Trends in Improving the Content of Secondary Education," *Soviet Education*, X (1967), No. 1, pp. 22-33.

Arsen'ev, A.M., and F. Korolev. "Metodologicheskie problemy marksistsko-leninskoy pedagogiki," *Narodnoe obrazovanie*, 1972, No. 4, pp. 6-11.

Asmus, V.F. "Mirovozzrenie Tolstogo," *Literaturnoe nasledstvo*, LXIX, Part I (1961), pp. 35-105.

Ayzerman, L.S. "Contemporary Literature Through the Eyes of Upper-Grade Pupils," *Soviet Education*, VII (1965), No. 3, pp. 3-16.

_____ . "K miru prekrasnogo," *Novy mir*, 1962, No. 11, pp. 211-15.

_____ . "K voprosu o prepodavanii teorii literatury v vos'miletney shkole," *Sovetskaya pedagogika*, November, 1961, pp. 11-16.

Bakhtin, M. *Problemy poetiki Dostoevskogo*. 2nd edition. Moscow, 1963.

Barsuk, A.I. *Pechatny seminarii po russkoy literature (1904-1963)*. Moscow, 1964.

Beketova, M.A. *Aleksandr Blok*. Peterburg, 1922.

Bel'chikov, N.F. *Puti i navyki literaturovedcheskogo truda*. Moscow, 1965.

Belen'kiy, G.I., and G.K. Bocharov, eds. *Rodnaya literatura. Khrestomatiya dlya 7 klassa*. Moscow, 1967.

186

Belen'kiy, G.I. "The Programme of the Communist Party of the Soviet Union and Some Problems in the Teaching of Literature," *Soviet Education*, IV (1962), No. 5, pp. 21-30.

_____. "Stat'i V.I. Lenina na urokakh literatury," *Literatura v shkole*, 1969, No. 4, pp. 12-28.

Belik, A. "O nekotorykh oshibkakh v literaturovedenii," *Oktyabr'*, 1950, No. 2, pp. 150-64.

Belinsky, V.G. *Polnoe sobranie sochineniy*. Vol. I. Moscow, 1953.

Bereday, George Z.F., and Bonnie B. Strech. "Political Education in the USA and in the USSR," *Comparative Education Review*, VII (1963), No. 1, pp. 9-16.

Bereday, George Z.F., ed. *The Changing Soviet School: The Comparative Education Society Field Study in the U.S.S.R.* Boston, 1960.

_____. *The Politics of Soviet Education*. London, 1960.

Bilinkis, Ya. "Narod i revolyutsionery v romane L.N. Tolstogo 'Voskresenie,' " in *O russkom realizme XIX veka i voprosakh narodnosti literatury: sbornik statey*. Moscow-Leningrad, 1960.

Blagoy, D.D., ed. *L.N. Tolstoy: sbornik statey. Posobie dlya uchitelya*. Moscow, 1955.

Blok, Aleksandr. *Sobranie sochineniy*. Vol. VII. Moscow-Leningrad, 1963.

Bogomolov, A. "Poleznaya diskussiya," *Voprosy literatury*, 1964, No. 4, pp. 185-88.

Boguslavsky, A.O., and L.I. Timofeev, eds. *Russkaya sovetskaya literatura: ocherki istorii*. Moscow, 1963.

Borisova, M.N., and A.N. Posadskaya, comp. *Russkaya literatura. Khrestomatiya dlya 5 klassa natsional'nykh shkol*. 6th edition. Moscow, 1967.

Brazhnik, N.I. *Izuchenie romana L.N. Tolstogo "Voyna i mir" v sredney shkole*. Moscow, 1959.

Britikov, A.F. "Iz nablyudeniy nad psikhologicheskim analizom v 'Tikhom Done,' " in V.A. Kovalev and A.I. Pavlovsky, eds., *Voprosy sovetskoy literatury*, VII (Moscow-Leningrad, 1958), pp. 437-53.

Brodsky, N.L., and V.V. Golubkov, eds. *Pushkin v shkole: sbornik statey*. Moscow, 1951.

Brown, E.J. *Russian Literature Since the Revolution*. New York, 1963.

Bursov, B.I. *Lev Tolstoy. Ideynye iskaniya i tvorcheskiy metod 1847-1862*. Moscow, 1960.

_____. *L.N. Tolstoy. Seminariy*. Leningrad, 1963.

_____. "Pered litsom Tolstogo," *Zvezda*, 1964, No. 12, pp. 204-11.

Bursov, B.I., ed. *Russkaya literatura: uchebnoe posobie dlya 9 klassa sredney schkoly*. Moscow, 1968.

Bychkov, S.P. "Roman 'Voyna i mir'—narodno-geroicheskaya epopeya (Problematika i osnovnye obrazy)," *Tvorchestvo L.N. Tolstogo. Sbornik statey*. Moscow, 1954.

Bychkov, S.P., ed. *L.N. Tolstoy v russkoy kritike*. N.p., 1949.

Chekhov, A.P. *Polnoe sobranie sochineniy i pisem*. 20 vols. Moscow, 1944-51.

Chistyakova, N.V. "Roman 'Voyna i mir' i desyatiklassniki," *Literatura v schkole*, 1966, No. 4, pp. 46-54.

Coleman, James S., ed. *Education and Political Development*. Princeton, N.J., 1965.

Counts, George S. *The Challenge of Soviet Education*. New York, 1957.

_____. *Krushchev and the Central Committee Speak on Education*. Commentary and analysis by George S. Counts. Pittsburgh, 1959.

Dement'ev, A.G., and others, eds. *Istoriya russkoy sovetskoy literatury. 1917-1929*. Vol. I. Moscow, 1967.

Dement'ev, A., and others. *Russkaya sovetskaya literatura*. 17th edition. Moscow, 1968.

DeWitt, Nicholas. *Education and Professional Employment in the U.S.S.R.* Washington, 1961.

_____. *Soviet Professional Manpower, Its Education, Training and Supply*. Washington, 1955.

Deyneko, M.M. *40 let narodnogo obrazovaniya v SSSR*. Moscow, 1957.

_____. *Public Education in the U.S.S.R.* Moscow, 1964.

Dokusov, A.M., and V.G. Marantsman. *Izuchenie komedii N.V. Gogolya "Revizor" v shkole*. Moscow-Leningrad, 1967.

Dostoevsky, F.M. *The Diary of a Writer*, translated and annotated by Boris Brasol. Vol. II. New York, 1949.

_____. *Sobranie sochineniy*. 10 vols. Moscow, 1956-58.

F. Dostoevsky v russkoy kritike. Sbornik statey. Moscow, 1956.

Eliutin, V.P. "Successfully Fulfill the Party's Design," *Soviet Education*, XIV (1972), No. 5.

Erlich, V. *The Double Image*. Baltimore, 1964.

Ermilov, V. *Tolstoy—khudozhnik i roman "Voyna i mir."* Moscow, 1961.

_____. *Tolstoy romanist. "Voyna i mir," "Anna Karenina," "Voskresenie."* Moscow, 1965.

Eykhenbaum, B. *Lev Tolstoy. 50-ye gody*. Leningrad, 1928.

_____. *Lev Tolstoy. 60-ye gody*. Leningrad-Moscow, 1931.

_____. *Lev Tolstoy. Semidesyatye gody*. Leningrad, 1960.

_____. *Molodoy Tolstoy*. Peterburg-Berlin, 1922.

_____. *Skvoz' literaturu. Sbornik statey*. 'S-Gravenhage, 1962. (Originally published in the series "Voprosy poetiki," Leningrad, 1924).

Fein, G.N. *Roman L.N. Tolstogo "Voyna i mir": tselostnyy analiz*. Moscow, 1966.

Florinsky, S.M. *Russkaya literatura. Uchebnoe posobie dlya sredney shkoly*. 13th edition. Moscow, 1967.

Friche, V.M., ed. *O Tolstom. Literaturno-kriticheskiy sbornik*. Moscow-Leningrad, 1928.

Friedberg, Maurice. *Russian Classics in Soviet Jackets*. New York, 1962.

Galkin, K.T. *The Training of Scientists in the Soviet Union*. Moscow, 1959.

————. *Vysshee obrazovanie i podgotovka nauchnykh kadrov v SSSR*. Moscow, 1958.

Glebov, B. "A Letter to the Editor," *Literatura v shkole*, 1970, No. 4, pp. 91-93.

Glezerman, G.E., M.N. Parkhomenko, and others, eds. *Voprosy teorii i praktiki kommunisticheskogo vospitaniya*. Moscow, 1962.

Gogol', N.V. *Sobranie sochineniy v semi tomakh*. Vol. VI. Moscow, 1967.

Golovanov, T.P. "Turgenev i sovetskaya literatura," *Russkaya literatura*, 1968, No. 4, pp. 20-33.

Golovenchenko, F.M. *Vvedenie v literaturovedenie*. Moscow, 1964.

Golubkov, V.V. and others, comp. *Rodnaya literatura. Khrestomatiya dlya 5 klassa*. 7th edition. Moscow, 1966.

————. *Rodnaya literatura. Khrestomatiya dlya 5 klassa*. 11th edition. Moscow, 1970.

Goncharov, N.K., ed. *Novaya sistema narodnogo obrazovaniya v SSSR: sbornik dokumentov i statey*. Moscow, 1960.

Grant, Douglas, ed. *The Humanities in Soviet Higher Education*. Toronto, 1960.

Grant, N. *Soviet Education*. Baltimore, 1964.

Gromtseva, S.N. "K ustnomu ekzamenu v X klasse," *Literatura v shkole*, 1969, No. 1, pp. 76-80.

Grossman, L. *Dostoevsky*. Moscow, 1962.

————. *Dostoevsky*. 2nd edition, Moscow, 1965.

Gudzy, N.K. "Kak prepodavat' literaturu v shkole," *Voprosy literatury*, 1961, No. 12, pp. 118-21.

————. *Lev Nikolaevich Tolstoy*. 2nd edition, Moscow, 1956, 3rd edition, Moscow, 1960.

Gukovsky, G.A. *Izuchenie literaturnogo proizvedeniya v shkole*. Moscow-Leningrad, 1966.

————. *Realizm Gogolya*. Moscow-Leningrad, 1959.

Gulyaev, N. "Literatura i vospitanie novogo cheloveka," *Voprosy literatury*, 1963, No. 8, pp. 155-60.

Gural'nik, U. "Dostoevsky i sovremennost'," *Novy mir*, 1971, No. 8, pp. 240-53.

Hingley, Ronald. *Chekhov*. New York-London, 1966.

Iezuitov, A.I. "V.I. Lenin o partiynosti literatury," Akademiya nauk SSSR. Institut russkoy literatury. *V.I. Lenin i voprosy literaturovedeniya*. Moscow-Leningrad, 1961, pp. 60-117.

"Instruction on the Procedure for Awarding Academic Degrees and Titles," *Soviet Education*, X (1968), No. 9, pp. 3-52.

Iovchuk, M.T. "O meste gumanitarnykh nauk v sisteme formirovaniya kommunisticheskogo mirovozzreniya molodezhi," *Voprosy filosofii*, 1959, No. 6, pp. 17-29.

Kairov, I.A., and others, eds. *Pedagogicheskaya entsiklopediya*. Vol. III. Moscow, 1966.

Kaminsky, V. "Problema khudozhestvennoy pravdy v literaturnykh otsenkakh V.I. Lenina," *Neva*, No. 4, pp. 159-66.

Kandiev, B.I. *Roman-epopeya L.N. Tolstogo "Voyna i mir."* Moscow, 1967.

Kanunova, R.Z. *Nekotrye osobennosti realizma Gogolya.* Tomsk, 1962.

Kaplan, I., and Ya. Nesturkh. "Zametki s ustnykh ekzamenov," *Literatura v shkole*, 1969, No. 5, pp. 48-58.

Kerimov, D.A., ed. *Voprosy vospitaniya i prepodavaniya v universitete.* Vol. II. Leningrad, 1967.

Khrapchenko, M.B. *Lev Tolstoy kak khudozhnik.* Moscow, 1963.

Khrestomatiya po dialekticheskomu i istoricheskomu materializmu dlya sistemy partiynoy ucheby. 2nd edition. Moscow, 1970.

Kirillov, M.I. "O nedostatkakh uchebnikov po literature," *Literatura v shkole*, 1960, No. 2, pp. 66-68.

Kogan, P.S. *Lev Tolstoy i marksistskaya kritika.* Moscow-Leningrad, 1928.

Korchagin, A. "Obuchat' po novumu," *Novy mir*, 1963, No. 9, pp. 273-75.

Korst, N.O. *Ocherki po metodike analiza khudozhestvennykh proizvedeniy.* Moscow, 1963.

Kostylev, O.L. *Kriticheskaya stat'ya na uroke literatury.* Leningrad, 1967.

Kosygin, A.N. *Direktivy XXIII s"ezda KPSS po pyatiletnemu planu razvitiya narodnogo khozyaystva SSSR na 1966-1970 gody.* Moscow, 1966.

Kovalev, V.A., and E.A. Maymin. "50-letie so dnya smerti L.N. Tolstogo. Tolstovedenie v vysshey shkole," *Vestnik vysshey shkoly*, VII (1960), No. 11, pp. 74-82.

Kovalev, V.A. "Puti izucheniya istorii russkoy sovetskoy literatury," *Russkaya literatura*, 1968, No. 1, pp. 73-80.

Krasnov, G. *Geroy i narod. O romane L'va Tolstogo "Voyna i mir."* Moscow, 1964.

Krasnov, N.F. "Vysshey shkole-dostoynoe popolnenie," *Vestnik vysshey shkoly*, 1969, No. 4, pp. 3-7.

Kravtsov, N.I., ed. *Istoriya russkoy literatury vtoroy poloviny XIX veka.* Moscow, 1966.

Kudryashev, N.I. "The Literary Course in the Secondary School," *Soviet Education*, VII (1965), No. 7 pp. 35-44.

_____. "Ob effektivnosti zanyatiy po literature," *Literatura v shkole*, 1970, No. 4, pp. 16-30.

Kudryashev, N.I., ed. *Za tvorcheskoe izuchenie literatury.* Moscow, 1968.

Kydryashev, N.E. "Literature in the New School," *Soviet Education*, I (1959), No. 7.

Kudryavtsev, Yu.G. *Bunt ili religiya.* Moscow, 1969.

Kuleshov, V.I., ed. *Sovetskoe literaturovedenie za pyat'desyat let.* Moscow, 1967.

Kunitsyn, G.I. "Klassovost' v literature," *Znamya*, 1968, No. 1, pp. 226-42.

_____. *V.I. Lenin o klassovosti i partiynosti literatury.* Moscow, 1960.

Kupreyanova, E.N. *Estetika L.N. Tolstogo.* Moscow-Leningrad, 1966.

Larmin, O.V. "Rol' iskusstva v esteticheskom vospitanii trudyashchikhsya," *Voprosy kommunisticheskogo vospitaniya: sbornik statey*. Moscow, 1961, pp. 104-31.

Lilge, F. "Lenin and the Politics of Education," *Slavic Review*, XXVII (June 1968), 230-57.

_____. "The Study of Literature in the Soviet School," U.S. Office of Education. *Studies in Comparative Education*. Vol. XI, 1959, pp. 30-40.

Leningradskiy universitet. *Spravochnik dlya postupayushchikh v 1965 godu*. Leningrad, 1965.

Lenin, V.I. *Collected Works*. Vols, V, XIV, XV, XVI, XVII. Moscow, 1961-63.

_____. *O literature i iskusstve*. Moscow, 1957.

_____. *Sochineniya*. 4th edition. Vols. V, X, XXVIII, N.p., 1946-50.

V.I. Lenin o L.N. Tolstom. Moscow, 1969.

Leont'ev, K. *Analiz, stil' i veyanie. O romanakh gr. L.N. Tolstogo*. Moscow, 1911.

Lesokhin, L.N. "O problemnosti uroka literatury," *Literatura v shkole*, 1965, No. 6, pp. 32-37.

Litvinov, V.V. "L.N. Tolstoy v shkole," *Literatura v shkole*, 1966, No. 4, pp. 68-71.

Lunacharsky, A. *Lenin i literaturovedenie*. Moscow, 1934.

_____. *On Literature and Art*. Moscow, 1965.

Makogonenko, G. "Russkaya klassicheskaya literatura v svete leninskoy kontseptsii osvoboditel'nogo dvizheniya," *Voprosy literatury*, 1968, No. 4, pp. 3-27.

Mal'tseva, K.V., and others, comp. *Russkaya literatura. Uchebnaya khrestomatiya dlya VII klassa natsional'nykh shkol*. 6th edition, corrected and revised. Moscow, 1967.

Matyushkin, A.M. "Teoreticheskie osnovy problemnogo obucheniya," *Sovetskaya pedagogika*, 1971, No. 7.

Merezhkovsky, D.S. *Polnoe sobranie sochineniy*. Vols. IX-XII. Moscow, 1914.

Meylakh, B.S. *A.S. Pushkin. Seminariy*. Leningrad, 1959.

_____. *Lenin i problemy russkoy literatury kontsa XIX-nachala XX vv.* Moscow-Leningrad, 1951.

_____. "Novye materialy o vzglyadakh Lenina na literaturu i iskusstvo," *Zvezda*, 1961, No. 4, pp. 186-91.

_____. "O khudozhestvennom myshlenii Dostoevskkogo," *Voprosy literatury*, 1972, No. 1, pp. 89-104.

Mirsky, D.S. *A History of Russian Literature from Its Beginnings to 1900*. New York, 1958.

Moos, E. "The Changes in Soviet Schools in September 1964," *Comparative Education Review*, VIII (1964), No. 3, pp. 264-68.

Naumova, N.N. *L.N. Tolstoy v shkole. Posobie dlya uchitelya*. Ed. by L.A. Sokolova. Leningrad, 1959.

Nesterenko, A.A. "Avtorskaya pozitsiya v proizvedeniyakh L.N. Tolstogo (po stranitsam 'Uchenykh zapisok')," *Nauchnye doklady vysshey shkoly. Filologicheskie nauki*, 1965, No. 2, pp. 182-90.

――――. "Ob izuchenii pozitsii pisatelya v khudozhestvennom proizvedenii (na primere tvorchestva L.N. Tolstogo)," *Vestnik moskovskogo universiteta, seriya X, filologiya* 2 (1966), pp. 52-66.

――――. "Tvorchestvo L.N. Tolstogo v 'Uchenykh zapiskakh,' " *Nauchnye doklady vysshey shkoly. Filologicheskie nauki*, 1964, No. 4, pp. 191-98.

Nikitina, E.I. *Rodnoe slovo. Kniga dlya chteniya v tret'em klasse.* 2nd, corrected edition. Moscow, 1971.

Nikol'sky, V.A. *Ocherki prepodavaniya literatury v sredney shkole. Posobie dlya uchitelya.* Moscow, 1958.

"Novoe Polozhenie o vuzakh," *Vestnik vysshey shkoly*, 1969, No. 3, pp. 3-7.

Nuykin, A. "Iskusstvo-ne arifmetika," *Voprosy literatury*, 1970, No. 3, pp. 40-50.

Odintsov, V. "Voennaya podgotovka uchashchikhsya," *Narodnoe obrazovanie*, 1969, No. 6, pp. 45-48.

Ogorodnikov, I.T. *Pedagogika.* Moscow, 1968.

"O grafike perekhoda na novye uchebnye plany i programmy," *Narodnoe obrazovanie*, 1969, No. 6, pp. 10-11, 91.

Opul'skaya, L.D. "Nekotorye voprosy izucheniya L. Tolstogo," *Voprosy literatury*, 1958, No. 9, pp. 56-63.

Palkin, M.A. *Voprosy teorii literatury.* Minsk, 1971.

Pennar, Jaan, Ivan I. Bakalo, and George Z.F. Bereday. *Modernization and Diversity in Soviet Education, with Special Reference to Nationality Groups.* New York, 1971.

Petrosyan, A. "Partiya i voprosy literatury," *Literatura v shkole*, 1953, No. 6, pp. 3-9.

Pinchukov, E.M., and V.A. Semin. "Na pervom soveshchanii dekanov fakul'tetov povysheniya kvalifikatsii prepodavateley," *Vestnik vysshey shkoly*, 1969, No. 6, pp. 55-58.

Plotkin, L. *Partiya i literatura.* Leningrad, 1960.

"Polozhenie ob aspiranture pri vysshikh uchebnykh zavedeniyakh i nauchno-issledovatel'skikh uchrezhdeniyakh," *Byulleten' ministerstva vysshego i srednego spetsial'nogo obrazovaniya* SSSR, 1969, No. 9, pp. 2-8.

Prokof'ev, M.A., and others, eds. *Narodnoe obrazovanie v SSSR. 1917-1967.* Moscow, 1967.

Pushkareva, M.D. and others, comp. *Rodnaya literatura. Uchebnoe posobie dlya IV klassa.* 3rd edition. Moscow, 1972.

Pushkareva, M.D., and Snezhnevskaya, M.A. "O zadachakh literaturnogo obrazovaniya v IV klasse," *Literatura v shkole*, 1970, No. 1, pp. 22-28.

Pushkin, A. *Polnoe sobranie sochineniy.* Vol. XI. Izdatel'stvo Akademii nauk SSSR, 1949.

Pustovoyt, P. "O nashem filologicheskom obrazovanii," *Voprosy literatury*, 1962, No. 3, pp. 179-87.

————. "V.I. Lenin o partiynosti literatury," *Literatura v shkole*, 1962, No. 2, pp. 3-7.

Reck, R.D. "The Politics of Literature," *PMLA of America*, LXXXV (1970), No. 3, pp. 429-32.

Revyakin, A.I. *O prepodavanii khudozhestvennoy literatury*. Moscow, 1968.

————. *Problema tipicheskogo v khudozhestvennoy literature. Posobie dlya uchitelya*. Moscow, 1959.

Reyser, S. "Evolyutsiya zhanra," *Voprosy literatury*, 1964, No. 4, pp. 182-85.

Rosen, Seymour Michael. *Education and Modernization in the USSR*. Reading, Mass., 1971.

————. *Higher Education in the U.S.S.R.: Curriculums, Schools, and Statistics*. Washington, 1963.

————. "Significant Aspects of Soviet Education," U.S. Office of Education. *Bulletin*, 1965, No. 15.

Russia. Tsentral'noe statisticheskoe upravlenie. *Vysshee obrazovanie v SSSR. Statisticheskiy sbornik*. Moscow, 1961.

Saburov, A.A. "Ob istorizme romana 'Voyna i mir,' " *Voprosy literatury*, 1958, No. 9, pp. 41-55.

————. *"Voyna i mir" L.N. Tolstogo. Problematika i poetika*. Moscow, 1959.

Safronova, E. "O sotsiologicheskom analize v literaturnoy kritike," Vil'nyuskiy gosudarstvennyy universitet. *Uchenye zapiski*, XXXI, Literatura II (1966), pp. 77-97.

Sarnov, B. "Glazami khudozhnika," *Novy mir*, 1964, No. 7, pp. 249-54.

Semanova, M. *Chekhov v shkole. Posobie dlya uchitelya*. Leningrad, 1949.

Semenikhin, V. "Uchit' i uchit'sya razumno," *Novy mir*, 1962, No. 11, pp. 106-10.

Semenovsky, O. *Marksistskaya kritika o Chekhove i Tolstom*. Kishinev, 1968.

Serbin, P.K. "Izuchenie poemy V.V. Mayakovskogo 'Khorosho!,' " in Ministerstvo prosveshcheniya USSR. *Metodika prepodavaniya russkogo yazyka i literatury. Respublikanskiy nauchno-metodicheskiy sbornik*. Vypusk II. Kiev, 1966, pp. 137-60.

Schepilova, L.V. *Vvedenie v literaturovedenie*. 2nd edition, Moscow, 1968.

Scherbina, V.R. "V.I. Lenin i problema ideynosti literatury," *Voprosy filosofii*, 1957, No. 3, pp. 61-71.

Shevchenko, P.A., and S.M. Florinsky, comp. *Rodnaya literatura. Khrestomatiya dlya 6 klassa*. 8th edition. Moscow, 1967.

Shifman, A.I. "Byl li Lev Tolstoy petrashevtsem?" *Voprosy literatury*, 1967, No. 2, pp. 53-73.

————. *Lev Tolstoy-oblichitel' burzhuaznoy kul'tury*. Tula, 1960.

Shishkina, A. "Podstupy k resheniyu vazhnoy zadachi," *Zvezda*, 1950, No. 4, pp. 167-73.

Shklovsky, V. *Lev Tolstoy*. Moscow, 1963, 2nd edition, Moscow, 1967.

_____. *Mater'yal i stil' v romane L'va Tolstogo "Voyna i mir."* Moscow, 1926.

_____. *Povesti o proze. Razmyshleniya i razbory*. Vol. II. Moscow, 1966.

_____. *Zametki o proze russkikh klassikov*. Moscow, 1955.

Shneidman, N.N. "The Russian Classical Literary Heritage and the Basic Concepts of Soviet Literary Education," *Slavic Review*, XXXI (1972), No. 3, pp. 626-38.

_____. "Soviet Approaches to the Teaching of Literature. A Case Study: L. Tolstoy in Soviet Education," *Canadian Slavonic Papers*, XV (1973), No. 3.

Sholokhov, M.A. *Sobranie sochineniy*. 8 vols. Moscow, 1956-60.

Shumilin, I.N. *Soviet Higher Education*. Munich, 1962.

Slonimsky, A. Introduction to N.V. Gogol', *Izbrannye proizvedeniya*, pp. 3-50, Moscow, 1963.

Smith, H.N. "Something Is Happening But You Don't Know What It Is, Do You, Mr. Jones?" *PMLA of America*, LXXXV (1970), No. 3, pp. 417-22.

Solodovnikov, A. "Ob otnoshenii k klassicheskomu naslediyu," *Kommunist*, 1968, No. 13, pp. 98-109.

Solov'eva, E.E., and others, eds. *Rodnaya rech'. Kniga dlya chteniya v I klasse nachal'noy shkoly*. 25th edition. Moscow, 1968.

_____. *Rodnaya rech'. Kniga dlya chteniya vo II klasse nachal'noy shkoly*. 24th edition. Moscow, 1967.

_____. *Rodnaya rech'. Kniga dlya chteniya v III klasse nachal'noy shkoly*. 21st edition. Moscow, 1965.

_____. *Rodnaya rech'. Kniga dlya chteniya v IV klasse nachal'noy shkoly*. 23rd edition. Moscow, 1966.

_____. *Rodnaya rech'. Kniga dlya chteniya v III klasse natsional'nykh shkol*. 26th edition. Moscow, 1970.

_____. *Rodnaya rech'. Kniga dlya chteniya vo II klasse natsional'nykh shkol*. 26th edition. Moscow, 1969.

Solzhenitsyn, A. *Cancer Ward*. New York, 1969.

Stakhov, V. "Esli ne zabyvat' o psikhologii uchenika (O problemakh prepodavaniya literatury v shkole)," *Zvezda*, 1968, No. 3, pp. 137-45.

Strezikozin, V. "Uchitel' i novaya programma," *Narodnoe obrazovanie*, 1969, No. 8, pp. 127-42.

Struve, Gleb. "Chekhov in Communist Censorship," *Slavonic and East European Review*, XXXIII (June 1955), No. 1. pp. 327-41.

Suslov, M. "Obshchestvennye nauki—boevoe oruzhie partii v stroitel'stve kommunizma," *Kommunist*, 1972, No. 1, pp. 18-30.

Svirsky, V.D., and E.K. Frantsman, eds. *Russkaya literatura. Uchebnaya khrestomatiya dlya IX klassa natsional'nykh shkol*. Moscow, 1967.

_____. *Russkaya sovetskaya literatura. Uchebnaya khrestomatiya dlya X klassa natsional'nykh shkol*. 4th edition. Leningrad, 1972.

Swayze, Harold. *Political Control of Literature in the U.S.S.R. 1946-1959.* Cambridge, Mass., 1962.

Tamarchenko, D. *Literatura i estetika.* Leningrad, 1936.

Tatuyko, A. "Za realisticheskiy podkhod," *Voprosy literatury*, 1963, No. 8, pp. 160-62.

Timofeev. L.I. "O poezii Aleksandra Bloka," *Literatura v shkole*, 1968, No. 5, pp. 21-26.

_____. *Osnovy teorii literatury.* Moscow, 1966.

Tolstoy, L.N. *Neizdannye teksty.* N.p., 1933.

_____. *Sobranie sochineniy.* 20 vols. Moscow, 1960-65.

"Tolstoy segodnya," *Voprosy literatury*, 1960, No. 11, pp. 3-13.

Tropin, V.I., ed. *Spravochnik dlya postupayushchikh v moskovskiy universitet.* Moscow, 1969, and Moscow, 1972.

Trotsky, L. *Literature and Revolution.* New York, 1957.

_____. *Sochineniya. Seriya VI. Problemy kul'tury.* Vol. XX. Moscow-Leningrad, 1926.

Trushchenko, E. "Kakim zhe on dolzhen byt' uchebnik po russkoy literature?" *Voprosy literatury*, 1967, No. 4, pp. 244-48.

Tsentral'noe statisticheskoe upravlenie pri Sovete ministrov SSSR. *Narodnoe khozyaystvo SSSR v 1969 godu.* Moscow, 1970.

Tsentral'nyy komitet KPSS i Sovet ministrov SSSR. "Postanovlenie ob organizatsii podgotovtel'nykh otdeleniy pri vysshikh uchebnykh zavedeniyakh," *Byulleten' ministerstva vysshego i srednego spetsial'nogo obrazovaniya*, 1969, No. 10, pp. 1-4.

Tseytlin, M.A. "Novoe o 'Voyne i mire,' " *Literatura v shkole*, 1965, No. 4, pp. 65-68.

_____. "O problemnon izuchenii romana L. Tolstogo 'Voyna i mir,' " *Literatura v shkole*, 1968, No. 1, pp. 24-39.

_____. "Urok o Natashe Rostovoy," *Literatura v shkole*, 1963, No. 2, pp. 41-47.

Tugarinov, V.P. "Nekotorye gnoseologicheskie problemy izobrazitel'nogo iskusstva," *Leninskaya teoriya otrazheniya i sovremennaya nauka.* Moscow, 1966.

24th Congress of the Communist Party of the Soviet Union. March 30-April 9, 1971. Documents. Moscow, 1971.

Ustyuzhanin, D., comp. *Russkaya klassicheskaya literatura. Razbory i analizy.* Moscow, 1969.

Utechin, S. "The Ferment Among Soviet Youth," *Soviet Surveys*, London, 1957, No. 12, pp. 1-16.

Vasil'eva, M.S., and others, comp. *Nasha rodina. Kniga dlya chteniya v tret'em klasse.* 2nd, corrected edition. Moscow, 1971.

Vayman, S. "A kto u nikh vel teoriyu?" *Voprosy literatury*, 1964, No. 4, pp. 168-70.

"V Ministerstve prosveshcheniya RSFSR," *Narodnoe obrazovanie*, 1969, No. 3, pp. 123-24.

Volkov, A.A. *Russkaya literatura XX veka*. Moscow, 1960.

————. *Russkaya literatura XX veka. Dooktyabr'skiy period*. 4th edition, revised and enlarged. Moscow, 1966.

Volkov, M.N. "Sovershenstvovat' attestatsiyu nauchnykh rabotnikov," *Vestnik vysshey shkoly*, 1968, No. 12, pp. 52-60.

Voytolovskaya, E.L., and E.M. Rumyantseva. *Prakticheskie zanyatiya po russkoy literature XIX veka*. Moscow-Leningrad, 1966.

Yarmolinsky, A. *Literature Under Communism*. New York, 1957.

Zel'dovich, M.G., and L.Ya. Livshits. *Russkaya literatura XIX v. Khrestomatiya kriticheskikh materialov*. 2nd revised edition. Moscow, 1964.

Zerchaninov, A.A. and D. Ya. Rayhkin. *Russkaya literatura. Uchebnik dlya sredney shkoly*. 25th edition. Moscow, 1967.

Zerchaninov, A.A., D.Ya. Raykhin, and B.I. Strazhev. *Russkaya literatura*. 10th edition. Moscow, 1951.

"Znat' i lyubit' literaturu" (Stenogramma soveshchaniya v MGU), *Voprosy literatury*, 1963, No. 1, pp. 159-82.

Newspaper Articles

Afanas'ev, K. "Stupen'yu vyshe-strozhe schet," *Uchitel'skaya gazeta*, June 6, 1970, p. 3.

Andrianov, G. "Tsel' nashykh urokov," *Uchitel'skaya gazeta*, December 2, 1969, p. 3.

Belov, P. "Tol'ko pri sochetanii," *Uchitel'skaya gazeta*, June 20, 1968, p. 2.

Boborykin, A., and others. "Vremya eksperimentov," *Uchitel'skaya gazeta*, May 16, 1968, p. 2.

Brezhnev, L.I. "Rech'na Vsesoyuznom s"ezde uchiteley," *Uchitel'skaya gazeta*, July 5, 1968, pp. 1-2.

Dzeverin, I. "Znamya revolyutsionnogo iskusstva," *Literaturnaya gazeta*, January 21, 1970, p. 5.

El'sberg, Ya. "Oblachivshis' v togu uchennogo," *Literaturnaya gazeta*, September 22, 1971, p. 2.

El'tseva, O. "Shablon," *Uchitel'skaya gazeta*, June 22, 1972, p. 3.

Gonchar, I. "Nereshennye problemy," *Uchitel'skaya gazeta*, August 2, 1969, p. 3.

Gudzy, N.K. "Nuzhny li obshchie kursy?" *Literaturnaya gazeta*, June 11, 1959, p. 3.

Klimov, A. "Aspiranty," *Uchitel'skaya gazeta*, July 16 and 18, 1968.

"Konkurs, student, ball," *Uchitel'skaya gazeta*, March 16, 1972, p. 2.

Mikhalkov, S. "Tvorchestvo eto bor'ba," *Literaturnaya Rossiya*, December 19, 1969, p. 4.

Prokof'ev, M.A. "O sostoyanii i merakh dal'neyshego uluchsheniya raboty sredney obshcheobrazovatel'noy shkoly," *Uchitel'skaya gazeta*, July 3, 1968, pp. 1-4.

196

Prussakova, I. "Vsegda v nastuplenii," *Uchitel'skaya gazeta*, September 20, 1969, p. 3.
Shcherbakova, I. "Plata za brak," *Uchitel'skaya gazeta*, August 9, 1969, p. 2.
"S pervykh dney," *Uchitel'skaya gazeta*, September 4, 1969, p. 1.
Tsentral'nyy komitet KPSS. "Postanovlenie o 50-letii VLKSM i zadachakh kommunisticheskogo vospitaniya molodezhi," *Uchitel'skaya gazeta*, October 8, 1968, p. 1.
Trembitskaya, S. "Vernemsya k Pushkinu," *Uchitel'skaya gazeta*, June 22, 1972, p. 3.
Vorob'eva, N., and S. Khitarova. "Nazad k 'istokam' ili ot 'istokov'—v budush-chee?" *Literaturnaya gazeta*, December 10, 1969, p. 4.

Educational Programs

Glavnoe upravlenie podgotovki uchiteley ministerstva prosveshcheniya RSFSR. *Programmy pedagogicheskikh institutov. Russkaya literatura XIX veka.* Moscow, 1954.
Glavnoe upravlenie vysshikh i srednikh pedagogicheskikh uchebnykh zavedeniy ministerstva prosveshcheniya RSFSR. *Programmy pedagogicheskikh institutov. Russkaya literatura XVIII veka.* Moscow, 1961.
_____. *Programmy pedagogicheskikh institutov. Russkaya literatura XIX veka.* Moscow, 1959.
_____. *Programmy pedagogicheskikh institutov. Russkaya literatura predo-ktyabr'skogo perioda (1890-1917 gg.).* Moscow, 1958.
Lietuvos TSR Švietimo Ministerja. *Vidurinio Mokslo Egzaminu, Bilietai 1967-1968 m.m.* Kaunas, 1968.
Ministerstvo prosveshcheniya Litovskoy SSR. *Programmy vos'miletney i sredney shkoly. Russkiy yazyk i literatura (V-XI klassy). Dlya shkol s litovskim yazykom obucheniya.* Kaunas, 1967.
Ministerstvo prosveshcheniya RSFSR. *Programmy sredney shkoly na 1965/66 uchebnyy god. Literatura.* Moscow, 1965.
_____. *Programmy vos'miletney i sredney shkoly na 1969/70 god. Russkiy yazyk i literatura.* Moscow, 1969.
_____. *Programmy vos'miletney shkoly. Russkiy yazyk i literatura.* Moscow, 1967.
Ministerstvo vysshego i srednego spetsial'nogo obrazovaniya SSSR. Ministerstvo prosveshcheniya RSFSR. *Programmy pedagogicheskikh institutov. Drevnyaya russkaya literatura.* Moscow, 1964.
_____. *Programmy pedagogicheskikh institutov. Russkaya literatura predo-ktyabr'skogo perioda (1890-1917).* Moscow, 1964.
_____. *Programmy pedagogicheskikh institutov. Russkoe narodnoe tvorches-tvo.* Moscow, 1963.

_____. *Programmy pedagogicheskikh institutov. Russkaya sovetskaya literatura*. Moscow, 1967.

Ministerstvo vysshego i srednego spetsial'nogo obrazovaniya RSFSR. *Programma po russkomu narodnomu tvorchestvu*. Moscow, 1960.

Ministerstvo vysshego i srednego spetsial'nogo obrazovaniya SSSR. Moskovskiy gosudarstvennyy universitet. *Uchebnyy plan spetsial'nosti 2001/V-I. Russkiy yazyk i literatura*. Moscow, 1964.

Ministerstvo vysshego i srednego spetsial'nogo obrazovaniya SSSR. *Programma po istorii russkoy literatury. Chast' I-ya. Drevnyaya literatura*. Moscow, 1963.

_____. *Programma po istorii russkoy literatury. Chast' 2-ya. XVIII v.* Moscow, 1963.

_____. *Programma po istorii russkoy literatury. Chast' 3-ya. XIX v.* Moscow, 1964.

_____. *Programma po istorii russkoy literatury. Chast' 4-ya. XX vek (do 1917 g.)*. Moscow, 1964.

_____. *Programma po istorii russkoy literatury. Chast' 5-ya. Sovetskaya literatura*. Moscow, 1964.

MGU. Kafedra russkoy literatury. Proekt. *Programma po kursu "Vvedenie v literaturovedenie" (dlya filologicheskikh fakul'tetov gosudarstvennykh universitetov)*. Moscow, 1960.

Programmno-metodicheskoe upravlenie ministerstva prosveshcheniya RSFSR. *Bilety dlya vypusknykh ekzamenov za kurs sredney shkoly na 1966/67 uchebnyy god*. Moscow, 1968.

_____. *Bilety dlya vypusknykh ekzamenov za kurs vos'miletney shkoly na 1967/68 uchebnyy god*. Moscow, 1968.

Programmy pedagogicheskikh institutov. Russkaya literatura (dlya gosudarstvennykh ekzamenov po spetsial'nosti "Russkiy yazyk i literatura"). Moscow, 1967.

Index

Index

About the Author

N.N. Shneidman was born in the city of Wilno, Poland and educated in Poland, the U.S.S.R., and Canada. He holds degrees in education, Russian and East European Studies, and a Ph.D. in Slavic Languages and Literatures from the University of Toronto. Dr. Shneidman published a number of articles and lectured on problems of education, physical education, Slavic languages and literatures in Europe and in North America. He is presently on the staff of the Department of Slavic Languages and Literatures of the University of Toronto in Canada.

Books Written Under the Auspices of the Centre for Russian and East European Studies, University of Toronto

Feeding the Russian Fur Trade. By James R. Gibson. (University of Wisconsin Press, Madison, Wisconsin, 1969)

The Czech Renascence of the Nineteenth Century: Essays in Honour of Otakar Odložilĭk. Edited by Peter Brock and H. Gordon Skilling. (University of Toronto Press, Toronto, 1970)

The Soviet Wood-Processing Industry: A Linear Programming Analysis of the Role of Transportation Costs in Location and Flow Patterns. By Brenton M. Barr. (University of Toronto, Press, Toronto, 1970).

Interest Groups in Soviet Politics. Edited by H. Gordon Skilling and Franklyn Griffiths. (Princeton University Press, Princeton, New Jersey, 1971)

Between Gogol' and Ševčenko. By George S.N. Luckyj. (Harvard Series in Ukrainian Studies. Wilhelm Fink Verlag, Munich, Germany, 1971)

Narrative Modes in Czech Literature. By Lubomir Doležel. (University of Toronto Press, Toronto, 1973)

Guide to the Decisions of the Communist Party of the Soviet Union. By Robert H. McNeal. (University of Toronto Press, Toronto, 1973)

Soviet Urban Politics. By Michael B. Frolic. (The M.I.T. Press, Cambridge, Massachusetts, forthcoming)

Leon Trotsky and the Politics of Economic Isolation. By Richard B. Day. (Cambridge University Press, Cambridge, England, 1973)

The Collective Farm in Soviet Agriculture. By Robert C. Stuart. (D.C. Heath and Company, Lexington, Mass., 1972).